The Lived Experiences of Muslims in Europe

This book unearths new knowledge and challenges existing paradigms in relation to the integration of minority communities. It comprehensively reflects upon the complexity of recognition experiences and integration challenges faced by Muslim individuals and groups in Europe. By focusing on universal recognition themes related to experiences within personal relationships, legal relations, religion and civil society, it makes an essential contribution to a deeper understanding of Muslim life in the West. It offers a reconsideration of the everyday lives of Muslims in Europe by drawing on the paradigm of recognition. Exploring universal themes, it demonstrates the complexity of recognitive relations by examining how Muslim individuals perceive the ways they are recognised, or misrecognised, within various spheres of everyday interaction. It sheds light on the ways in which forms of recognition affect identity formation and social relations more generally, and the broader ramifications that arise from such forms of misrecognition. This book draws on Honneth's critical social theory of recognition to frame a range of grassroots interviews and focused discussion groups. Grounded in qualitative research and with an emancipatory intent, *The Lived Experiences of Muslims in Europe* challenges both the assumption that minority groups simply seek to have their particular culture and associated beliefs endorsed by a majority, and the security paradigm that narrowly views Muslims in Europe through the lens of political extremism.

Des Delaney is Postdoctoral Researcher at Dublin City University (DCU), Ireland, where he completed his doctorate on the subject of recognition at the School of Law and Government. His research interests are the synthesis of philosophy and empirical sociology, particularly in relation to recognition, power, social struggle, and integration issues.

Routledge Studies in Social and Political Thought

141 Politics through the Iliad and the Odyssey
Hobbes writes Homer
Andrea Catanzaro

142 Social Change in a Material World
Theodore R. Schatzki

143 Hubris and Progress
A Future Born of Presumption
Carlo Bordoni

144 Work: Marxist and Systems-Theoretical Approaches
Stefan Kühl

145 The Social Life of Nothing: Silence, Invisibility and Emptiness in Tales of Lost Experience
Susie Scott

146 A Politics of Disgust
Selfhood, World-Making and Ethics
Eleonora Joensuu

147 The Lived Experiences of Muslims in Europe
Recognition, Power and Intersubjective Dilemmas
Des Delaney

148 Ethical Politics and Modern Society
T. H. Green's Practical Philosophy and Modern China
James Jia-Hau Liu

For a full list of titles in this series, please visit www.routledge.com/series/RSSPT

The Lived Experiences of Muslims in Europe
Recognition, Power and Intersubjective Dilemmas

Des Delaney

LONDON AND NEW YORK

First published 2020
by Routledge
2 Park Square, Milton Park, Abingdon, Oxon OX14 4RN

and by Routledge
52 Vanderbilt Avenue, New York, NY 10017

Routledge is an imprint of the Taylor & Francis Group, an informa business

© 2020 Des Delaney

The right of Des Delaney to be identified as author of this work has been asserted by him in accordance with sections 77 and 78 of the Copyright, Designs and Patents Act 1988.

All rights reserved. No part of this book may be reprinted or reproduced or utilised in any form or by any electronic, mechanical, or other means, now known or hereafter invented, including photocopying and recording, or in any information storage or retrieval system, without permission in writing from the publishers.

Trademark notice: Product or corporate names may be trademarks or registered trademarks, and are used only for identification and explanation without intent to infringe.

British Library Cataloguing-in-Publication Data
A catalogue record for this book is available from the British Library

Library of Congress Cataloging-in-Publication Data
Names: Delaney, Des, 1979- author.
Title: The lived experiences of Muslims in Europe : recognition, power and intersubjective dilemmas / Des Delaney.
Other titles: Recognition, power and intersubjective dilemmas
Description: Abingdon, Oxon ; New York, NY : Routledge, 2019. | Series: Routledge studies in social and political thought | Includes bibliographical references and index.
Identifiers: LCCN 2019024113 (print) | LCCN 2019024114 (ebook) | ISBN 9781138497825 (hardback) | ISBN 9781351017756 (ebook)
Subjects: LCSH: Muslims–Europe–Social conditions. | Recognition (Philosophy)–Social aspects–Europe. | Europe–Ethnic relations.
Classification: LCC D1056.2.M87 D45 2019 (print) |
LCC D1056.2.M87 (ebook) | DDC 305.6/97094–dc23
LC record available at https://lccn.loc.gov/2019024113
LC ebook record available at https://lccn.loc.gov/2019024114

ISBN: 978-1-138-49782-5 (hbk)
ISBN: 978-1-351-01775-6 (ebk)

Typeset in Times New Roman
by Taylor & Francis Books

Firstly, this book is dedicated to my wife and children. Their love and support made this book possible. Secondly, it is dedicated to the memory and influence of my parents, P.J. and Helen Delaney, may they Rest-In-Peace. I would also like to dedicate this book to my nieces and nephews, who bring a renewed sense of joy, happiness and hope for the future.

Contents

List of illustrations viii
Acknowledgements ix
List of Abbreviations x
Foreword xi

1 Introduction 1
2 Muslims in Europe: divergent perspectives 14
3 Recognition and power 43
4 Societal relations 72
5 Spiritual relations 114
6 Intergenerational relations 143
7 Resolving recognitive-power dilemmas 162
8 Conclusion 186

Appendix 197
Index 199

Illustrations

Figure

3.1 The movement of recognition   47

Tables

3.1 Honneth's structure of relations of recognition   48
3.2 The structure of relations of recognition (amended)   67
A.1 Pseudonyms and attributes of interviewees   197
A.2 Pseudonyms and attributes of discussants   198

Acknowledgements

This book was ten years in the making and it could not have been completed without the love and encouragement of friends and family as well as the advice and valued input of numerous colleagues. I would like to give a big thank you to my amazing wife for her incredible love and support over the years as well as a special thank you to Anne and Paschal Robinson and Mary Morris.

I would like to thank, in particular, Dr Cillian McBride, Dr Danielle Petherbridge, Dr Eoin O'Malley, Dr Michael Breen, Rob Delaney, Nicola Foxe, John Delaney, Joe Brennan, Juan Portillo, Eamonn McConnon, Ian Kelly, Míde Ní Súilleabháin and Peter McCrossan.

It is important to acknowledge that this research project would not have been possible without the valued input received from all the Muslim research participants. I would like to thank all the interviewees and discussants, who took the time to share their personal experiences. With immense gratitude and indebtedness, I would also like to thank Professor Axel Honneth for his prodigious and influential work on critical social theory, in particular, recognition theory, which greatly inspired and formed this research.

List of Abbreviations

Cit	Citizen
CSO	Central Statistics Office
DCU	Dublin City University
Den	Denizen
DIS	Dublin Islamic Society
ESS	European Security Strategy
EU	European Union
F	Female
FDG	Focused Discussion Group
FGM	Female Genital Mutilation
GDP	Gross Domestic Product
GIP	Information Group on Prisons
ICCI	Islamic Cultural Centre of Ireland
IFI	Islamic Foundation of Ireland
ICI	Immigrant Council of Ireland
IR	International Relations
IRCHSS	Irish Research Council for Humanities and Social Sciences
JMMA	Journal of Muslim Minority Affairs
LGBT+	Lesbian, Gay, Bisexual, Transsexual, plus
M	Male
NCCRI	National Consultative Committee on Racism and Interculturalism
RTE	Raidió Teilifís Éireann
SSI	Semi-Structured Interview
SfR	Struggle for Recognition
TG4	Teilifís na Gaeilge
UK	United Kingdom
US	United States of America
UCC	University College Cork
1st Gen	1st Generation
2nd Gen	2nd Generation

Foreword

The Lived Experiences of Muslims in Europe by Des Delaney is an important and timely book. At a historical juncture when Muslim populations are open to vilification and othering by anti-immigration prejudice and populist movements, and subject to the security apparatus of surveillant states throughout Europe, *The Lived Experiences of Muslims in Europe* provides an alternative narrative. It is a study that challenges the one-dimensional focus on a dangerous 'other' that needs to be policed in terms of surveillance and integrated in the face of putative discontent, risk to national life, and violence. For Delaney, this one-dimensional focus misrepresents and overlooks a much more complex state of affairs for European Muslim immigrant populations.

Through nuanced empirical investigation undertaken by way of interviews with Irish-Muslims (particularly second-generation immigrants), the book demonstrates that a complex and successful series of negotiations take place at the everyday level for Muslims living in Europe. The result is an emerging sense of Muslim-civic identity that sits in between two worlds simultaneously and combines a Muslim identity with a sense of civic pride and responsibility based on the norms of diversity, tolerance and recognition. The study makes clear that older arguments in European politics and public culture that posit a divide between either religious beliefs, attitudes and practices, on the one hand, or secular ones that indicate a divide between religion and modernity on the other, are no longer representative or operable.

In this spirit of a new way of looking at contemporary problems, Delaney's work sits within the tradition of Critical Theory and takes up its approach to social research with an emancipatory intent. As the German critical social theorist Jürgen Habermas has noted, Europe is facing a new series of experiences that have previously been confronted by New World settler societies to the extent that they can be described as 'post-secular' and are able to accommodate a diverse range of beliefs and practices in the context of modern norms of tolerance and recognition. Initially taking inspiration from Habermas' work on citizenship, the public sphere and debates about post-secularism, Delaney identifies a social space of negotiation between the normative ideals of a diverse and cosmopolitan Europe and what he terms the everyday recognition experiences of Muslims in European national contexts.

Notwithstanding the important currents taken from Habermas's work, the book's main research framework is informed by the critical theory of Axel Honneth. In the tradition of interdisciplinary critical social research, the study skilfully brings together Honneth's recognition theory with substantive evidence to provide a nuanced and sophisticated account of the lives of Muslims in Europe. As Honneth has noted, there are always struggles for recognition in a series of complex settings and *The Lived Experiences of Muslims in Europe* indicates that these struggles are not necessarily negative but can result in selective and positive reassessments of tradition and modernity that inform and reshape both. Delaney's study provides insights into the recognition dynamics that Muslims experience and create in the spheres of societal recognition, legal recognition, spiritual recognition and in the affective sphere of love, thereby demonstrating the ways in which recognition theory provides an important framework for qualitatively structured empirical social research.

Although informed by Honneth's recognition theory, Delaney also seeks to develop a more complex account of power that can account not only for systemic and hierarchical forms of power indicative of the security state, but action-theoretic ones that take the form of individual and collective action, which can contest and stand apart from those that are 'top-down' or imposed. Delaney's argument is that our understanding of this contemporary state of affairs – let alone recognition theory itself – needs to be augmented by a more complex notion of action-theoretic or constitutive power if we are to adequately explain the everyday experiences of Muslims in a post-secular Europe. Through his extensive interviews with Irish-Muslim youth, Delaney's work shows that this form of active subject-constituting power often occurs simultaneously within two normatively rich contexts: both religious and civic ones. Delaney's research reveals particularly salient insights in relation to the self-formation of Irish-European Muslim youth, through which they forge and embrace religion and personal relations, civic identity and citizenship, legal relations and civil society in their everyday lives.

The Lived Experiences of Muslims in Europe demonstrates that the experience of Muslim immigration should not be considered a challenge to European identity nor a challenge to Europe's survival. Rather, as a new generation contributes to European societies and participates in local schools, jobs and professions, as well as the broader associations and institutions of civil society, a new identity is being forged. This new identity is summed up by Delaney as a Muslim-civic one. Such a civic identity balances Muslim beliefs and practices with participation in forms of civil society that foster civic culture at the most basic everyday level in terms of forms of recognition, politeness and tolerance. Instead of civic norms disappearing in such contexts, this study reveals that they become stronger and less fragile. Muslim forms of civic identity enable immigrants not merely to cope with the exigencies of being outsiders, aliens or denizens, but of being new citizens in their adopted homelands, irrespective of whether they have experienced forced or voluntary exile, often due to war or civil unrest.

Delaney's qualitative research, through which the notion of Muslim-civic identity resonates, forms the most significant core of the book and results in important conclusions. This is particularly evident in discussions of education, women's participation, good citizenship, reconstructions of identity, and the recognitive-power dilemmas that Muslim immigrants constantly and productively negotiate. A significant finding of Delaney's research is that the narratives of his research participants show a resistance to existing integration policies in Europe that demand and promote either total assimilation, like France's secularism policy, or the separatism and isolationism of a particular form of 'multiculturalism' that can result in ghettoization. Rather, Delaney's research participants advocate for a form of integration without compromising or diluting their core identities. This is not simply a defensive strategy. Delaney's research participants indicate that Muslim immigrants want to keep and strengthen valued identities and, at the same time, productively interact, rather than simply integrate, with society more generally. In fact, an Islamic-civic identity better facilitates more open-ended interactions by mobilising broad-based recognitive forms, while protecting valued identities from dilution or even extinction. Delaney's book argues that the concerns and opinions of new immigrants should be taken into account if local, national or even pan-European policies of integration are to be effective. This entails that what appears as passive or even dormant lived, everyday experiences should become visible in ways that retrieve and advocate these at all policy levels throughout Europe. As Delaney's book suggests, the everyday narratives of Irish-Muslims can demonstrate to policy-makers how their intersubjective or recognitive needs could be met.

The Lived Experiences of Muslims in Europe demonstrates that against a background of civil unrest in the country of origin, civic life and culture is a fundamental part of a new life that remains open rather than closed and is receptive to new ways and new cultures within emerging immigrant societies. *The Lived Experiences of Muslims in Europe* is an important work that provides an alternative to the predominance of negative assessments and critiques of Europe's new immigration experiences.

Dr. Danielle Petherbridge,
School of Philosophy,
University College Dublin (UCD).
Dublin, May 2019

1 Introduction

Introduction

There is a common perception that democracy continuously moves in a positive direction towards higher forms of progress. However, as continuously highlighted by history and its events, this is not always the case and regressions are possible. A clear example of this is when unregulated capitalism faltered leading to the devastating 2008 economic crash and the Great Recession. As everyday people suffered, trust towards bankers, politicians as well as globalisation generally declined allowing extremist views to re-emerge, gain momentum in the mainstream and fill a political vacuum. Throughout the world, but particularly in the West, an alt-right politics has come to prominence. It is a politics that mirrors 1930s populism by similarly advocating for international isolationism, fervent nationalism, aggressive trading and security prioritisation. Examples of this politics in action include the surge in support and influence of far-right political parties throughout Europe, the divisive politics and mindset that led the United Kingdom (UK) to disconnect from the European Union (EU), and the increasingly hostile partisan politics played out between political actors and parties in the United States (US).

In domestic politics, to find majority support among the populace and garner legitimacy for divisive policies, alt-right leaders and administrations must still justify their actions. To do so, they utilise the power of fear. This fear works by connecting minorities to security risks, i.e. the risk of terrorism as well as economic and cultural harm. When the mechanism of fear is initiated to gain political capital, it is Muslims, legal and illegal immigrants, refugees and people viewed as different, who become the political pawns and scapegoats required to legitimise and sell ideological policy. Such regressions in democratic societies show the precariousness of belonging to a minority and being different from what is considered the dominant identity standard of a nation.

The use of the Muslim stereotype to produce fear and legitimise ideological policy is not a new phenomenon. Its origins date back as far as the time of the Crusades. However, in the 1980s, as alt-right ideas were being resown, there was a resurgence in the view that Islam and Muslims pose a potential security risk to Western societies. As the Cold War threat dissipated, a gap emerged in the manufacture and production of fear. With the communist enemy fading into history, a new threat was required. This led to Islam replacing the Soviet foe. The Islamic religion, its countries and people became a new enemy. Through political rhetoric and media propaganda with a simplistic focus on jihadism; Islam and Muslims generally became perceived as something to fear, a renewed justification for unpopular policies and security measures in the West. Then in 2001, the September 11 attacks occurred and the Muslim threat entered centre stage. Throughout the world, Muslims became suspect, potential terrorists. This blanket misrepresentation and misrecognition struck Muslims living in the West hard. The generalised stereotype linking Muslims to terrorism flowed through politics, media and academia. Research about Western Muslims adopted a defensive security lens that concentrated on studying issues related to Islamic terrorism, youth radicalisation as well as immigration and border control. The lived reality experienced by these Muslims was demoted in importance and left unacknowledged were the positive contributions Islam and Muslims make to Western culture and society. Through the adoption of this one-dimensional perspective, the humanity of Islam and Muslims became obscured and was replaced by a reified risk-assessment to safeguard Western civilisation. The fixation on security has had dire consequences for the 20 million plus Muslims living across Europe, whose lives and identities are tarnished, risk-assessed and seen as a potential threat to be contained. In essence, Muslims in Europe, and throughout the world, have become *Othered*. Jensen (2011) has clarified the concept of Othering and how it relates to

> discursive processes by which powerful groups, who may or may not make up a numerical majority, define subordinate groups into existence in a reductionist way, which ascribe problematic and/or inferior characteristics to these subordinate groups. Such discursive processes affirm the legitimacy and superiority of the powerful and condition identity formation among the subordinate.
>
> (Ibid., p.65)

Alongside this irrational fear which has crossed into the twenty-first century, large numbers of Muslim immigrants and refugees have left war-torn or poverty-stricken home countries and risked their lives to enter Europe in the hope of attaining a better life. These migrants bring with them religious and cultural ideas and practices that run counter to Christian-influenced traditions and secular ways of being in Europe. Consequently, such a mass influx of people into Europe exacerbates the already tense secular-religious divisions present on the continent as well as creating tensions in politics, culture and everyday life within and between European states. This complex situation raises pertinent questions relating to how best to integrate people of difference into European cultural life as well as how to ensure that European nation states do not regress back into an anti-immigrant and undemocratic nativist politics. To ease such tensions and create a cohesive pan-European society that benefits from harmonious co-operation and solidarity, it has been argued by pre-eminent European scholar, Jürgen Habermas, that it is imperative for Europe as a whole to overcome its secular-religious divisions so that people of difference and the constructed Other can be integrated inclusively into European democratic culture.

Habermas and bridging the secular-religious divide

To understand the European secular-religious divide the work of renowned German intellectual, Jürgen Habermas, is vital considering he has written extensively on the topic. Habermas' academic career spans sixty years. He is a leading figure in the critical theory tradition primarily concerned with emancipation through transformational processes in society and his writings have covered pertinent topics, including his celebrated work on the development and transformation of the European democratic public sphere (Habermas 1994), communicative action and discourse ethics (1984, 1987, 1990) as well as post-nationalism (2001). Although his work primarily tackles problems in his home country of Germany, its universal application has enabled such work to be transferred and applied by others to the wider European context.

In the 1990s, Habermas tackles legal and societal issues relating to constitutional law, citizenship, immigration and the EU supranational project. He understands the conflict surrounding immigration, in that his home country of Germany, once a country of emigration, has for a number of decades been going through a process of 'being painfully transformed into a nation of immigrants' (Habermas 1996, p.122). However, with that, Habermas also acknowledges that it is from the ranks of second and third generation immigrants that 'fellow countrymen and women are created' (Ibid., p.123). For conflict to be avoided, he argues that immigrants 'must now become citizens, in the legal sense as well as in the political-cultural sense of citizenship' (Ibid.). Running in contrast to the persistent perception in Germany that being a citizen is integrally part of an ethnic German identity and community, Habermas advocates for German citizens to be viewed as a legal community to create harmony and internal equality (Ibid., p.129). It is this critical analysis that leads to groundbreaking work advocating for 'the emancipatory protocols of a community under the rule of law' (Ibid., p.141). By reflecting on the disintegrating influence of nation states, he comes to identify the need for a federal and legally based European project in law in which citizens, devoid of nationalist tendencies, can proclaim their trust and loyalty. He calls this new citizenship-based allegiance, *constitutional patriotism*. The benefit of European citizens looking towards the constitution of a post-national entity is that it enables the balancing of 'ethnic tensions within a multicultural association of citizens' (Ibid., p.493) and thereby eases tensions and social conflict surrounding the issue of immigration into Europe. Habermas is keen to point out that nationalism's ability to embody in people a sense of extreme pre-political inherited loyalty and self-sacrifice is based on its appropriating the republican notion of citizenship, which does not see identity 'in ethnic or cultural commonalities but in the practise of citizens, who actively exercise their rights to participation and communication' (Ibid., p.495). Habermas advocates for the purity of republican citizenship to rise to the foreground and empower citizens of all creeds, races and religions to move beyond nationalism and its corresponding identifications (Ibid.). In the Habermasian argument, filling the void of the nation state will be a constitutional patriotism in which citizens pledge allegiance to the law of a supranational entity.

As stated above, Habermas is adamant that the political community 'depends primarily on legal principles anchored in the political culture and not in ethnical-cultural forma of life as a whole' (Ibid., p.514). It is this understanding of political community that informs how he views European immigration policy in an era defined by the mass movement of people towards economic and democratic centres. He advocates for European nations to adopt 'a liberal immigration policy' (Ibid.), meaning European societies should expect that immigrants 'engage in the political culture of their new home, [but] without necessarily abandoning the cultural life specific to their country of origin' (Ibid.). This implies that there should not be totalistic assimilation or isolation of immigrant cultures and identities. For Habermas, being political and participating as a citizen in the republican tradition does not by default imply that a person's ethnic or cultural affiliations be discarded and replaced by an assimilated version of the dominant culture and identity.

In his book *The Inclusion of the Other* (1998), Habermas delves further into the contradictions inherent between republican citizenship and the nationalist tendency to Other minorities. He once again advocates that 'the romantically inspired idea of the nation as an ethnically based community of culture and historical destiny' (Ibid., p.xxxvi) is an ideological conception paving the way for such nationalist states to 'support questionable attitudes' such as claiming a 'right to national self-determination, the corresponding hostility towards multiculturalism and a politics of human rights, and a distrust of the transfer of sovereign rights to supranational organisations' (Ibid.). Habermas describes how the nation state constituted itself. Nationalism or popular national self-consciousness enabled *subjects* to become *citizens* and, for the first time, enter into a collective belonging with strangers. Through this process, the nation state solved recurrent problems regarding legitimation and social integration (Ibid., p.111). However, in creating modern citizens, the ideology of national consciousness and belonging to the same people, crystallised into the notion of common ancestry, language and history, to the exclusion of others (Ibid.). Alternatively, Habermas sees another way to foster inclusiveness, which is made possible by the 'progressive extension of citizenship to the whole population' (Ibid., p.132). This provides secular legitimation and facilitates social integration through the abstract neutrality of law (Ibid.). Through this alternative democratic route, the Other can become citizen, and direct his or her patriotic feeling towards a European constitution.

However, by the late 2000s, Habermas had become disillusioned with a faltering European Union project (2009). A pan-European constitution did not materialise as nation states remained firmly in control, thereby exasperating the democratic deficit felt by ordinary European citizens towards the EU's large unwieldy technocratic bureaucracy. For an academic viewed as an ardent secularist and whose work is a continuation of the Enlightenment tradition, Habermas, in this period, makes concerted efforts to breakdown these assumptions by focusing specifically on unravelling the intricacies of the secular-religious divide in Europe. He does this by paying close attention to the communicative interaction between post-secular societies and Islam (Ibid., Chapter 5). The fact that Habermas' work begins to focus on Islam in Europe shows the importance of the debate surrounding the role of religion in a Europe commonly perceived as fully secularised. It also highlights the need for more in-depth analysis and understanding about this topic. Together with acknowledging the steady decline of religious adherence in Europe since the end of World War II, Habermas defines Europe today as moving from secularism towards a post-secular society. By this he means that the presence of Muslims and other faiths keeps religion consistently in the public sphere and tests the universal awareness that Europe is a secular society. He states in relation to this point:

> The Muslim next door ... forces the Christian citizens to confront the practise of a rival faith ... [and also] prompts a keener awareness among the secular citizens of the phenomenon of the public presence of religion.
> (Ibid., p.64)

A post-secular society is one in which the public role of religion retains its influence and relevance in public forums and the totalising secular mentality that Europe as a whole has moved beyond religion is tested. On this point, Habermas states:

> [In post-secular societies] religion retains a certain influence and relevance, while the secularistic certainty that religion will disappear everywhere in the world as modernisation accelerates is losing ground.
> (Ibid., p.65)

In this new context, Habermas argues that the 'end of religion' narrative, adopted by extreme secularist ideology, has been forced to change in European society due to three factors. Firstly, the 'media-generated perception' that global strife is primarily caused by religious turmoil. Secondly, the increased religious influence in national public spheres due to vibrant advocacy of established churches and by 'foreign religions' in the civil public sphere. And lastly, the entrance of immigrants into European societies invoking 'confessional schisms' and problems of integration throughout Europe (Ibid., pp.63–64). By uncovering the dogmatic falsehoods of totalising European secularism, Habermas proposes two questions to be debated by the citizenry of all European states in relation to the interaction between secularism and religion. Firstly, as members of a post-secular society, how do people define themselves and relate

6 *Introduction*

to others? Secondly, in pluralistic democratic societies that should enable the growth of new and varied cultures and religions, how can social relations remain cohesive and civil?

In line with his past work, Habermas answers such topical questions by turning to constitutionalism and the recognitive power of the universal citizen. In this regard, the evolution from the early modern secular state to the democratic constitutional state is pivotal. Whereas the early modern state eased religious tensions by creating a secular separation between Church and state, over time, the modern constitutional state has been able to 'guarantee its citizens equal freedom of religion only under the proviso that they no longer barricade themselves up within the self-enclosed lifeworlds of their religious communities' (Ibid., pp.67–68). This implies that the everyday practise of full participatory citizenship, under the umbrella of constitutional law, enables individuals and groups enclosed in religious communes to venture out of their protective communities into the expanse of civil society. For Habermas, the concept of the legal citizen is closely connected to recognition in the political community:

> All subcultures, whether religious or not, are expected to loosen their hold on their individual members so that the latter can recognise each other reciprocally as citizens in civil society, hence as members of one and the same political community. In their role as democratic citizens, they give themselves those laws which enable them as private citizens to preserve their identity in the context of their own particular culture and worldview and to respect each other.
>
> (Ibid., p.67)

As a form of recognition, toleration is another key component for Habermas. Not only should it be practised in the practical application and enacting of laws but also in daily life. In Habermas' understanding, toleration 'means that believers, members of other religions and non-believers must concede each other's right to observe convictions, practises and ways of life which they themselves reject' (Ibid., p.69). Essentially, toleration is a form of 'mutual recognition' that bypasses 'repugnant dissonances' (Ibid.). The above can only take place if the citizen is given primary reference as the glue that connects many differing identifications in society. To put this in the context of Muslims in Europe, a young Muslim may protect his different Islamic identity and yet utilise the sameness of his citizenship to interact in society on a level playing field with other citizens. Although Habermas' solution may be viewed as too utopian and idealistic, it is important to clarify that he remains aware that a transformation in political culture towards more inclusiveness is also required alongside the equal redistribution of material conditions, such as 'full integration in kindergartens, schools and universities in order to offset social disadvantage and equal access to the labour market' (Ibid.).

Overall, Habermas' work is commendable due to his adamant prognosis that the universal value of his critical theory does not impede but compliments the plurality and recognition of difference already present in Europe. As he declares himself, he is 'primarily concerned with the image of an inclusive society in which equal citizenship and cultural difference complement each other in the correct way' (Ibid.). However, in the German context in which he lives, he also acknowledges issues involving Muslim immigrants being barricaded in isolationist religious communities and not utilising the universal value of citizenship. He argues that as long as a substantial proportion of German citizens of Turkish origin and Muslim faith take their political orientation and identity from the home country rather than from Europe, the political impetus needed to expand and correct the values and perspectives of the dominant political culture will be lacking in the public sphere and at the ballet box. Without the inclusion of active minorities in civil society, two complimentary processes will not be able to develop. Namely, the opening-up of the political community to a difference-sensitive inclusion of foreign minority cultures, on the one hand, and on the other, the liberalisation of minority subcultures to a point where they internally encourage their individual members to exercise their equal rights as citizens and participate in the political life of the larger community (Ibid., p.70).

In conclusion to his discussion on Islam, Habermas stresses that all citizens, whether secular or religious, have something to learn from each other. Although an agnostic academic, he is concerned about extreme secularist tendencies that devalue religion and the repercussions this has for a post-secular society. This extreme secular ideology can be compared and paralleled to forms of religious fundamentalism. Notably, Habermas is against all extreme ideations taking hold in civil society. He hopes and normatively advocates for a civil society that strives to provide a good life for all through the concept of equal citizenship and not through the partisanship of 'hard' religious or secularist tendencies. He views 'changes in mentality' in civil society as the 'result of a learning process' (Ibid., p.75), which can be painful, but must be carried out by both religious and secular communities under the aegis of an ethics of citizenship embedded in constitutional democracy. Habermas is adamant that religious communities must align their religious principles to the secular order of democracy. For example, Muslim communities throughout Europe will need to develop a more flexible Islam that is faithful to the Islamic sources yet complementary to the European context. He states in relation to an Islamic reformation taking place in Europe:

> Religious communities must do more than merely conform to the constitutional order in a superficial way. They must appropriate the secular legitimation of constitutional principles under the premises of their own faith. It is a well-known fact that the Catholic Church embraced liberalism and democracy only with the Second Vatican Council in 1965. It is no different with the Protestant churches in Germany. Many Muslim communities still have to undergo this painful learning process. Certainly, the realisation is also dawning in the Islamic world that today a historical–hermeneutic approach to the teaching of the Qur'an is necessary. However, the discussion concerning a desirable Euro-Islam alerts us once again to the fact that it is

the religious communities themselves that will decide whether they can recognise their true faith in a reformed faith.

(Ibid.)

Alongside reforms by religious communities, the dominant powers in secular Europe must take part in this 'complementary learning process' (Ibid., p.76). To do so, Habermas suggests that European secularists must come to the realisation that the neutrality of the state against old and new religions does not also necessitate the secularisation of the democratic public sphere. Therefore, individuals and groups belonging to religious communities have an active and political role to play in civil societies throughout the European landscape and should not be tied to the private sphere as demanded by advocates of laicism (Habermas 2011, pp.23–24). Habermas stresses that deliberative democracy 'is as much a product of the public use of reason on the part of *religious* citizens as on that of *non-religious* citizens' (Ibid., p.24). In his opinion (2009), all the constitutional state's 'enforceable legal norms must be capable of being formulated and publicly justified in a language intelligible to all citizens' (2009, p.76). By doing this, the neutral state maintains a non-biased linguistic approach to all religions, yet at the same time, it 'does not speak against the permissibility of religious utterances within the political public sphere' (Ibid.). This is providing that a separation remains between the institutions and organs of the state and those of religious communities. In line with Rawls, Habermas is adamant that 'the secularisation of the state is not the same as the secularisation of society' (2011, p.23) and he calls on secularists in the European sphere to give respect and toleration, that is to say, recognition, to religious groups in the democratic public sphere. Stressing the importance of the democratic citizen, the balancing act proposed by Habermas in civil society is based on the mutual recognition of common citizenship and this presents the following advice for secular citizens living in a post-secular environment:

> Secular citizens who encounter their fellow [religious] citizens with the reservation that the latter cannot be taken seriously as modern contemporaries because of their religious mindset would regress to the level of a mere modus vivendi and abandon the basis of mutual recognition constitutive for shared citizenship. Secular citizens should not exclude a fortiori that even religious utterances may have semantic contents and convert personal intuitions capable of being translated and introduced into secular discourse. Thus, if all is to go well, each side must accept an interpretation of the relation between faith and knowledge from its own perspective, which enables them to live together in a self-reflective manner.
>
> (Ibid., p.76)

Having experienced Nazi ideology and conflict as well as witnessing firsthand the destruction of his home country during World War II, Habermas is keenly aware of how Europe's democratic progress carries the potential to regress into fervent and isolating nationalism. He is aware that in such contexts, the person who is Othered, who differs from the dominant identity standard, becomes a potential target and victim of ideological culture. With this in mind, Habermas has theorised a solution that involves the development of a pan-European legal framework that accentuates the participatory role of the citizen. This alternative solution shows how nationalist and ethno-cultural tension and the secular-religious divide can be eased and traversed. It thus enables differing people to come together through the practice of their universal civic identities and by projecting loyalty and patriotism to an abstract European constitution. Certainly, with the rise of populist politics and immigration being a contested political issue, Habermas' civic and democratic solution to bridging the secular-religious divide and integration issues still provides valuable insights and a visionary model that can aid Europe in reaching a brighter more cohesive culture.

The aim of the research

The work of Habermas on the secular-religious divide in Europe highlights issues related to integration and how people from differing cultures and identities can practise better communication and recognition towards each other in a secular European environment. Such interaction is needed for Europe to be cohesive, cosmopolitan and to overcome the cultural hangovers of the past. With the above in mind, pertinent questions come to the fore that may indicate if we are any closer to realising Habermas' ideal of civic integration. Have any bridges been built by non-Muslims and Muslims that cross the secular-religious divide in Europe? What are the everyday recognition and integration experiences of Muslim individuals and groups in the European context and are these experiences perceived in positive or negative terms? If perceived negatively, what impact does this have on Muslim identity and integration? And are Muslims utilising citizenship and a civic identity to aid recognition and integration processes in Europe.

When taking the above into account, a research gap emerges centring around the recognition experiences of Muslims in Europe. The aim of this study is to empirically expand Habermas' reflections on the themes of recognition and intersubjectivity by unearthing new knowledge about Muslim experiences in Europe. The research in this book sets out to understand how Muslims in Europe perceive the everyday *recognition order*. As Zurn (2015) states, a recognition order is the 'reigning set of interpretations of the specific principles that society uses to accord respect and esteem' (p.133). By taking on and fulfilling this task, this research aims to excavate new knowledge in relation to the dynamics surrounding recognition relations and a number of related integration themes such as intersubjective communication, identity, solidarity and power.

This is an interdisciplinary study, the first of its kind, that combines and synthesises critical social theory and empirical investigation to better understand Muslim recognition experiences. Surprisingly, the theme of recognition is an area of study absent from the European Muslim studies literature, despite its importance to Muslim individuals and communities. The research is framed and highly influenced by Axel Honneth's (1995) theory of the Struggle for Recognition, which philosophically explores the grounded universal dynamics of recognition in multiple spheres of everyday life, i.e. in the sphere of love, legal respect and social esteem. In line with Honneth's work and critical social theory more generally, this study advocates and enacts an emancipatory intent. The theory is empirically complemented by the case study of Ireland in which narrative sociology is deployed to explore everyday Muslim recognition experiences in different social spheres. It is important to emphasise that this book is not solely about Muslim experiences in Ireland by the fact that it focuses on the universal dynamics of recognition, which ensures that the findings of the case study translate to the wider European context. Furthermore, this research is unique. By combining recognition theory and empirical sociology to unearth new knowledge about Muslim experiences in Europe, it presents the first extensive study representing *Applied Recognition Theory*.

But why study recognition? It can be said that uncovering new knowledge about these relations is important for European society generally in that it unearths a more nuanced understanding about the experiences and interactions between the secular and the religious in Europe. It develops a better insight into integration processes that emerge from below and generates a fuller appreciation of how recognition and respect matter in everyday social life, especially in foreseeing and limiting the rise of suffering and conflict. Furthermore, recognition dynamics indicate the degree of democratic freedom and non-domination available, which indicates the degree to which individuals and groups are able *to be* themselves in multiple spheres of life. By linking the theme of recognition with an empirical investigation of everyday life, this study gives a more rounded account of the experiences of Muslims in Europe and openly challenges the dominant security paradigm that narrowly views Muslims through the lens of political extremism. With the above in mind, the aim of the research is:

> To gain a detailed holistic understanding of the universal recognition relations experienced by Muslims in the Irish-European context in three distinct spheres of everyday interaction, and by doing so, to develop and unearth knowledge that can be translated back to the wider European context. Taking everyday Muslim perspectives seriously as a means to uncover new knowledge, the spheres of interaction to be examined are:
>
> - relations to the non-Muslim community when interacting as particular individuals in the wider social sphere of public interaction and as citizens in the legal sphere
> - relations to an abstract spiritual deity
> - and relations between the first and second generations in the Muslim community with particular attention on familial and communal interactions.

Empirical methodology

The research in this book is qualitative and relies on empirical narrative sociology. This methodology involved the design, collection and analysis of narratives about recognition experiences in different social spheres that provide a more nuanced and holistic understanding of everyday Muslim life in the Irish-European context.

The fieldwork was collected over a period of twenty-nine months between the years 2011 and 2013. Firstly, sixteen preliminary pilot interviews were conducted. Although not presented in this study, these informal interviews focused the research onto the prominent theme of recognition. With the research theme identified, Honneth's theory of recognition was fully examined and utilised to frame the questions asked of the research participants in further qualitative data collection stages. The empirical narratives presented in this study were attained through the conduction of two further data collection stages involving twenty-five formal semi-structured interviews (SSIs) followed by four focused discussion groups (FDGs) comprising thirty-two participants. In total, this study presents the viewpoints of fifty-seven research participants out of a total of seventy-three.

After the data collection was completed, the narratives were transcribed and reflectively analysed using qualitative data analysis software, NVivo. This software enabled effective management and extensive iterative coding of large volumes of narrative data, while simultaneously, protecting the integrity of the source material. Each interview and focused discussion group could be continuously coded leaving the original source material intact. Each source document was extensively free-coded into nodes based on observable themes and related small stories. These are presented in the empirical chapters in the form of *streams of narrative*, which mix similar viewpoints from both the interviews and focused discussion groups. Just as Walter Benjamin, an early member of the Frankfurt school, had once hoped to write a book solely based on quotations so as to reach an objective higher reality (Jay 1973, p.200), the narrative technique used in this book aims to combine subjective narratives together to create a central perception of truth. With that said, it is important to clarify that such narratives are not taken as totalising truths but are presented as perceptions of experience, which have the capacity to give a variety of reflective insights into the everyday life of individuals and groups, who belong to a minority religious community in Europe.

Of note is that the research narratives are presented in this book verbatim. Pseudonyms have been used in place of the real names of the research participants to ensure privacy and confidentiality. Furthermore, in the main text of the empirical chapters, relevant attributes for each participant are stated. For example, Abdul (1st Gen, M, Cit, FDG), identifies a 1st generation male, who is an Irish citizen that participated in a focused discussion group. Likewise, Isra (2nd Gen, F, Den, SSI), identifies a 2nd generation female, who is a denizen or long-term resident that took part in a semi-structured interview. Throughout the empirical chapters, participants from the semi-structured interviews are referred to as *interviewees*

12   *Introduction*

and the participants of the focused discussion groups are referred to as *discussants*. Please refer to the Appendix for tables listing the pseudonyms and attributes of each research participant.

Structure of the book

This book comprises eight chapters. After this introduction, Chapter 2 investigates how Muslims are viewed and represented in the European academic literature. It does so by identifying and critically assessing two opposing paradigms, that is, the security perspective alongside the advocacy and participatory perspective. These two paradigmatic views have come to define and permeate the research about Muslims in Europe. This chapter then outlines the characteristics and development of the Muslim community in the Irish case study and constructively critiques the research output emanating from the nascent field of Irish Muslim studies.

Chapter 3 examines Axel Honneth's theory of recognition, which has deeply influenced and framed this study. After a critique of Charles Taylor's recognition model, this chapter then outlines in detail Honneth's structured multi-dimensional typology of recognition. Such an exploration highlights the theory's core insights, advantages and development over time. The chapter then explores the varying criticisms directed towards Honneth's theory and pinpoints the ongoing and unresolved concerns in relation to the role and formation of power.

Chapters 4 to 6 are the empirical chapters of this study that focus on the Irish case study and, through a *streams of narrative* technique, recount the everyday recognition experiences of Muslims. All three empirical chapters identify forms of negative recognition in various interactive social spheres and assess its impact upon Muslim individuals and groups. In particular, Chapter 4 explores how Muslims relate to the non-Muslim community they interact with daily. This chapter identifies forms of misrecognition in the wider sphere of social interaction and in the legal sphere of citizenship. Chapter 5 focuses on developing a deeper empirical understanding of spiritual recognition, particularly in relation to how religious practise and identity offers support and regulates everyday action. Chapter 6 explores intergenerational relations in terms of how 1st and 2nd generation Muslims critically perceive and relate to each other. It is important to note that all of the empirical chapters offer insights into the universality of intersubjective relations, which can be transposed to the European context, especially in terms of identifying prevalent social dilemmas in everyday interaction, the impact and influence of differing forms of power in multiple social spheres as well as gaining a comprehensive and grounded understanding of identity construction, formation and maintenance.

Chapter 7 is a discussion chapter that examines the most pertinent points and findings that emerge from this philosophical-empirical study. This chapter concisely combines the information from preceding chapters into a cohesive picture by exploring what the research has unearthed and by assessing the relationship that exists between recognition and power.

Introduction 13

Chapter 8 concludes the book by positioning this study in the context of the rise of populist politics and assessing the continuing role and influence of critical social theory. The chapter then briefly summarises the new knowledge and understandings unearthed by this study. It also clarifies how this research contributes to the existing philosophical and Muslim Studies literature as well as giving a general assessment of the influence this study has on integration policymakers and policy in Europe. Lastly, recommendations for future research are listed and the book ends with some concluding remarks befitting the overarching insights of the research.

References

Habermas, Jürgan. 1984 [1981]. *The Theory of Communicative Action, Volume 1: Reason and Rationalisation of Society.* Boston, MA: Beacon Press.
Habermas, Jürgan. 1987 [1985]. *The Theory of Communicative Action, Volume 2: Lifeworld and System: A Critique of Functionalist Reason.* Boston, MA: Beacon Press.
Habermas, Jürgan. 1990. *Moral Consciousness and Communicative Action.* Cambridge: Polity Press.
Habermas, Jürgan. 1994 [1962]. *The Structural Transformation of the Public Sphere.* Cambridge: Polity Press.
Habermas, Jürgan. 1996. *Between Facts and Norms.* Cambridge: Polity Press.
Habermas, Jürgan. 1998. *The Inclusion of the Other: Studies in Political Theory.* Cambridge: Polity Press.
Habermas, Jürgan 2001. *The Postnational Constellation: Political Essays.* Cambridge: Polity Press.
Habermas, Jürgan. 2009. *Europe: The Faltering Project.* Cambridge: Polity Press.
Habermas, Jürgan. What is meant by a 'post secular society'? A discussion on Islam in Europe. Chapter 5, IN: Habermas, J. 2009. *Europe: The Faltering Project.* Cambridge: Polity Press.
Habermas, Jürgan. 'The political': The rational meaning of a questionable inheritance of political theology. Chapter 1, IN: Mendieta, E. and Vanantwerpen, J. (eds.). 2011. *The Power of Religion in the Public Sphere.* Colombia: Colombia University Press.
Honneth, Axel. 1995 [1992]. *The Struggle for Recognition: The Moral Grammar of Social Conflicts.* Cambridge: Polity Press.
Jay, Martin. 1973. *The Dialectical Imagination.* Oakland, CA: University of California Press.
Jensen, Sune Qvotrup. 2011. Othering, identity formation and agency. *Qualitative Studies.* 2(2), pp.63–78.
Zurn, Christopher F. 2015. *Axel Honneth: A Critical Theory of the Social.* Cambridge: Polity Press.

2 Muslims in Europe: divergent perspectives

Introduction

In the 1950s, after the catastrophe of World War II that devastated much of Europe, many European countries replenished stocks of working individuals by facilitating mass emigration from former colonies. Britain looked towards India, Pakistan and the West Indies, France enticed allied war veterans from Algeria, and West Germany introduced a guest worker program to ensure a steady flow of temporary Turkish workers into its refurbished industrial economy. The majority of transnational migrants who entered Europe during this time, originated from postcolonial territories that had large Muslim populations. For the first time in European history, large numbers of Muslim immigrants were accepted into Europe for the purpose of labour. Although the filling of these quotas was viewed as meeting a short-term goal, such migratory flows had long-term and permanent repercussions for European nation states, who entered into a new period of pluralistic development, which brought with it the need for significant social and cultural change.

As a consequence of these immigration policies, European nation states have had to come to terms with the permanent pluralistic transformations that have become rooted in their societies. In terms of Islamic immigrants, such issues have centred upon how to integrate and communicate with Muslim communities, how to promote participation of these communities in local and national politics, as well as how to safeguard society against the ills of Islamic fundamentalism and youth radicalisation.

Since the 1970s, academics in Europe have proposed solutions to key integration issues relating to isolation, participation and security. This research tends to fall into two paradigmatic perspectives. On the one hand, there are those who take an advocacy and participatory perspective and aim their sociological work towards learning and understanding more about Muslim communities and their everyday experiences. This work aims to enhance civic society by advocating for mutual interaction. It looks beyond stereotypes and generalisations. Such research takes an emancipatory view by advocating for Muslim communities and wider society to interact, communicate and participate together to build trust and meet shared societal goals. On the other hand, since the late 1980s, with the deepening of conservatism and growth of Islamic terrorism, there is another identifiable paradigm in the literature, the security perspective, which narrowly focuses on the threat posed by global Islamic extremism and the risk of Muslims being radicalised into performing terrorist actions in Europe. This perspective aims to protect European society but can easily slip into overprotection that ends up viewing the Muslim as the reified Other and curbing democratic freedoms. Muslim individuals and communities in Europe become suspect, something to be tracked, risk-assessed and contained. When this ideological perspective becomes all-encompassing, it tarnishes how different individuals and communities are recognised.

The security perspective

With the withdrawal of Soviet forces from Afghanistan in 1988 and the return of trained Muslim jihadists to their countries of origin, Western academia, particularly the field of International Relations (IR), focused its attention on the rise of Islamic militant fundamentalism and political Islam. The impact of the Persian Gulf War in 1990 and the Bosnian war in 1992 concentrated attention on the rise of Islamic fundamentalism. Key texts published in this period include Esposito's (1992) account of the characteristics of Islamic fundamentalism and its associated myths, Fukuyama's (1992) argument that humankind has reached the pinnacle of political evolution in a liberal democratic model followed by Huntington's (1996) positivist metatheory, which proposed that the ideological contrasts between socialism and capitalism ended with the conclusion of the Cold War and humanity has entered the ultimate Clash of Civilisations between Christian-West and Islamic-East. Huntington suggests that 'in the post-Cold War world, the most important distinctions among people are not ideological, political and economic ... [but] cultural' (Ibid., p.21). He places significant emphasis on the religio-cultural clash between the predominantly Muslim people of the East and Christian people of the West. It is suggested that where these two groups live beside each other, in border areas, conflict has often occurred or is expected to continue more frequently into the future. A good example of a civilisational faultline would be the Balkan region and the disintegration of Yugoslavia. Huntington identifies the growth and revival of Islam, especially among the youth, by stating that 'Muslims in massive numbers ... [are] turning toward Islam as a source of identity, meaning, stability, legitimacy, development, power and hope' (Ibid., p.109). However, he is also highly sceptical and pessimistic about any positive interaction between the two main religio-cultural civilisations, which have strong historical geopolitical demarcations:

> The underlying problem for the West is not Islamic fundamentalism. It is Islam, a different civilisation, whose people are convinced of the superiority of their culture and are obsessed with the inferiority of their power.
> (Ibid., p.217)

16 *Muslims in Europe: divergent perspectives*

Since the 1990s, influenced by Huntington's hypothesis, numerous academic works have given considerable attention to Islamic fundamentalism and the development of political Islam in the Middle East and around the world (Maddy-Weitzmann and Inbar 1997, Esposito 1997, Gerges 1999). The 9/11 attacks on the US together with numerous attacks on various European cities over the last fifteen years, have prompted governing powers, security services and academic research institutes to focus and fund research on Islamic fundamentalism and political Islam so as to learn more about the threat of such terrorist networks. This has resulted in a plethora of studies on terrorism, its associated fundamentalist ideology, and in a broad sense, political Islam. (Kepel 2002, Gunaratna 2002, Tibi 2002, Fuller 2003, Hafez 2003, Milton-Edwards 2004, Delong-Bas 2004, Burgat 2008, Varady 2008, Bawer 2010, Kassam and Farage 2017, Kepel and Jardin 2017).

The continuation of terrorist attacks on European cities has seen a staggering growth in research and publications that follow the security perspective and explore European security issues, Islamic fundamentalism and youth radicalisation (Gartner and Cuthbertson 2005, Bawer 2006, Amghar, Boubekeur and Emerson 2007, Jones 2007, Deliso 2007, Coolsaet 2008, Pargeter 2008, Rabasa and Benard 2014, Nesser 2018). For example, Gartner and Cuthbertson (2005) focus on the common intergovernmental European Security Strategy (ESS), which 'seeks to improve EU coherence in foreign and security policy' and to prevent further terrorist attacks in Europe (p.23). In the same anthology, Steinhausler (2005, p.63) stresses the general security concerns that exist in modern Europe, a continent that has transformed significantly, in demographic terms, through large scale transnational migration. His risk assessment recommends improvements in intelligence gathering, physical protection of sensitive sites, as well as research and development in technical countermeasures. Pargeter (2008) and Coolsaet (2008) provide accounts of the continuing rise of Islamic fundamentalism, particularly among the younger Muslim generations residing in European states. As Pargeter states:

> Traditions and cultural norms imported from the Islamic world are often still applied even within the second and third generation ... Isolation and marginalisation within Europe and the individual's response to Western society are repeatedly cited as the main drivers behind the radicalisation process.
> (Pargeter 2008, p.109 and p.206)

For example, to tackle the issue of terrorism and youth radicalisation in the UK, the British government set up the Prevent programme, which identifies and intervenes in the lives of immigrants, mostly Muslim children and teenagers, who show tendencies towards radicalisation. This programme has been highly criticised by human rights advocates due to its reliance on legislation requiring public servants (in education, health and local communities) to report on children and by the fact that it targets pre-criminal extremism, enabling the undemocratic and unjustified security surveillance of everyday thought and action. At the other end of the spectrum in relation to IR, this securicrat perspective has even widened its remit to concentrate on securitising development aid to Muslim home countries. As McConnon (2018) has shown, Western governments, for example, the US, the UK and Canada have promoted close co-operation between security and development actors as a risk management strategy to prevent, at source, the growth of Islamic fundamentalism and radicalisation that could potentially blow back upon developed countries.

Although development aid and actions can be directed, the Internet and its impact is much harder to regulate and control. With the advent and pervasiveness of social media, large research funding grants have been issued to investigate violent online political extremism, with a particular focus on jihadi terrorism and Muslim youth radicalisation. The VOX-Pol research network (Gill, Corner, Thornton and Conway 2015, Conway and Dillon 2016, Mahlouly and Winter 2018), based at Dublin City University (DCU), is a prime example of a well-funded European Union research project aiming to gather information and analyse how extremist ideology is disseminated online. Although such research programmes are important for learning more about extremist ideologies and how they are disseminated by a small minority of anonymised people online, there is the serious concern that the lives, actions and viewpoints of everyday civic people, particularly those in Muslim communities, become overshadowed by sensationalism and the fetishisation of terrorism. Paradoxically, such projects give undeserving attention and recognition to extremist ideology and violent action rather than striving to learn more about the grounded everyday sociological experiences and civic actions of Muslim individuals and communities in the European context.

Spurred on by the fear instilled by ongoing terrorist attacks in Europe, the security perspective has become pervasive and well-funded. Although its focus is on the containment of ideologies and actions of a minority, it has come to view all Muslim communities as a possible security threat or *suspect* community to be contained (Hickman, Thomas, Silvestri and Nickels 2011). Reflecting the experience of other minorities in different European contexts, like the Jews and Irish, Muslims have become the go-to suspects, the Other. It can be argued that the majority of academic accounts have to a large extent been too narrowly concerned with viewing Muslims in Europe through the lens of political extremism. As a consequence, the everyday is an aspect of Muslim life in Europe commonly lost from sight when the security lens is active.

With that said, not all research has taken on the security perspective. There is sociological work that takes a more nuanced approach by aiming to understand the grounded everyday experiences of Muslim individuals and communities in Europe. Unlike the security perspective, which distances itself from the reality of Muslim everyday life in Europe, the advocacy and participatory perspective advocates for an understanding of these actualities and reflects upon the positives of civic participation. This emancipatory paradigm, rooted in the critical social theory tradition, unearths new knowledge by researching the complexities of everyday intersubjective interaction, processes of integration, and the struggle to be oneself in society.

The advocacy and participatory perspective

In opposition to the security perspective, which tends to fall into the trap of rigidly viewing Muslims in Europe as potential threats to the status quo of European life, another research approach has been identified that aims to learn more about everyday Muslim life in Europe. This is the advocacy and participatory paradigm, which was pioneered by a sociologist of Pakistani origin, Muhammad Anwar (1979, 1985, 1994, 1998, 2008, 2009), who dealt specifically with the everyday experiences of the growing number of Pakistani immigrants in the UK. Anwar produced important work that focused on the everyday experiences and evolution of this community from its state-sponsored migratory origins from the Kashmir region to detailing how these migrants gained access to British society through employment, education or participating in the political system. Anwar exposed the *Myth of Return* (1979) by bringing into sight issues of discrimination and elaborating on how the biraderi-kinship system aided political mobilisation and challenged far-right extremism. In his later work, he acknowledged the growing role of Islamic identity, particularly after the Rushdie affair. Alongside highlighting the issues faced by ethno-Muslim communities in the UK, he also stressed that the plight of Muslims in mainland Europe was, in all likelihood, worse, given that a considerable number of these people lacked legal recognition as citizens:

> Many Muslims face multiple discriminations as they belong to ethnic groups as well as to a religious group. Second, if British Muslims as British citizens face all the issues ... then what is the situation of Muslims in the rest of Western Europe where a vast majority of them are not yet citizens of their home countries of residence. All the available evidence shows that their legal and socio-economic situation is generally worse compared to British Muslims. The recent debate about wearing the headscarf by Muslim girls in French state schools is a good example in this context.
> (Anwar 2008, pp.134–135)

The aim of the advocacy and participatory research paradigm is to develop a holistic understanding of the everyday experiences of Muslim populations in Europe. Although this form of research does analyse security issues, such as radicalisation and integration, overall the work tends to take an emancipatory position and stands in stark contrast to the neorealist security-orientated agenda. It aligns with critical social theory by striving to understand Muslim populations in their everyday relationships and interactions. By extracting the negative and positive aspects of this relationship, common themes arise in the literature, such as detailing experiences of discrimination and Islamophobia, access to education and the formation of Islamic schools, access to employment and social service provisions, and the development of political participation and community representation.

Some of the literature takes a broad perspective. Goody (2004) explores the positive historical influence of interactions between Eastern Islam and the Western European continent. Hellyer (2009) attempts to understand the Muslim experience at a higher European level and defines Muslim populations in Europe as 'Othered' (p.3). He states that with increasing terrorist attacks, the 'idea of a dangerous Muslim Other [has] become ever more entrenched' (Ibid.) but that maintaining such a conception also has long-term ramifications for 'the development of European civilisation and, consequently, [for] European identity' (Ibid., p.177). Hellyer is highly critical of the exploitation of the Muslim Other for nationalist political gain:

> The rise of the extreme right-wing, whether in Holland or in Britain, may use the Muslim communities as scapegoats for various issues, but the issue at the root of their collective obsession is not really the 'Muslim Other'. Rather, just as in many situations where the 'Other' is emphasised, the real issue is the 'us', a concept of 'Self', perceived as withering and emaciating before European eyes. European identity has been challenged on several fundamental levels in the last fifty-years and, as yet, the ambiguity has not been clarified.
>
> (Ibid., p.179)

Other work is state-centric by dedicating itself to understanding Muslim populations living and residing in specific European states. This approach enables academics to explore the relationships that Muslim populations have within a particular nation state and then cross-compare against experiences in other European states (Nielsen 1999, 2004, 2013, Shadid and von Koningsveld 1996a, 1996b, Hunter 2002, Klausen 2005). Of note is that extensive priority and research focus has been given to larger core European states (or a combination of these) such as France (Kepel 1997), Great Britain and Germany (Fetzer and Soper 2005) that have large Muslim populations. The experiences of Muslim populations residing in the main cities of these states have also been explored in detail (Bemelmans and Freitas 2001, Open Society Institute 2009). Research is beginning to refocus its attention to the experiences of minority Muslim populations residing in peripheral European states, which share common characteristics such as a history of colonialism and emigration as well as the relatively late immigration of Muslims into these regions. Despite academic research considering the Muslim populations in these areas too small to be worthy of attention, it is becoming acknowledged that these marginal states are in a position to learn from the past mistakes of the core countries and, considering their characteristics, they also carry the potential to innovate in the area of integration and the treatment of long-term residents and refugees (Larsson and Sander 2007, Martikainen, Mapril, and Khan 2019).

With the continuation of civil strife in the Middle East and parts of Africa (e.g. in Libya, Syria, Iraq and Sudan) research has also taken an interest in the correlation between such conflicts and the rise of Islamic radicalisation among a small proportion of European Muslim youth, who have or intend to leave Europe to participate in conflicts abroad. In the advocacy and participatory paradigm, research has aimed to explore how the second generation Muslim youth in Europe are negotiating identity issues (Phalet, Fleischmann and Stojčić 2012). Although such issues may seem to be strongly positioned in the remit of the security paradigm, two studies by Tariq Ramadan and Konrad Pędziwiatr give a nuanced insight and understanding in relation to Muslim youth identity issues and how such complex dynamics relate to religion, citizenship and cultural experience.

Tariq Ramadan's (1999) theoretical advocations in his seminal book, *To be a European Muslim*, have opened up new ways to view the experience of Muslim youth in Europe and how such youth will develop into the future. He examines how the identity of the younger Muslim generation is transforming its relationship to the Islamic religion and citizenship. He advocates that Muslim youth should return to the Islamic sources, i.e. the Qur'an and the Sunna to contextualise and interpret Islam for a European environment. He determines that such action will be aided by the newly revived concept of *ijtihad* (critical reasoning to resolve an issue when the Islamic sources are silent), which is gaining more traction among various Islamic scholars, who regulate Islamic jurisprudence (Ibid., p.43). In other words, Ramadan is proclaiming that Islam is not a rigid and immutable system of belief that is entrenched in time but one that can be flexibly interpreted for a European context, without compromising the religion in terms of creating excessive innovation. He is highly critical of the Othering of Muslims in Europe (Ibid., p.113) as well as catch-22 identity options offered to Muslim youth by secular European societies to either assimilate or isolate themselves. For Ramadan, Muslim youth are living 'in Europe [yet] out of Europe' (Ibid., p.188).

To counter the above, Ramadan advocates for more participation among second generation Muslim youth, especially the educated, who he determines have the ability to find a balance between the interpretation and practice of a salient Islamic identity and European citizenship. Through such civic participation, Muslim youth can develop confidence, respect and esteem as citizens in the European polity by contributing to the wider social sphere, and at the same time, hold onto and enhance their Islamic identities. As Ramadan states on the second generation experience in Europe:

> The youth are coming back to an Islam which is purified from the accidents of its traditional teaching. For the more educated, it is no more an Islam of Moroccan, Algerian or Pakistani countryside but a return to the basics of Islamic teaching through an immediate contact with the sources, Qur'an and the Sunna. This is a fundamental development for it sets the seal on the break-up between, on the one hand, Islam, and its actualisation

in North Africa or Asia and, on the other, the way it should be thought, adapted and lived in the West.

(Ibid., p.115)

The second study of importance relates to Konrad Pędziwiatr's (2010) sociological cross-comparative study of young educated Muslim elites in London and Brussels, which empirically confirms Ramadan's theoretical advocations. Through in-depth interviews, this research identifies narrative evidence that young educated Muslims in both cities, aged between 18 and 36, are fusing their salient Islamic identities with the notion of participatory civicness. This process of synthesising identity and action aims to find a middle ground between maintaining a salient Islamic identity and enabling wider societal civic participation. Pędziwiatr identifies the distinct advantage Muslim youth have over their immigrant parents in terms of having full citizenship and utilising their social capital comprising 'tacit knowledge, competences and taken-for-granted assumptions' (Ibid., p.10) that enable them to actively use their citizenship to participate in and change the culture of society.

By socially engaging, these young Muslims become key players in the representation of their identities to society. Pędziwiatr determines that these young Muslims have taken on the societal role of 'new religious brokers' (Ibid., pp.17–20 and pp.412–417). In other words, the second generation are developing what Pędziwiatr calls 'Muslim civicness' in that they are in the process of defining a new identity, a 'high Islam', that is based around active citizenship as well as a perceived to be normative Islamic faith and identity that challenges securitised notions of Muslims as suspect. In contrast to this Islamic-civic identity, Pędziwiatr associates anti-nationalist and geopolitical forms of radical Islamist identity with the term 'uncompromising Muslim'. For Muslim youth, the Islamic-civic conception of identity transforms existing power structures by challenging the social norms that delineate outsiders from the established in society and in so doing challenges ethno-cultural influences and the 'low Islam' emanating from the immigrant first generation (Ibid., pp.42–45). In terms of participation, Pędziwiatr suggests that the process of rediscovering and practising the Islamic religion, particularly during the teenage years or as adults in third-level education, ensures that young Muslims attain a more participatory aspect to their identity. Pędziwiatr states the following in relation the authority of the Islamic sources and how it positively engages civic agency:

> by subjecting themselves to [the authority of] Islam they have not only become much more assertive religious subjects, but also societal subjects. In other words, subjecting themselves to the religious authority did not deprive them of agency, but on the contrary, [it] stimulated it positively. Islam, in their case, did not constitute a barrier for interactions with non-Muslim Belgians and Britons, but the opposite of it: it encouraged and facilitated such interactions ...Their practise of Islam enabled them

to generate both bonding and bridging social capital [to the wider societal sphere].

(Ibid., p.397)

Pędziwiatr reaffirms the challenges that await young European Muslims, who are determined to self-invent and develop their civic identities. By enhancing their religious identity through practise they are enabling a more potent struggle against stigmatising and stereotypical caricatures of Islam and Muslims still widely prevalent across Europe:

> The improvement of the situation of the Muslim communities in Europe will depend not only on the effective struggle against at least some of the forms of exclusion and disadvantage faced by the members of these communities, but also on the results of the Muslims' efforts to reinvent and position themselves as citizens and full members of the European polities. The latter objective is particularly difficult to attain. Before European Muslims achieve this goal they will need to work tirelessly to reconstruct popular images, assumptions and representations of their religion and their communities within wider societies.
>
> (Ibid., p.426)

It has been identified that the field of European Muslim studies, in broad terms, tends to follow two paradigmatic perspectives, i.e. a security or an advocacy and participatory approach. Fuelled by a realist agenda and by sporadic Islamic attacks in various European cities, the security paradigm's prime focus is on researching the continuing War on Terror, tracking the social media propaganda of jihadi groups and trying to prevent Muslim youth radicalisation in Europe. Such issues are topical, well-funded and verge on sensationalism. By adopting a security perspective, where averting risk and enhancing security is core, the less sensationalist but equally as important topic of Muslim everyday life and participatory existence in the European context recedes into the background, despite the valuable civic knowledge it has the potential to bring forth and make known. Instead, by being used as subjects of research, Islam and Muslims in Europe are more often than not perceived as a security risk, as a suspect community, Othered. History repeats in variations and like so many minorities before them, Muslims in Europe have become scapegoats, a potential risk to be evaluated and tracked so as to ease the anxiety of a European polity worn down by economic recession and political malaise.

In line with the work of Anwar, Ramadan and Pędziwiatr, who are critical towards the security perspective, the research undertaken in this book has an emancipatory intent that utilises an advocacy and participatory perspective. It does so by reaching out to Muslim communities and individuals in the Irish-European context to learn about their everyday lives. It brings to the fore previously unknown knowledge about Muslim life by collecting and presenting narratives in relation to universal recognition experiences and identity issues that translate to other contexts across Europe and enable a wider audience to learn and appreciate what it is like to be Muslim in the European context as the War on Terrorism continues into the twenty-first century.

The unknown community: Muslims in Ireland

The empirical data collected in this research emanates from Muslims in Ireland, primarily in the capital city of Dublin. It is therefore important to give some background details about the Irish context as well as evaluate the current Irish Muslim studies literature.

The Muslim population in Ireland

Since the 1950s, in similarity to other countries in the European continent, the Republic of Ireland's population demographic has slowly transformed into a multicultural environment, spurred on by the Celtic Tiger economic boom of the 1990s and by economic globalisation generally. This process has seen Ireland move away from being an extremely homogenous Caucasian society, dominated by a conservative Catholic ethos, to one of increasing population heterogeneity in race, religion and culture. In the twentieth century, a portion of the new entrees into the Irish community were of the Muslim faith and of a variety of ethno-cultural backgrounds that differed from Irish cultural norms. Although remaining for many decades inconspicuous, the Muslim community has become more visible by continuing to increase in size. Examples of this include elite recognition of the Muslim population, the construction of facilities by the new community, and the establishment of social provisions such as Islamic education, provision of halal food in public institutions, and the demarcation of burial sites. Unlike the stressed multiculturalism in the UK or France's well-known advocation of secularism in public life, Ireland's local and national integration policy is firmly based around the premise of interculturalism and interreligious interaction (Office of the Minister of Integration 2008). Despite sounding progressive and innovative by suggesting an intersubjective dialogue between groups, in reality, this policy is a coined phase with little to no practical application. In fact, with the economic crash of 2008 followed by a decade of recession, many societal organisations and advocacy groups, for example, the National Consultative Committee on Racism and Interculturalism (NCCRI), who aimed to advance this policy, suffered funding cuts and closure leaving an innovative integration policy in the realms of mere talk.

In the new contemporary Ireland, the visibility of different people signifies a new transformed society that runs parallel to the globalising tendencies, which are manifest throughout the rest of Europe and the world (Ferriter 2005, O'Malley 2011). This study aims to explore such processes through the lived experience of individuals emanating from the grassroots of a minority religious group that finds itself at the apex of cultural fluctuations. Academics interested and cognisant of such social and economic change, such as Kuhling

24 Muslims in Europe: divergent perspectives

and Keohane (2007), have reclassified the Irish nation as, 'Cosmopolitan Ireland'. Although critical of Ireland's transformation in terms of the continuing persistence of economic inequality and the 'short-sightedness of Irish immigration policy', they recognise that since the 1990s the Irish republic has experienced:

> Major social and cultural changes, which in some ways has secularised, liberalised and cosmopolitanised Ireland: emigration was reversed, which facilitated a 'new multiculturalism', divorce and homosexuality were legalised, the shift from the rural to urban patterns of living accelerated. Most significantly, Ireland was effectively transformed from a premodern, peasant rural community to a postmodern, high-technology urbanised society. The period coincided with the Peace Process in Northern Ireland, culminating in the Belfast Agreement in 1998, the decommissioning of IRA weapons in 2005, and the emergence (albeit fragile) of a post-nationalistic political discourse.
>
> (Ibid., p.1)

The latest descriptive statistics from the Central Statistics Office (CSO) give a valuable insight into the growth and development of the Muslim community in Ireland. At the same time as the proportion of Irish Catholics has fallen since 2011 from 84.7 per cent to 78.3 per cent, the Muslim population has continued to rise. There was 3,875 in 1991, 19,147 in 2002, 32,539 in 2006, 49,204 in 2011 and 63,443 in 2016. Of note is that the Muslim population has increased 28.9 per cent since the previous census and nearly doubled since 2006. Furthermore, the population is quite young with 25.8 per cent aged between five and eighteen, with the average age being just twenty-six years old. Of the total Muslim population, 55.6 per cent are Irish nationals, 11.4 per cent are Pakistani and 3.4 per cent UK nationals. In terms of ethnicity, a 42.2 per cent majority declared themselves to be Asian. According to the 2016 census, Muslims are less likely to be single and more likely to be married, with divorce being less prevalent. The census recorded 129 males per 100 females and that 27.4 per cent of Muslim women aged 15 and over were homemakers, which is significantly higher than the national average of 14.9 per cent (CSO 2016).

It must be acknowledged that the Muslim population in Ireland is extremely heterogeneous, composed of over fifty different nationalities and incorporating regional links to Europe, (South) Asia, Africa and the Middle East. The Sunni sect of Islam is by far the most populous group. Also present are a few thousand Shia and a growing Sufi population. In parallel with other European countries, immigration to Ireland was initiated due to economic and professional necessity. The first migrants to Ireland were medical students, practising doctors, aircraft mechanics and businessmen. However, it must be borne in mind that discriminatory practices in the South African apartheid regime acted as a catalyst for South Africans of Pakistani origin to immigrate to Ireland in the 1950s in search of better social and economic opportunities. The latest census shows that 23 per cent of Muslim respondents declared themselves as having professional occupations with 12 per cent of these in medical professions and 12.7 per cent in skilled trade occupations such as in the health, sales, restaurant and personal/child care services (CSO 2016).

The institutional establishment of Ireland's Muslim community traces its origins back to the late 1950s, when a small group of South African students attending the Royal College of Surgeons (RCSI), established an Islamic committee, known as the Dublin Islamic Society (DIS), to organise religious needs for the Muslim holidays and weekly prayers on Fridays. After many years of national and international fundraising, the DIS changed its name to the Islamic Foundation of Ireland (IFI) and established the first Islamic centre on the southside of the city known as the Dublin City Mosque. However, the Muslim community remained a small, relatively invisible, community in Ireland until the early 1990s, when the country's economic fortunes began to change:

> The Irish economy grew by an average 6.8 per cent per annum, peaking at 11.1 per cent in 1999. Unemployment fell from 18 per cent in the late 1980s to 4.2 per cent in 2005, and the Irish Debt/GDP ratio fell from 92 per cent in 1993 to 38 per cent in 1999. This rapid economic growth meant that labour market demand began to exceed what the Irish labour market could supply, which encouraged the Irish government actively to seek to encourage migrant workers to relocate to Ireland.
>
> (Ibid., p.54)

As the Irish economy transformed throughout the 1990s, the Muslim population increased dramatically due to an influx of political refugees, particularly from Bosnia, Somalia and Albania, who were fleeing their war-torn countries. By the end of the decade, there was a substantial increase in asylum-seeker applications from individuals emanating from Africa and the Middle East due to the 9/11 attacks and the subsequent invasions of Afghanistan and Iraq. This increase brought with it practical and logistical issues relating to physical and religious space, i.e. the limits of space in existing mosques and the lack of Islamic education and corresponding facilities. In November 1996, the second purpose-built mosque in Ireland (the first being the Ballyhaunis mosque, built in 1987), the Islamic Cultural Centre of Ireland (ICCI) was officially opened. This large mosque, located in the middle-class Dublin suburb of Clonskeagh, was initially administered by the IFI but was then subsequently managed by the al-Maktoum Foundation, which is closely linked to and receives funding from authorities in the United Arab Emirates.

Since the 1990s, advances have been made in opening and increasing the space available for the Muslim community not only in Dublin but throughout the whole island of Ireland. At present, there are four large mosques, i.e. the Ballyhaunis Mosque, Dublin City Mosque (IFI), Ahlul Bayt Islamic Centre (Shia Hussainia), and the Clonskeagh (ICCI) mosque complex. Three of the larger mosque complexes and many of the smaller prayer halls are located in Dublin while the Ballyhaunis mosque and at least sixteen small prayer halls are located in major towns and cities throughout the country.

Outside of Dublin, Muslim communities have developed in towns that contain regional economic resources and associated opportunities. For example, Cavan town has a Muslim population, who benefit from close proximity to a hospital that provides medical services for the wider provincial area. Also in County Kerry, the small town of Tralee has a significant Muslim population, who avail themselves of the important tourist industry in which sales and services thrive. Interestingly, over a decade ago, a local newspaper published an article on the Muslim population increase in the town by stating that 'in the county capital [Tralee], Islam has overtaken Protestantism to become the second most practised religion in the town' (The Kerryman 2007).

The Muslim population in Dublin

Dublin has a rapidly growing and permanent Muslim community, which is composed of multiple and identifiable generations, the first generation, being immigrants that settled in Ireland and their offspring, the second generation, being those who were born or primarily raised in Ireland. It must be acknowledged that there are significant differences between the lives and experiences of the various Muslim populations inside the metropolitan area of Dublin and those outside the capital city. These fundamental differences can be broken down into three distinct elements to consider: (1) the demographic and geographic spread, (2) the differences in levels of institutional completeness, and (3) the differences in economic and social power concentration.

Firstly, in terms of demographic and geographic spread, the census figures of 2016 indicate that Muslims are highly concentrated in urban areas with more than four out of ten living in Dublin city and its various suburban districts. Of note is that only 5.8 per cent live in rural areas. Overall, just under half or 47.5 per cent of Muslims in Ireland lived in the county of Dublin as compared to other counties. Of these, 15.5 per cent resided in Dublin City, 13.1 per cent in South Dublin, 12.8 per cent in Fingal, and 5.9 per cent in Dún Laoghaire-Rathdown (CSO 2016). It must be acknowledged that the Muslim population residing outside of the Dublin area is geographically spread throughout a variety of city and town locations. There are significant differences between Dublin and the rest of the country in terms of the geographic spread and concentration of their respective Muslim populations.

Secondly, the institutional completeness of the Muslim community is strong primarily in the Dublin region and very much weaker outside of the metropolitan area. For example, on the one hand, the capital city contains the three largest mosques and affiliated organisations, the main Muslim educational facilities in the country plus the majority of the economic resources, as well as close access to pre-existing social and political opportunity structures that have historically resided in the Irish capital. On the other hand, the small Muslim communities outside of Dublin are institutionally incomplete and lack access to religious, social and educational facilities such as those found in Dublin (Delaney and Cavatorta 2011).

Lastly, the institutional superiority of the Dublin Muslim community (particularly the large Sunni population) ensures that the economic and political power base remains concentrated in the capital. Consequently, many of the regional Muslim communities are dependent and reliant upon Dublin-based mosque organisations for religious, political and economic support. Overall, it can be stated that the Dublin Muslim community, in similarity to Islamic communities based in other large European cities, has far more social and political opportunities for recognition than their fellow Muslims in more rural areas. In terms of the research, such opportunities lead us to infer that the *recognition order* in metropolitan Dublin is more diverse, complex and inter-subjective due to the concentration of people, institutions and power. Such concentrated structures and opportunities imply that the grassroots of the Muslim community in Dublin have greater access to necessary resources to participate fully in political and social life.

Irish Muslim studies: a constructive critique

In contrast to the focus on Muslim populations in core European countries, research output on Muslim communities in Ireland is scant. A common reason for this has been the suggestion that Irish Muslim communities are too small to facilitate and contribute new insights to the wider Muslim experience in Europe. However, as the size of the Islamic population has grown, the Irish government and academics have taken more interest in trying to understand this unknown community. The field of Irish Muslim studies is at an early developmental stage. The research output has beneficially produced new knowledge and insights yet, at the same time, it has also suffered limitations, particularly in relation to synthesising theory, methodology and empirical data into a cohesive holistic research project. Also of note is that the research output to date has not explicitly explored the recognition dynamics and experiences that reside in different spheres of Muslim everyday life nor fully engaged with the grassroots of the community, particularly with the second generation's recognition experiences and identity issues.

An emerging field

In 2006, both the first academic journal and book studying the Muslim community in Ireland were released, thereby initiating the emergence of a new Irish academic field of study. Flynn (2006) produced the first journal article to take account of the Muslim community in Ireland. In this work, he outlines the development of the Muslim population in Ireland from the 1950s to the present day. As well as outlining the institutional development of the community in the Dublin region, he also touches on topics such as educational institutions, the arrival of political refugees in the 1990s, and the coming of age of the Muslim community in Ireland. Although relatively descriptive, this article is the first academic attempt to seriously analyse and understand the Muslim community in Ireland. His overall viewpoint is one in which the Irish republic's historical development has been overwhelmingly positive for the Muslim community. Flynn stresses the fact that the Muslim community 'is coming of age [and] is no longer becoming established or trying to survive but is an important and integral part of the social and religious environment of Irish society' (Ibid., p.236). His positive assessment of the relationship between Irish society and Islam continues by placing emphasis on how Irish society 'provides an environment where Muslim identity can flourish and develop' to the point where Ireland 'provides a home for Islam' and where 'community, inclusion and hospitality' are valued (Ibid.).

Sakaranaho (2006) published the first book on the Muslim population in Ireland. This research compared the Muslim educational experience to that of Finland with particular attention to the topics of religious freedom, multiculturalism and Islam. The primary aim was to challenge the persistent allegation that Islam 'constitute[s] a problem for religious freedom as it is understood and implemented in a multicultural Europe' (Ibid., p.8). In similarity to Flynn, Sakaranaho views Irish historical development, in terms of the Catholic legacy of denominational confessional education and the public recognition of religion, as a significant developmental benefit for the Islamic community in Ireland. However, she criticises the Irish approach to the new realities of pluralism as 'constituting a paradox of friendly discrimination' (Ibid., p.16). Despite the lack of focus on the grassroots of the community and the fixation on educational experiences, Sakaranaho's work is significant because it recognises the institutionalisation of the Muslim community in Ireland as exemplified by the establishment of mosques, schools and community organisations.

By 2009, the Irish government began to take an interest in understanding the Muslim communities residing within its borders. Under the guidance of Oliver Scharbrodt and Adil Khan of University College Cork (UCC), the Irish Research Council for Humanities and Social Sciences (IRCHSS) and the Department of the Taoiseach initiated a research project entitled *History of Islam in Ireland* with the aim of providing an 'in-depth survey and discussion of the historical evolution of the Muslim community in Ireland, from the first wave of Muslims in the 1950s to the present'. Unfortunately, this project lacked coherence, theoretical underpinning, and did not engage with the Muslim grassroots. The project's output was devoid of an overarching research agenda and was marked by descriptive repetitions of how various Muslim institutions developed historically, which unfortunately left unexplored how the Muslim grassroots experience everyday recognition in different spheres of life in Ireland (Scharbrodt 2011a, Scharbrodt, Sakaranaho, Khan, Shanneik and Ibrahim 2015).

Alongside the government funded project, a special edition of the *Journal of Muslim Minority Affairs* (JMMA 2011) was issued, which presented a broad spectrum of the existing research that focuses on the Muslim community in Ireland. This special edition presented the developments in the field since Flynn and Sakaranaho's first publications. For example, Adil Khan's (2011) detailed empirical research gives a nuanced insight into the influences that transformed the leadership of the main Muslim mosques and organisations in Dublin into transnational political components of larger Islamic umbrella organisations in Europe, under the aegis of the ideology of the Muslim Brotherhood. On the other hand, the JMMA special edition also showed limitations in the research output. For example, Scharbrodt and Sakaranaho's (2011) tendency to repetitively describe Muslim migration to Ireland and the evolution of various mosques and Islamic organisations, leaving unexplored a more nuanced understanding of Islam in Ireland and brushing over the everyday lived complexities of the Muslim experience in the Irish context and how it can be translated to connect with the European situation. Furthermore, the special edition brings to the fore the propensity to narrowly focus on Muslim subgroups. For example, Shanneik's (2011) article focuses on the preconversion lives of Salafi female converts and Scharbrodt's (2011b) article on the self-representation of Shi'a Muslims moderation in the Irish Muslim community. Although such research into 'minorities within minorities' is interesting, the lack of an overarching research agenda is apparent. Such siloed research does not develop a comprehensive understanding and knowledge of the overall Muslim experience in the Irish context and therefore leaves a holistic research agenda only as a recommendation for future research to undertake.

An ideological turn: a critique of Carr's research

As shown above, the initial output produced by the emerging field of Irish Muslim studies could be improved further to meet higher academic standards, particularly in the area of producing holistic research that is designed to synthesise theory, methodology and empirical insight. Despite such design deficits, there have been positive signs of advancement in the field's output. Such progression can be traced to the work of James Carr, who has explored societal discrimination against Muslim communities in Ireland using a holistic research approach.

Through his academic and public advocacy work, Carr (2010, 2011) identifies and rails against discrimination by advocating for the Irish state to utilise its administrative power and structures to collect disaggregated statistical data on occurrences of racism and Islamophobia so as to impede discriminatory forms of interaction in Irish society. His research is a progression upon previous output in the field in that it utilises a Foucauldian theoretical framework alongside a mixed methodology to attain and analyse narrative empirical data in relation to discrimination experienced by Muslims in the Irish context. Carr must be highly commended for confronting the issue of racism and Islamophobia in Ireland as well as for highlighting how such pernicious societal pathologies negatively impact upon Muslim individuals and communities. His goal is to impede the Othering of Muslims and prevent them from being negatively labelled and perceived as suspect. The overarching aim of his work is positive and emancipatory in that it aims to transform Irish society and the lives of minority individuals and communities for the better.

However, while there are positive aspects to Carr's research output, upon a closer reading of his work, serious concerns come to the fore in relation to how his work contains and perpetuates a negative dialectic, i.e. the positive aim of impeding discrimination becomes a counterproductive blame game against macro-level state institutions and their role in regulating micro-sociological processes of discrimination. The institutions Carr takes aim at include An Garda Siochana, the Central Statistics Office, the Equality Authority and Tribunal as well as the Economic and Social Research Institute. His work has also focused on discrimination in public services such as in the Irish educational and transport systems. The dialectic manifests and is fuelled by his ideological position and viewpoint that the Irish state and its institutions are racist supplicants of neoliberalism. As he states in this regard: 'Ireland is clearly an exemplar of a state intoxicated by neoliberalism and the practises of Irish governmentality' (Carr 2015, p.147). Stretching this viewpoint even further, he states that such negativity reaches down to the micro-social level of the individual and 'pervades and informs how one should be an ideal citizen' (Ibid.). For Carr:

> Neoliberal rationalities have seeped into the process of belonging and notions of ideal Irishness at the level of the individual and of state policies.
> (Ibid., p.133)

Carr's viewpoint has no basis in empirical reality but is fuelled by his ideological agenda, which unfortunately regressively impacts upon his emancipatory work of confronting discrimination against Muslims in Ireland. The question must be asked, is the Irish state neoliberal? When looked at objectively and empirically, the answer is negative. Neoliberalism is an economic philosophy, which favours a greater role for free market capitalism and espouses values related to privatisation, deregulation, free trade, a reduction in government spending and bureaucratic oversight. The evidence concretely verifies that the Irish state and its institutions are not and never have been neoliberal. Despite the limited outsourcing of some functions to non-governmental organisations and private health businesses, the Irish state and its institutions remain large and unwieldy bureaucratic entities tasked with regulating and administering public monies and societal institutions. To determine that the Irish state and its varied institutions are neoliberal is fantasy and to link a theory of economic practices to institutional and everyday discrimination is untenable without concrete empirical evidence to support such a claim.

In Carr's work one finds an explicit ideological position and argument, which is unsubstantiated. Despite advancing the field in terms of conducting holistic research by synthesising theory, methodology and empirical research, his ideological position and reasoning is concerning and represents a step forward then back for the field of Irish Muslim studies. Spurred on by a conspiratorial ideological viewpoint, in Carr's work, there are two primary issues of concern, which are (1) the tendency to conceptually conflate racism and Islamophobia, and (2) his understanding of power and positioning of vulnerability.

Conflating racism and Islamophobia

An identifiable concern in Carr's work is his conflation of key sociological concepts and terminology. In sociology, as it has developed for over a century, the identification of concepts and their parsing out has been important for understanding issues and actions in everyday life, especially discrimination. This involved the scientific practice of recognising, identifying and labelling varieties of discriminations that target race (i.e. racism), religion (i.e. anti-Semitism and Islamophobia), gender (i.e. sexism and misogyny), as well as cultures and countries (i.e. ethnocentrism and xenophobia). This differentiation enables a deeper understanding of discriminatory acts, especially in terms of developing insights into why and how such discriminations manifest in the course of everyday interaction. However, although Carr advocates for apparatuses of the Irish state to take responsibility and confront discrimination more successfully by conducting 'the systematic collection of disaggregated data that illuminates the levels of Islamophobia that exist in society' (Carr 2011, p.575), he simultaneously conflates racist discrimination (i.e. racism) with the discrimination of the Islamic religion and Muslim identity (i.e. Islamophobia) by proposing that such acts and experiences are more comprehensively understood as 'anti-Muslim racism' (Ibid., p.578).

Adopted from Chris Allen's (2010) work on Islamophobia in the UK, Carr defines this term used throughout his work as 'exclusionary practises of hostility and discrimination informed by Islamophobic discourses' (Carr 2016, p.80). Surprisingly, although the majority of his published articles have 'Islamophobia' in the title, he views this terminology, commonly used by sociologists and Muslims in their everyday lives, as 'not fit for purpose' (Carr 2015, p.53) as it has been used as a 'tool' by neoliberal regimes to 'suit their own ends' (Ibid.). His reasoning for preferring and utilising the term 'anti-Muslim racism' is that it has 'greater utility' (Ibid., p.33) as well as an 'emotional resonance' that has 'a stronger purchase in the public mind-set [thereby] capitalising on the established foothold that the term racism already has' (Ibid., p.33 and p.44). Carr has presented a weak argument for downgrading a term regularly and successfully used by sociologists and everyday people to recognise and identify forms of discrimination against Islam and Muslims. Carr's deconstruction of Islamophobia and replacement with a new racialised term is an instrumental action on his behalf, which enables him to shoehorn discrimination against Muslims into his overarching ideological argument that the Irish state is neoliberal and racist. Ismail Patel (2016), who reviewed Carr's (2015) book publication, is also highly sceptical of the use of the term 'anti-Muslim racism'. On this issue, Patel states the following:

> Islamophobia as a term will survive as long as it is able to address issues more successfully than other alternatives. However, when it eventually

fails to achieve this, then a further shift in paradigm will ensue. Islamophobia is not a panacea, but as a paradigm it has emerged to 'name' something better than 'racism' could.

(Patel 2016, p.107)

Agreeing with Patel, Islamophobia remains the most useful term to describe discrimination against Islam and a Muslim identity. Not only is the term utilised successfully and broadly in academia, but it is also deployed by Muslims themselves to identify and categorise discriminatory experiences directed against their religion and identity. Would Carr also be willing to deconstruct and racialise the term anti-Semitism and does he think this would be acceptable to Jewish communities around the world? Instead of acknowledging the complexity of varying forms of discrimination, Carr instrumentally combines racism and Islamophobia (with racism taking the primary position), and by doing so, he falls into an epistemological empirical error. Also, how does Carr know that such racism is informed by Islamophobic discourses? Where is the empirical evidence to support such a claim? Does racialising religious discrimination accurately reflect actual Muslim experience? Surprisingly, and in contradiction to much of his persistent terminological conflations and emphasis on race, Carr verifies in relation to his research participants that 'religious identity was a decisive factor in their experience [of discrimination]' as well as highlighting that 'Muslims in Ireland are selectively identified and profiled on the basis of their religious identity' (Carr 2015, p.136).

Certainly, some events are linked to anti-Muslim sentiment and populist anti-Islamic discourses; yet Carr's research seems to connect all incidents of misrecognition to (primarily) racial or a religious identity, when other variables, such as ethnocentrism or misogyny, may also be possible causal explanations. It is not convincing that conflating distinct forms of discrimination, i.e. racism and Islamophobia, helps or aids victims, researchers or society as a whole to understand the complexity of such abuse in everyday life. While Carr gives priority to Muslim discriminatory experiences in the wider societal sphere, many individuals and groups, whether Muslim or not, suffer discriminations, which manifest in other social arenas such as in the family, the local community as well as in the legal sphere, e.g. the experience of denizens in gaining full citizenship in various European states. Without doubt, racism and Islamophobia exist and interact in the Irish context. From an ethical standpoint, such pathologies must be identified, confronted and prevented. However, to conflate two distinct social pathologies into a single highly dubious concept is unhelpful for diagnosing the complexity of discriminations that Muslims encounter in Ireland and throughout Europe.

Power, vulnerability and ideology

Throughout his work, Carr (2015) presents an interpretation of Foucault's theory of power (Foucault, 2002) to link Islamophobia to domineering and racist neoliberal state power. He is interested in how power and discrimination interact and has the view that power at a high level, from government and/or state institutions, is a neoliberal domineering force in the lives of everyday people enabling racism to fester in society and go unchallenged. Carr's viewpoint is that discrimination continues in society because top-down powers, emanating from the 'duplicitous neoliberal state' (Ibid., p.99), shirk responsibilities to monitor what he calls 'anti-Muslim racism' by not collecting disaggregated data. In Carr's opinion, the state is confirmed to be racist and domineering yet the technologies of such governmental powers remain neutral and can be utilised in both negative and positive ways. Carr (2010, p.53) states in this regard, 'the technologies of state are blind to racism'. Following this, he argues that if the Irish state utilised and collected more statistical data, in a more effective (neoliberal) way, then domineering power constellations would transform into positive forms of constitutive developmental power that, in turn, would protect and enable citizens to be themselves in society.

Carr ideologically determines, without empirical evidence, that the Irish state is neoliberal and racist because its institutions and civil servants shirk responsibility to collect more nuanced statistical data about everyday discrimination (Ibid.). As he states, 'inadequate recording of religiously aggravated crime and discrimination against Muslims in Ireland is tantamount to institutional racism' (Ibid.). Certainly, in line with European standards, the Irish state has a responsibility to record all forms of discrimination. Not doing so is ethically wrong. However, there is no evidence brought forward by Carr to prove that such clerical deficiencies and maladministration is a confirmation of racism and connects directly to an all-powerful neoliberal conspiracy.

In terms of the use of Foucault's theoretical understanding of power, especially governmentality, Carr does not understand, or has self-interpreted, Foucault's theoretical insights in relation to power. This detrimentally impacts his research output and emancipatory goals. Contrasting Carr's interpretation of Foucault with that of Amy Allen, his ideological viewpoint leads to a loose and confusing inference that neoliberal (yet at the same time bureaucratic) top-down power is racist. However, Allen (1999, 2008, 2010, McNay 1994, Hoffman 2013) has provided a more comprehensive interpretation of Foucault's thoughts and actions (2002) in relation to power by showing that the famous French theorist teased out the complexity of power as power-over others in terms of being negatively *domineering* and positively *constitutive* of identity and action as well as acknowledging bottom-up *resistive* power, i.e. an individual's power to resist top-down forces by gaining strength collectively with others. With this in mind, it can be stated that Foucault had an immensely complex understanding of power that covers forms of positive and negative power-over others as well as elucidating bottom-up resistive power in everyday life.

Yet, discrepancies arise when we compare such a complex view of power to Carr's narrow ideological interpretation. A one-dimensional view of power ultimately leads Carr to identify and blame so called neoliberal state institutions for anti-Muslim discrimination. In his articles, *Measuring Islamophobia*

(2010) and *Regulating Islamophobia* (2011), Carr presumes that apparatuses of the Irish state are innately disciplinary and domineering. However, he has no evidence to support this claim apart from referencing the unsubstantiated position of Lentin (2007) that the Irish state is racist and by highlighting the intentional (yet paradoxically also unintentional) administrative bureaucratic deficiencies by state institutions to collect disaggregated statistical data (Carr 2011, p.585). Once again, these contradictory statements show that Carr has fallen into another epistemological empirical error. How does he know that the Irish state is domineeringly racist, in the first instance, and that collecting disaggregated data will somehow temper and transform such a force into something more civically amenable and democratic?

In contrast to the Foucauldian view that high power can be both negatively domineering and positively constitutive, Carr takes the view that the Irish state is, in the first instance, domineering and can only develop a positive constitutive capacity by following his resistive reasoning and advocations. It becomes apparent that Carr acknowledges resistive power or 'counter-conducts' but only as emanating from his own academic output (Ibid., p.576). He views his book as 'clearly identifying the manner and space for resistance and change' (Ibid., p.147) and that:

> Research such as this, working with those whose voices are silenced, can act as insurrections of subjugated knowledges, in this case anti-Muslim racism, and provide a platform from which the aforementioned counter-conducts can be vitalised.
>
> (Ibid., p.140)

Carr claims to want to hear and give access to a diversity of voices yet the resistive voices of Muslim individuals and communities remain dormant in his work. Their 'counter-conducts' remain silent and unknown. Carr's reading and self-interpretation of Foucault's theory of power blinds him to everyday resistive power and strips his own research participants of agency. He fails to recognise that Muslim people have the ability and capability to forge their own forms of resistive power against the domineering and constitutive powers over them, not just in relation to the wider societal domain (including state influence), but in other spheres of life such as in the family, the local community and the legal sphere. In other words, Muslims as individuals (and collectives) have the power to struggle and change situations that impact upon them and to conjoin their resistive power to struggle for mutual emancipatory aims. In Carr's work, his research participants are presented as vulnerable subjugated beings, who lack agency and silently suffer discrimination.

In a report prepared on behalf of the Immigrant Council of Ireland (ICI), *Islamophobia in Dublin* (2016), which utilises everyday narrative more extensively than previous work, Carr's research participants express concern at being presented as vulnerable and for the research to simply 'retell racism' without expressing the complexity of everyday life and how victims tackle discrimination by utilising their agency and capacity to resist (Carr 2016, pp.60–69). These narratives against 'retelling racism' are a resistance against sociological work that denies the agency of research participants and instead utilises them as *subjects*. It is also a resistance against research that has an overly ideological focus and is willing to use everyday narratives to perpetuate blame at a higher level.

In his work, Carr consistently presents Muslims as vulnerable. Their narratives are examples of 'subjugated knowledge' (Carr 2011, p.147). In *Regulating Islamophobia*, he states that 'Muslims are increasingly vulnerable to racism' (Ibid., p.586). Later in *Islamophobia in Dublin* (Op. cit.), he claims that he does not mean to show Muslims as vulnerable, yet the majority of narratives presented in this report 'retell racism' and position Muslims as vulnerable. Resistive power can be identified as emanating from the research participants themselves, who reject Carr's instrumental representation of their lives and emphasise their wish in the publication not to be pigeonholed as vulnerable but to be seen publicly as different yet also the same as others. In other words, although their racial and cultural traits should be respected in public, they also expect to be seen as human beings with a universal civic status enshrined by their legal status as Irish citizens. A narrative from Fatima in *Islamophobia in Dublin* illustrates such agency and resistance:

> I don't want to be promoted as someone who is vulnerable. Because when [you] show people that we're vulnerable then they'll treat us in a way ... it could be good and bad ... I don't want to be treated like I'm someone special, because I'm not. I'm just human ... I just want to be treated as a normal person, simply, you know.
>
> (Carr 2016, p.69)

Despite such clarifications by the research participants, Carr does not elaborate on bottom-up resistances. Instead, mainly due to his persistent ideological stance that views the Irish state as neoliberal and racist, he persists in 'retelling' how domineering powers upon high facilitate 'anti-Muslim racism' (Ibid., p.16 and p.68).

Alongside conflating core sociological concepts, simplifying Foucault's complex theory of power, and positioning resistive capacity away from his own research participants, Carr also makes a profound error in his attempt to empirically verify his ideological stance. His approach relies on the tactic of blame by utilising negative perceptions of everyday experiences from individuals to infer to the higher systems-level that the state and its institutions are racist for allowing and enabling discrimination to occur in Irish society. This is a misuse of sociological narrative. Without doubt, large state bureaucratic entities should have ethical procedures and ensure discriminatory behaviour is identified and impeded. In certain circumstances, individual actions can be reflective of an institutional culture of prejudice, however, Carr's narrative examples do not empirically substantiate the existence of such a culture and/or policy of discrimination against Muslims generally. In *Islamophobia in*

Dublin, he presents narrative examples of 'possibly discriminatory' (Carr 2016, p.43) institutional racism by teachers and public transport staff. However, many of these examples are dubious in providing concrete evidence for the existence of institutional racism against Muslims in the Irish context. One such example is from a Muslim woman, Nahla, who narrates her experience of being on a bus and the driver not stopping to let her off (Ibid.). The woman may have perceived this as a racist experience and carry negative feelings towards it, but this narrative is not an example of institutional racism. Alternatively, it could also have been an honest mistake on the part of the bus driver. Such an example is reflective of much of Carr's work that continuously presents siloed perceptions of possible acts of discrimination, which do not empirically verify the presence of macro-level institutional racism and its inferred link to the ideology of neoliberalism.

Carr misuses narrative for his own ideological ends. An issue very much evident in his report, *Islamophobia in Dublin* (2016), where he makes unsubstantiated inferential claims from the everyday micro-level and then transposes them to the systems macro-level to validate his ideological opinions in relation to power and racism. Such a use of narrative is irresponsible. He is blind to the examples of positive Muslim recognition afforded by the Irish state and its institutions and how this positively benefits self-confidence and action. Furthermore, he fails to acknowledge that large apparatuses of the state, i.e. universities, the police force, the school system, public transport services etc., are managed and run by employees, by citizens, who provide a civically oriented service to others and that his misuse of narrative tarnishes the reputation of the majority of working citizens, who provide each day a public service for others irrespective of differing characteristics and traits. Certainly, such services are not perfect and require reform and development over time. Unfortunately, not only does Carr present Muslims as lacking resistive agency, he indirectly blames and accuses public service companies and their employees for facilitating or being racist. He ignores the good that such companies and employees do each day and views them ideologically as mere instruments for filtering neoliberalised and racist ideology down to the level of everyday life.

From an advocacy and participatory perspective, tackling and struggling against all forms of discrimination is a concern for all European citizens, who live in an increasingly cosmopolitan heterogeneous democratic sphere. However, it must also be stated that academics, who aim to struggle against discrimination, have a civic and ethical responsibility to produce research that does not free fall into ideology and find itself in a counterproductive blame game. Unfortunately, Carr's work falls into such a trap. Carr's use of narrative, especially in his paper *Islamophobia in Dublin*, is highly irresponsible. Most unfortunately, his positive struggle against discrimination spirals into the negativity of blame, which then detrimentally impacts upon the overall ethical goal of his research.

Carr's work and the field of Muslim studies in Ireland, more generally, should make concerted efforts to show greater attention to how individuals and groups have and utilise resistive power to struggle against forms of discrimination and avoid infusing ideology into research. As the research in this book aims to show, there is empirical evidence from Irish Muslim individuals and groups that convey resistive experiences against forms of top-down power in different spheres of life. Such narratives in turn promote and aid the general struggle against social pathologies and humanise religious minorities to the general public.

Conclusion

This chapter has facilitated the positioning of this study in the broader context of research conducted in the field of Muslim studies in Europe and more narrowly in the Irish context. In terms of the European literature, it was broadly identified that the Muslim studies literature in Europe can be positioned into two opposing perspectives, i.e. the security paradigm, which negatively views Muslims in Europe as a suspect community that pose a potential security risk to European society, and secondly, the advocacy and participatory perspective that is critical of the repercussions of the securitised lens and aims to sociologically understand the everyday actions, experiences and emotions of Muslims in Europe, particularly in terms of how an Islamic identity interacts with a civic identity producing positive results in terms of societal participation and contribution.

We then moved to the Irish case, where we learned about the historical development of the Irish Muslim population and how Dublin differs from rural areas in Ireland in terms of having a higher population concentration of Muslims, a higher prevalence of established Islamic institutions and how the Islamic social and economic power base is firmly located in Ireland's capital city. Alongside learning about the development of the Muslim population in Ireland, we also learned that the field of Irish Muslim studies is still in its infancy. The literature is scant and of varying quality. The work tends to be overly descriptive involving repetitions recounting the development of Muslim institutions, and it leaves unexamined empirical research into Muslim everyday life and the second generation experience. Furthermore, although Carr's work on anti-Muslim racism is holistic research and represents an advancement in the field of Irish Muslim studies, upon closer scrutiny it is also a step back due to its instrumental conflations of racism and Islamophobia alongside presenting, through an ideological train of thought, a biased empirically unsubstantiated argument that not only misuses narrative to harvest blame but also derails a complex understanding of power and vulnerability.

With the above taken into account, the research in this book is highly critical of the security perspective that marginalises and Others Muslim communities and individuals. It therefore aligns itself with the advocacy and participatory perspective of Anwar, Ramadan and Pędziwiatr, which shares a critical emancipatory intent and aims to learn and unearth more about the positives and negatives of Muslim everyday experiences in the Irish-European context. Taking an ethical perspective has determined that the voices of Muslim participants, presented as *streams of narrative* experience, take priority and course through the book leading to its findings and conclusions.

By taking such a grounded approach, rooted in the critical social theory tradition, this extensive study also aims to advance the field of Irish Muslim studies by synthesising theory and empirical narrative sociology to move beyond the repetitive descriptions and ideological machinations of prior work and constitute a more complex grounded sociological understanding of Muslim recognition experiences and identity issues in the Irish context, which can be universally translated to other national contexts in Europe and beyond.

The next chapter, Chapter 3, gives a detailed overview of Axel Honneth's critical social theory of a Struggle for Recognition, which frames and gives structure to the empirical aspects of the study.

References

Allen, Amy. 1999. *The Power of Feminist Theory: Domination, Resistance, Solidarity.* Boulder, CO: Westview Press.
Allen, Amy. 2008. *The Politics of Our Selves: Power, Autonomy, and Gender in Contemporary Critical Theory.* New York: Columbia University Press.
Allen, Amy. 2010. Recognizing domination: recognition and power in Honneth's critical theory. *Journal of Power.* 3(1), pp.21–32.
Allen, Chris. 2010. *Islamophobia.* London: Routledge.
Amghar, Samir, Boubekeur, Amel and Emerson, Michael. (eds.). 2007. *European Islam: Challenges for Society and Public Policy.* Brussels, Belgium: Centre of European Policy Studies.
Anwar, Muhammad. 1979. *The Myth of Return: Pakistanis in Britain.* London: Pearson Education.
Anwar, Muhammad. 1985. *Pakistanis in Britain: A Sociological Study.* London: New Century Publishers.
Anwar, Muhammad. 1994. *Race and Elections: The Participation of Ethnic Minorities in Politics.* Monograph in Ethnic Relations No. 9. Warwick: Centre for Research in Ethnic Relations.
Anwar, Muhammad. 1998. *Between Cultures.* London: Routledge.
Anwar, Muhammad. 2008. Muslims in Western States: The British experience and the way forward. *Journal of Muslim Minority Affairs.* 28(1), pp.125–137.
Anwar, Muhammad. 2009. *Ethnic Minorities and Politics: The British Electoral System.* Germany: Lambert Academic Publishing.
Bawer, Bruce. 2006. *While Europe Slept: How Radical Islam is Destroying the West from Within.* New York: Doubleday.
Bawer, Bruce. 2010. *Surrender: Appeasing Islam, Sacrificing Freedom.* New York: Anchor Books.
Bemelmans, Yvonne and Freitas, Maria Jose. 2001. *Situation of Islamic Communities in Five European Cities: Examples of Local Initiatives.* Netherlands: European Monitoring Centre on Racism and Xenophobia.
Burgat, François. 2008. *Islamism in the Shadow of Al-Qaeda.* TX: University of Texas Press.
Carr, James. 2010. Measuring Islamophobia. *Socheolas: Limerick Student Journal of Sociology.* 2(2), pp.39–57.

Carr, James. 2011. Regulating Islamophobia: The need for collecting disaggregated data on racism in Ireland. *Journal of Muslim Minority Affairs.* 31(4), pp.574–593.

Carr, James. 2015. *Experiences of Islamophobia: Living with Racism in the Neoliberal Era.* London: Routledge.

Carr, James. 2016. *Islamophobia in Dublin: Experiences and How to Respond.* Dublin: Immigrant Council of Ireland (ICI).

Central Statistics Office (CSO). 2016. Volume 8: Irish Travellers, Ethnicity and Religion. *National Census 2016.* Dublin: Stationery Office.

Conway, Maura and Dillon, Joseph. 2016. *Future Trends: Live-Streaming Terrorist Attacks.* Dublin: VOX-Pol.

Coolsaet, Rik. (ed.). 2008. *Jihadi Terrorism and the Radicalisation Challenge in Europe.* Farnham, UK: Ashgate Publishing.

Crowley, Una, Gilmartin, Mary and Kitchin, Rob. Vote yes for commonsense citizenship: paradoxes at the heart of Ireland's 'céad mile fáilte'. IN: Kuhling, C., and Keohane, K. 2007. *Cosmopolitan Ireland: Globalisation and Quality of Life.* London: Pluto Press.

Crul, Maurice, Schneider, Jens, and Lelie, Frans. (eds.). 2012. *The European Second Generation Compared: Does the Integration Context Matter?* Amsterdam, Netherlands: Amsterdam University Press.

Delaney, Des and Cavatorta, Francesco. The exclusion of denizens within the Irish social and political opportunity structure: the cosmopolitan case of Muslims in the Republic of Ireland. Chapter 8. pp.123–153, IN: Sinclair, K., and Egholm-Feldt, J. (eds.). 2011. *Lived Space: Reconsidering Transnationalism among Muslim Minorities.* Hamburg, Germany: Peter Lang.

Deliso, Christopher. 2007. *The Coming Balkan Caliphate: The Threat of Radical Islam to Europe and the West.* Santa Barbara, CA: Praeger Security International.

Delong-Bas, Natana J. 2004. *Wahhabi Islam.* Oxford: Oxford University Press.

Esposito, John L. 1992. *The Islamic Threat: Myth or Reality.* Oxford: Oxford University Press.

Esposito, John L. 1997. *Political Islam: Revolution, Radicalism or Reform.* London: Lynne Rienner.

Ferriter, David. 2005. *The Transformation of Ireland 1900–2000.* London: Profile Books.

Fetzer, Joel S., and Soper, J.C. 2005. *Muslims and the State in Britain, France and Germany.* Cambridge: Cambridge University Press.

Flynn, Kieran. 2006. Understanding Islam in Ireland. *Islam and Christian-Muslim Relations.* 17(2), pp.223–238.

Foucault, Michel. 2002. *Power: The Essential Works of Michel Foucault 1954–1984.* Volume 3. London: Penguin.

Fukuyama, Francis. 1992. *The End of History and the Last Man.* New York: Free Press.

Fuller, Graham E. 2003. *The Future of Political Islam.* London: Palgrave MacMillan.

Gartner, Heinz and Cuthbertson, Ian M. (eds.). 2005. *European Security and Transatlantic Relations after 9/11 and the Iraq War.* London: Palgrave MacMillan.

Gerges, Fawas A. 1999. *America and Political Islam: Clash of Cultures or Clash of Interests?* Cambridge: Cambridge University Press.

Gill, Paul, Corner, Emily, Thornton, Amy, Conway, Maura. 2015. *What are the Roles of the Internet in Terrorism? Measuring Online Behaviours of Convicted UK Terrorists.* Dublin: VOX-Pol.

Goody, Jack. 2004. *Islam in Europe.* Cambridge: Polity Press.

Gunaratna, Rohan. 2002. *Inside Al-Qaeda: Global Networks of Terror*. New York: Columbia University Press.
Hafez, Mohammed M. 2003. *Why Muslims Rebel*. London: Lynne Rienner.
Hellyer, H.A. 2009. *Muslim of Europe: The 'Other' Europeans*. Edinburgh: Edinburgh University Press.
Hickman, Mary J., Thomas, Lyn, Silvestri, Sara and Nickels, Henri. 2011. *'Suspect Communities'? Counter-Terrorism Policy, the Press, and the Impact on Irish and Muslim Communities in Britain*. London: London Metropolitan University.
Hoffman, Marcelo. 2013. *Foucault and Power: The Influence of Political Engagement on Theories of Power*. London: Bloomsbury.
Hunter, Shireen T. (ed.). 2002. *Islam, Europe's Second Religion: The New Social, Cultural and Political Landscape*. London: Preager.
Huntington, Samuel. 1996. *The Clash of Civilisations and the Remaking of World Order*. London: Simon and Schuster.
Jones, Seth G. 2007. *The Rise of European Security Co-operation*. Cambridge: Cambridge University Press.
Journal of Muslim Minority Affairs (JMMA). 2011. 31(4). Abingdon, UK: Taylor & Francis.
Kassam, Raheem and Farage, Nigel. 2017. *No Go Zones: How Sharia Law Is Coming to a Neighbourhood Near You*. Washington, DC: Regnery Publishing.
Kepel, Gilles. 1997. *Allah in the West: Islamic Movements in America and Europe*. Cambridge: Polity Press.
Kepel, Gilles. 2002. *Jihad: The Trail of Political Islam*. London: IB Tauris.
Kepel, Gilles and Jardin, Antoine. 2017. *Terror in France: The Rise of Jihad in the West*. Princeton, NJ: Princeton University Press.
Khan, Adil H. 2011. Transnational influences on Irish Muslim networks: From local to global perspectives. *Journal of Muslim Minority Affairs*. 31(4), pp.486–502.
Klausen, Jytte. 2005. *The Islamic Challenge: Politics and Religion in Western Europe*. Oxford: Oxford University Press.
Kuhling, Carmen and Keohane, Kieran. 2007. *Cosmopolitan Ireland: Globalisation and Quality of Life*. London: Pluto Press.
Larsson, Göran and Sander, Åke. 2007. *Islam and Muslims in Sweden: Integration or Fragmentation? A Contextual Study*. Germany: Lit Verlag.
Lentin, Ronit. 2007. Ireland: Racial state and crisis racism. *Ethnic and Racial Studies*. 30(4), pp.610–627.
Maddy-Weitzmann, Bruce and Inbar, Efraim. (eds.). 1997. *Religious Radicalism in the Greater Middle East*. London: Routledge.
Mahlouly, Dounia and Winter, Charlie. 2018. *A Tale of Two Caliphates: Comparing the Islamic State's Internal and External Messaging Priorities*. Dublin: VOX-Pol.
Martikainen, Tuomas, Mapril, José, and Khan, Adil H. (eds.). 2019. *Muslims in the Margins of Europe: Finland, Greece, Ireland and Portugal*. Leiden, Netherlands: Brill.
McConnon, Eamonn. 2018. *Risk and the Security-Development Nexus: The Policies of the US, the UK and Canada*. London: Palgrave Macmillan.
McNay, Lois. 1994. *Foucault: A Critical Introduction*. Cambridge: Polity Press.
Milton-Edwards, Beverly. 2004. *Islam and Politics in the Contemporary World*. Cambridge: Polity Press.
Muslim Population in Kerry Doubles in Four Years. 2007. *The Kerryman*. 5 December.
Nesser, Petter. 2018. *Islamist Terrorism in Europe*. Oxford: Oxford University Press.

Nielsen, Jørgen S. 1999. *Towards a European Islam*. London: Palgrave.
Nielsen, Jørgen S. 2004. *Muslims in Western Europe*. Edinburgh: Edinburgh University Press.
Nielsen, Jørgen S. 2013. *Muslim Political Participation in Europe*. Edinburgh: Edinburgh University Press.
Office of the Minister of Integration. 2008. *Migration Nation: Statement on Integration Strategy and Diversity Management*. Dublin: Stationery Office.
O'Malley, Eoin. 2011. *Contemporary Ireland*. London: Palgrave Macmillan.
Open Society Institute. 2009. *Muslims in Europe: A Report on 11 EU Cities*. London: Open Society Institute.
Pargeter, Alison. 2008. *The New Frontiers of Jihad: Radical Islam in Europe*. London: IB Tauris.
Patel, Ismail. 2016. James Carr – Experiences of Islamophobia: Living with racism in the neoliberal era [book review]. *ReOrient*. 2(1), pp.104–107.
Pędziwiatr, Konrad. 2010. *The New Muslim Elites in European Cities: Religion and Active Social Citizenship amongst Young Organized Muslims in Brussels and London*. Germany: VDM Verlag.
Phalet, Karen, Fleischmann, Fenella, Stojčić, Snežana. Ways of 'being Muslim', IN: Crul, M., Schneider, J., and Lelie, F. (eds.). 2012. *The European Second Generation Compared: Does the Integration Context Matter?* Amsterdam: Amsterdam University Press.
Rabasa, Angel and Benard, Cheryl. 2014. *Eurojihad: Patterns of Islamist Radicalisation and Terrorism in Europe*. Cambridge: Cambridge University Press.
Ramadan, Tariq. 1999. *To be a European Muslim*. Markfield, UK: The Islamic Foundation.
Sakaranaho, Tuula. 2006. *Religious Freedom, Multiculturalism, Islam: Cross-reading Finland and Ireland*. Leiden, Netherlands: Brill.
Scharbrodt, Oliver. Islam in Ireland: organising a migrant religion. Chapter 17, IN: Cosgrove, O., Cox, L., Kuhling, C., and Mulholland, P. (eds.). 2011a. *Ireland's New Religious Movements*. Cambridge: Cambridge Scholars Publishing.
Scharbrodt, Oliver. 2011b. Shaping the public image of Islam: The Shiis of Ireland as 'moderate' Muslims. *Journal of Muslim Minority Affairs*. 31(4), pp.518–533.
Scharbrodt, Oliver and Sakaranaho, Tuula. 2011. Islam and Muslims in the Republic of Ireland. *Journal of Muslim Minority Affairs*. 31(4), pp.469–485.
Scharbrodt, Oliver, Sakaranaho, Tuula, Khan, Adil H., Shanneik, Yafa and Ibrahim, Vivian. 2015. *Muslims in Ireland: Past and Present*. Edinburgh: Edinburgh University Press.
Shadid, Wasif and von Koningsveld, Sjoerd. (eds.). 1996a. *Muslims in the Margins: Political Responses to the Presence of Islam in Western Europe*. Kampen, Netherlands: Kok Pharos.
Shadid, Wasif and von Koningsveld, Sjoerd. (eds.). 1996b. *Political Participation and Identities of Muslims in Non-Muslim States*. Kampen, Netherlands: Kok Pharos.
Shanneik, Yafa. 2011. Conversion and religious habitus: The experiences of Irish women converts to Islam in the pre-Celtic Tiger era. *Journal of Muslim Minority Affairs*. 31(4), pp.503–517.

Steinhausler, Freidrich. Strategic terrorism: threats and risk assessment, IN: Gartner, H., and Cuthbertson, I.M. (eds.). 2005. *European Security and Transatlantic Relations after 9/11 and the Iraq War.* London: Palgrave MacMillan.

Tibi, Bassam. 2002. *The Challenge of Fundamentalism: Political Islam and the New World Order Disorder.* Oakland, CA: University of California Press.

Varady, David. 2008. Muslim residential clustering and political radicalism. *Housing Studies.* 23(1), pp.45–66.

3 Recognition and power

Introduction

This research aims to gather knowledge and learn about Muslim experiences in Europe by synthesising philosophy with empirical narrative sociology. Therefore, this chapter outlines and discusses the theory underpinning the research. The theory utilised in this study is Axel Honneth's (1995) critical social theory of recognition as detailed in his highly acclaimed work *The Struggle for Recognition* (SfR). This theory is crucial for this study as it inspires the content and structure of the empirical work and frames the insights that emerge. Firstly, the chapter begins by conducting a critique of the recognition model advocated by Charles Taylor. This critique enables a strong justification for utilising Honneth's more structured multidimensional typology. Then the chapter takes an in-depth look at Honneth's original theoretical insights on recognition, its advantages and development over time. In particular, the tripartite structure of the theory, which provides a deeper understanding of the interconnected forms of recognition, relation-to-self and misrecognition that manifest in the spheres of love, legal respect and social esteem. The last section explores the varying criticisms directed towards Honneth's work, and through the work of Petherbridge, Allen and McBride, pinpoints the ongoing and unresolved concerns in relation to the role of power. This constructive critique provides the necessary room to identify more complex power formations such as top-down domineering and constitutive power as well as bottom-up individual and collective resistive power. Such a nuanced understanding of power is more in line with the realities of everyday Muslim experience in a post-traditional Europe.

Taylor's Recognition model

Recognition has been a concept of importance for philosophers and academics over hundreds of years going back to Rousseau (Neuhouser 2008), Fichte (Williams 1992) and most productively by Hegel (Williams 1997). Over the last thirty years, the concept of recognition has come back to the fore again, spurred on by Charles Taylor's (1992) essay *The Politics of Recognition*. In this work, Taylor reinvigorates the intersubjective concept of recognition by exploring its ontological and internalised links to identity and how forms of non-recognition and misrecognition can inflict harm by 'imprisoning someone in a false, distorted and reduced mode of being' (Taylor 1992, p.25). Taylor identifies three forms of recognition to do with relations in the private intimate sphere as well as relations in two public spheres that he refers to as the 'Politics of Universalism and Difference' (Ibid., p.37). On the one hand, the 'Politics of Universalism' relates to citizenship and how all people should be the same in terms of having equal rights and obligations to each other as citizens. On the other, the 'Politics of Difference' relates to the human need to be recognised for one's individual and group uniqueness. Taylor's argument is that by acquiring such forms of recognition, people gain a close proximity to an authentic self by increasing the potential to reach self-fulfilment and self-realisation (Ibid., p.31).

In his work, Taylor is highly critical of how the procedural notion of the uniformal application of individual equal rights negates and becomes 'inhospitable to difference' (p.60). While this liberal model does not seek to abolish cultural difference, Taylor maintains that it is not culturally neutral and lacks respect for the survival of collective cultures of difference. Taylor takes a strong communitarian stance in that he stresses the need to respect minority cultures in a multicultural environment, which will enable such cultures to reasonably 'defend themselves', have their worth respected and survive into the future (p.64). He advocates for a non-procedural liberalism that is committed to equal concern for others but not uniform treatment. Fundamentally for Taylor, all cultures deserve a degree of respect. He states in this regard:

> The claim is that all human cultures that have animated whole societies over some considerable stretch of time have something important to say to all human beings.
>
> (Ibid., p.66).

This recognition model has been criticised. Simon Thompson (2006) is highly critical of Taylorian recognition theory for not being systematically presented as a structured typology. Although the theory comprises an intimate private sphere and two public spheres of dialogic recognition, such dimensions could have been explored further and structured into a viable typology that draws on Hegelian philosophy (Ibid., p.184). By expanding the detail relating to each sphere, Taylor would have avoided the zero-sum rivalry he enacts between the 'Politics of Universalism' and the 'Politics of Difference', where a gain for one sphere is a loss for the other (Ibid., p.55). Furthermore, Thompson identifies that Taylor makes a significant error by emphasising the need to respect both universalism and difference but does not distinguish between respect in the universal sphere and esteem in the sphere of difference (Ibid., pp.54–55).

In terms of Honneth's stance towards Taylorian recognition theory, he has proposed that cultural struggles may constitute a 'fourth recognition principle' (Fraser and Honneth 2003) understood as revolving around the 'mutual respect for the cultural particularities of groups or collectivities' (Ibid., p.159). However, he added the caveat that such forms of recognition inevitably lay claim to the 'principle of legal equality' (Ibid., p.165), which pressures the state to eliminate denigrating and humiliating obstacles that 'unjustifiably disadvantage or have disadvantaged a social group in carrying on its cultural way of life relative to the majority culture' (Ibid.). Importantly, Honneth stresses that individuals or groups cannot meaningfully demand esteem for a particular culture 'for its own sake' (Ibid., p.167) but that certain traits, abilities and achievements, which emanate from within a particular culture, can be valued for their contribution to a society's continually evolving value-horizon. This point is emphasised in the following statement:

> Certainly, cultural minorities can nurture hopes or have expectations of being especially valued by the majority for the achievements reflected in the fact of developing a distinct language and value orientation.
> (Ibid., p.168)

There has been some confusion as to exactly what the term 'traits' relates to. It is important to note that distinguishing characteristics or surface-level traits can be divided into two subgroups, genetic and constructed. Naturally determined genetic traits relate to attributes such as sex, race and ethnicity while socially constructed traits relate to attributes such as gender and religion. A development of interest has been the contestation of such attributes by fluid individuals and movements. Such recognition struggles are in the early stages of development and it remains to be seen how they will progress into the future. Of note is that in this particular study, the term 'traits' relates to both genetic and constructed aspects of identity held simultaneously by individuals.

Honneth, critical social theory and the Frankfurt School

Taking the above criticisms of Taylor's recognition theory into account, this research turns to the structured typological recognition framework developed by Axel Honneth. Although nearly thirty years old, Honneth's theory of recognition is a more structured philosophical approach to the issue of recognition and a significant development to preceding thought on the matter, especially considering its groundedness in everyday life and sociological application. With the rise of neoconservative nationalists and alt-right populism in America and Europe, the universal theme of recognition is gaining new momentum with the continuation and politicisation of identity politics alongside the conduct of old and new struggles for recognition by a variety of minority groups in many post-traditional societies, such as LGBT+, the Black Lives Matter movement and Traveller communities in Ireland.

Before proceeding, an important clarification is needed before delving deeply into Honneth's theory of recognition. It must be acknowledged that Honneth's work is broad in nature by encompassing cultural and economic considerations (Zurn 2015). This research has purposely narrowed its focus to the cultural dimension of recognition and endorses Honneth's view that struggles for recognition, particularly in the case of ethno-religious minorities, are best understood as struggles for respect and esteem.

Honneth's theory of recognition is associated with the diverse and varied paradigm of critical social theory (Tyson 1998), which traces its lineage back to the works of Hegel and Marx, and firmly roots itself in the heterogeneous and interdisciplinary Frankfurt School tradition. Joel Anderson (2011) has assessed the development of this tradition through three successive generations of academics, who have applied and developed a critical theoretical perspective in their work. For example, as Rush (2004) has outlined, first generation Frankfurt school theorists (Horkheimer, Adorno, Fromm, Lowenthal and Marcuse) focused on exposing social pathologies such as totalitarianism, alienation and reification whereas the second generation (Habermas, Schmidt, Apel and Offe) primarily concerned themselves with linguistically understanding 'the possibilities of democratic politics ... [and] the task of revealing the distortions of contemporary politics' (Anderson 2011, p.35, Wiggershaus 1994).

For Anderson, there is a new third generation, with Axel Honneth as the figurehead, that specifically focuses on social pathologies of misrecognition. Three central themes of importance highlight the direction of this new wave. Firstly, influenced by Hegel, conflicts and struggles for recognition are deemed to be the motor of progress that elevates history towards higher ethical values and a pluralistic conception of a good life. Secondly, these theorists are interested in topics such as integration, cultural identity and nationalism and have a 'greater openness to the Other' (Anderson 2011, p.51). Thirdly, unlike past generations, this new generation is interested in subjective and intersubjective experiences.

A major difference between the new wave in comparison to older generations is their relationship to normativity. The first generation suffered from a 'normative deficit' (Ibid., p.52), which led the second generation to focus on 'universalistic principles of morality, justice and truth' (Ibid.). However, in reaction to the position of the previous generations, the third generation are 'skeptical about the abstractness and uniformity' of an idealistic approach (Ibid.). Instead, the new generation gives much more attention and weight to individual lived experiences of respect and disrespect, leading to investigations of moral claims and social struggles (Ibid.). As Zurn has stated, despite such differences in approach, all the generations are linked together by the tradition of utilising an 'interdisciplinary social theory with emancipatory intent' to diagnose social pathologies that negatively impact upon individual freedom (Zurn 2015, pp.92–126).

Honneth's theory of a Struggle for Recognition

Honneth's theory focuses on interpretations of embodied experience and aims to explore the existence of a basic need to be recognised that precedes communicative action (Deranty 2009). He philosophically rethinks, illustrates and operationalises the movement of recognition, which takes place in different

Recognition and power 47

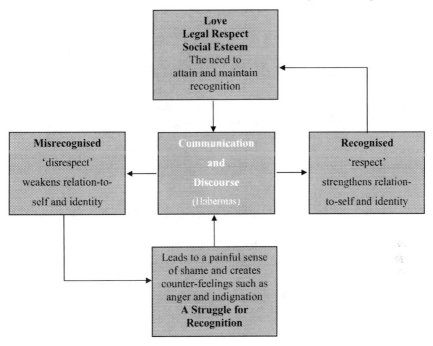

Figure 3.1 The movement of recognition

spheres of life as people attempt to gain recognition from others and how they respond and are impacted when such recognition is not forthcoming. The need for recognition is actioned through a communicative transaction, which leads to either *recognition,* or the opposite result, *misrecognition*. The relationship is then defined in positive or negative terms, with the negative aspect having the potential to lead towards a struggle for recognition. Figure 3.1 above illustrates the movement of recognition and how it relates to communication.

By reconstructing Hegel and Mead (1972), Honneth developed a theoretical key to unlock three modes of recognition, i.e. (1) love, (2) legal respect, and (3) social esteem. These three modes systematically correspond to three forms of disrespect or misrecognition, i.e. (1) abuse and rape, (2) denial of rights and exclusion, and (3) denigration and insult. The experiencing of negative misrecognition directs social actors into a *struggle for recognition* to regain a positive relation-to-self corresponding to (1) self-confidence, (2) self-respect, and (3) self-esteem. Table 3.1 below presents Honneth's original typology.

The rest of the chapter will detail Honneth's recognition theory with attention being paid to its tripartite multidimensional structure as outlined in SfR. To aid the reader, a concise outline of the theory is given to ensure that the theoretical frame is clearly understood. Furthermore, efforts are made throughout to contextualise amendments Honneth has made to his theory over the years and Table 3.2 compiles all revisions to the theory at the end of the chapter.

Table 3.1 Honneth's structure of relations of recognition

Mode of recognition	emotional support	cognitive respect	social esteem
Dimension of personality	needs and emotions	moral responsibility	traits and abilities
Forms of recognition	primary relationships (love, friendship)	legal relations (rights)	community of value (solidarity)
Developmental potential	—	generalization, de-formalization	individualization, equalization
Practical relation-to-self	basic self-confidence	self-respect	self-esteem
Forms of disrespect	abuse and rape	denial of rights, exclusion	denigration, insult
Threatened component of personality	physical integrity	social integrity	'honour', dignity

Source: Honneth, Axel. 1995. *The Struggle for Recognition*. Cambridge: Polity Press, p.129.

Love recognition

For Honneth, love relationships are defined and confined to primary relationships between small groups of people. In his opinion, love recognition 'represents a symbiosis refracted by mutual individuation' (Honneth 1995, p.107), which in essence means that recognition is a mutual double process by the fact that each social actor in a love relationship is released in his or her own individuality yet also inextricably tied or limited by the individual he or she loves. For Honneth, love recognition is 'an affirmation of independence that is guided – indeed supported – by care' (Ibid.). The double process of freedom and constraint to others through care is seen as an essential element for the production and development of individual self-confidence and participation in public life (Ibid.). Hegel's work on love reciprocity and recognition proved to be pivotal for the development of Honneth's theoretical work. This point is confirmed by Honneth when he states that

> For Hegel, love represents the first stage of reciprocal recognition, because in it subjects mutually confirm each other with regard to the concrete nature of their needs and thereby recognise each other as needy creatures ... The key for translating this topic into a context of scientific research is represented by Hegel's formulation, according to which love has to be understood as being oneself in another'.
>
> (Ibid., p.96)

As with Hegel, Honneth views love relationships as primary relationships in which there are 'strong emotional attachments among a small group of people' (Ibid., p.95). However, unlike Hegel, who concentrated and prioritised the institution of the family, Honneth broadens his conception of love to include not only familial relations but also love between friends and erotic lovers. Love relationships are bound together through the mutual recognition of need. In other words, 'subjects know themselves to be united in their neediness, in their dependence on each other' (Ibid.). For this reason, it can be stated that love relationships are based on complex interactions between dependency and independency. In terms of defining boundaries, love is kept within a bounded space by the fact that its intersubjective and mutual content to people close to us ensures that such caring relations do not extend outwards to cover a large group of people (Ibid.). To support this, Honneth moves away from the work of Mead towards Winnicottian object relations theory to provide empirical evidence and support for the development of intersubjective relations of dependent attachment and independence.

Honneth defines object relations theory as a 'therapeutic analysis of relational pathologies' that investigates 'the conditions that can lead to a successful form of emotional attachment to other persons' (Ibid., p.96). The post-Freudian work of Spitz (1965), Winnicott (1988, 1991, 2005, 2006) and Benjamin (1988) provides the evidence that enables Honneth to argue that intersubjective relations are important from the early stages of life. In opposition to the structured Freudian model of child development that focuses on the drives of the 'id', 'ego' and its influence on libidinal instincts, the Middle School of psychoanalysis provides evidence that the disconnection of the intersubjective relationship between mother and child at an early stage can cause 'severe disturbances in the behaviour of the infant' (Honneth 1995, p.96). Object relations theory provides the key argument that through intersubjective social interaction, children develop a sense of their independent capabilities through affective relations they have to other individuals, particularly primary caregivers. This theory provides an intersubjective account of human development that specifically relates to forms of recognition. In Honneth's opinion, object relations theory is well suited to advancing recognitive theory in that

> it can convincingly portray love as a particular form of recognition only owing to the specific way in which it makes the success of affectional bonds dependent on the capacity, acquired in early childhood, to strike a balance between symbiosis and self-assertion.
>
> (Ibid., p.98)

The work of Winnicott (1988, 1991, 2005, 2006) proves to be extremely important for Honneth's theory in that it provides an empirical base on which to ground the intersubjective aspects of his theory. Winnicott's work primarily focused on the mother and child relationship, which over time transforms and develops from a strong symbiotic attachment to one of individual independence. In relation to Winnicott's work, Honneth states that 'since both subjects [the primary caregiver and child] are initially included in the state of symbiotic oneness', they must recognitively 'learn from each other how to differentiate themselves as independent subjects' (Honneth 1995, p.98). Correspondingly, for both Winnicott and Honneth, the recognitive relationship between primary caregiver and child represents the first form of 'being oneself in another' and therefore 'represents the model of all more mature forms of love' (Ibid., p.100).

However, it must be kept in mind that this intersubjective relationship is not static but develops over time from dependency to independency. The primary caregiver will find independence by returning to his or her social field and the child will find independence in the ability to be alone in the world. Although there is a growth of independence, intersubjective recognition is maintained so as to build confidence and trust in and between both subjects. For Honneth, this dual process of dependence and independence through intersubjectivity is central to Winnicott's work in that

> the ability to be alone is dependent on the child's trust in the continuity of the 'mother's' care. [Winnicott's thesis] provides some insight into the type of relation-to-self that one can develop when one knows oneself to be loved by a person that one experiences as independent and for whom one, in turn, feels affection or love ... If the mother's love is lasting and reliable, the child can simultaneously develop, under the umbrella of her intersubjective reliability, a sense of confidence in the social provision of the needs he or she has, and via the psychological path this opens up, a basic 'capacity to be alone' gradually unfolds in the child.
> (Ibid., pp.103–104)

In his work, Winnicott focused predominantly on the child's ability to cope with the transformation from symbiotic dependency to a degree of independence. By studying this phase of intersubjective growth, Winnicott developed the concept of 'transitional objects', in which children become obsessive about specific environmental objects (e.g. toys, string, blankets and the child's own thumb and fist) that are either loved with tenderness or destructively abused (Caldwell and Joyce 2011). These could be termed 'comfort objects' as they provide a sense of calm to the user by easing stress and anxiety. As Honneth states in relation to Winnicott's concept, 'there are grounds for supposing that they [transitional objects] represent surrogates for the "mother", who has been lost to external reality' (Honneth 1995, p.102). In other words, it is through such objects that young children negotiate the fear and trauma of inner and outer reality. Ontologically, transitional objects enable the child to mediate between their perceptive feeling of omnipotence yet creatively and playfully interact with the overwhelming scope of reality.

John Rundell has suggested that Honneth's use of Winnicott's work has given recognition theory an 'imaginary turn' in which imagination, creative play and reflexivity 'are outcomes of a developmental process rather than constitutive dimensions of the human being ... the creation of meaning and mutual recognition stands in homologous relation with one another' (Rundell 2001, p.68). As

Winnicott states about transitional objects 'this object can become vitally important and can have value as an object intermediate between self and the outside world' (Winnicott 2006, p.18).

Winnicott and Honneth agree that this mediating sphere between playfulness and reality is the human solution to persistent ontological dilemmas 'that people face throughout their lives' (Honneth 1995, p.103). Being playfully lost in interaction, whether that is through culture (Kuhn 2013) or religion, enables people to appease the ontological fear of omnipotent reality (Young 1994). As Parker (2011) has explored, Winnicott was highly influenced in his youth by his family's adherence to Wesleyan Methodist religious tradition. Although he claimed that he eventually 'grew up, out of' his religious observance, Winnicott maintained that religious adherence could have a positive as well as negative impact upon individuals and groups. Winnicott commonly compared the beneficial mental and emotional aspects of religious adherence to the practise of psychoanalysis (Parker 2011).

Relating the above back to love recognition, Honneth emphasises that the original experience of dependence and independence sets the stage for the formation of love relationships. Love is a relationship in which individuals are attached yet separate, the same yet different. Love is the 'the recognition of the other as an independent person' (Honneth 1995, p.105). In the work of Benjamin (1988), the significance of the early relationships is explored in terms of its impact on adult relationships, particularly in terms of the development of sexual pathologies such as masochism and sadism. She states the following on the relationship between intersubjectivity and recognition:

> My premise is that recognition of the other is the decisive aspect of differentiation. In recognition, someone who is different and outside shares a similar feeling, different minds and bodies attune. In erotic union this attunement can be so intense that self and other feel as if momentarily 'inside' each other, as part of a whole. Receptivity and self-expression, the sense of losing the self in the other and the sense of being truly known for oneself all coalesce ... the simultaneous desire of loss of self and for wholeness (or oneness) with the other, often described as the ultimate point of erotic union, is really a form of the desire for recognition. In getting pleasure *with* the other and taking pleasure *in* the other, we engage in mutual recognition.
> (Benjamin 1988, p.126)

Self-confidence

In SfR, Honneth (1995) develops the concept of love recognition by discussing how the recognition of love mutually benefits individuals by enabling them to 'acquire basic self-confidence in themselves' (Ibid., p.106). This original form of relation-to-self is the premise upon which he states that love recognition is 'both conceptually and genetically prior to every other form of reciprocal recognition' (Ibid.). Love recognition is given a leading role. Love is needed by individuals first and foremost because it is through it that individuals develop a relation-to-self in which a basic level of self-confidence is attained. It enables individuals to confidently interact in the culture of public life. As Honneth states, love generates within all human beings, 'the psychological foundation for trusting one's own sense of one's needs and urges' (Ibid., p.118). Self-confidence enables an individual to interact as an independent and autonomous unit outside of the comforting sphere of love. For Honneth, the 'intersubjective experience of love helps [constitute] ... the psychological precondition for the development of all further attitudes of self-respect' (Ibid., p.107). It is an important factor that invigorates people to participate in public life (Ibid.). In other words, the dynamics of love recognition have a powerful influence on an individual's capacity to interact productively in the wider legal and societal spheres. Of note is that Honneth has amended his theory to acknowledge that love relations and their corresponding institutions have developed and transformed through history, in similarity to legal respect and social esteem (Honneth 2014).

Love and its disrespect

In terms of disrespect related to the recognitive sphere of love, Honneth determines that physical abuse or 'forms of practical maltreatment' (Honneth 1995, p.132) represent a form of misrecognition. Disrespect can detrimentally affect a person's relation-to-self. For Honneth, by being physically maltreated,

> a person is forcibly deprived of any opportunity freely to dispose over his or her own body [and this] represent[s] the most fundamental sort of personal degradation.
>
> (Ibid.)

Taking control of another person's body against their will causes humiliation. The victim feels a sense of shame in that their own worth is reduced. For Honneth, this form of disrespect against an individual's physical integrity, commonly associated with rape, spousal abuse or torture, detrimentally impacts upon a person's relation-to-self (Ibid.). It is the most destructive form of disrespect that can be directed towards a person's identity because it is physical pain combined with psychological control. Victims feel a sense of defencelessness and insecurity related to the impending psychological fear of coming under physical abuse. Honneth's model argues that such forms of disrespect do immense 'damage to one's basic self-confidence [learned through love] that one can autonomously co-ordinate one's own body' (Ibid.) In contrast to such disrespect, the norms of love nurture the relationship between emotions and the physical body, thereby building a sense of trust in oneself and others. For Honneth, the destruction of physical integrity breaks what love enabled and such suffering leads to a 'dramatic breakdown in one's trust in the reliability of the social world' and brings about 'a collapse in one's own basic self-confidence' (Ibid., p.133).

Legal recognition

The next social sphere is the universal recognition of rights. Honneth takes from Hegel and Mead the point that rights and obligations are formulated, understood and practised through the utilisation of mutual recognition by the fact that social actors can only come to understand themselves as legal persons and the validity of their claimed rights by taking 'the perspective of the generalised other' (Honneth 1995, p.108). In SfR, Honneth clarifies that legal relations are constituted by mutual recognition and that through the process of historical development such relations contain a transformative character. The development of equal legal rights was founded on rational agreement between individuals and modern communities under the regulation of law and is grounded 'on the assumption of the moral accountability of all its members' (Ibid., p.114). Under the law, if all individuals are seen as morally responsible entities, the tools for the transformative potential of legal recognition is provided for, in that such individuals are consistently working towards the betterment of legal content and advocating for the expansion of the scope of individual rights in the administration of collective living. Honneth states on this point:

> As a result of the introduction of the principle of equality into modern law, the status of a legal person was not only gradually broadened with regard to its content, in that it cumulatively incorporated new claims, but was also gradually expanded in the social sense that it was extended to an ever-increasing number of members of society.
>
> (Ibid., p.118)

Reflecting on legal recognition, Honneth makes an important differentiation between social esteem in both the legal sphere and in the wider societal sphere of recognition. Through legal respect, individuals garner self-respect by the fact that the individual is recognised by others in society as a morally responsible person with rights claims and the power to advocate for expansions to rights in society. This self-respect must be differentiated from esteeming people, which is a more particular and individualist form of recognition. As Honneth states:

> What makes esteeming someone different from recognising him or her as a person is primarily the fact that it involves not the empirical application of general, intuitively known norms but rather the graduated appraisal of concrete traits and abilities.
>
> (Ibid., p.113)

Honneth illustrates the strong connection between law and recognition by referring to Hegel and Mead, who both viewed law and its development as a form of mutual recognition in which we 'can only come to know ourselves as the bearers of rights' (Ibid., p.108) to the extent that 'we have taken the perspective of the "generalised other", which teaches us to recognise the other members of the community as the bearers of rights' (Ibid.). Honneth connects respect to legal recognition by stating that

> [legal recognition is a] situation in which self and other respect each other as legal subjects for the sole reason that they are both aware of the social norms by which rights and duties are distributed in their community.
> (Ibid.)

Legal recognition is formed through historical processes of development, which Honneth identifies as progressing from traditional law (in which membership of a community and legal entitlement is intrinsically connected to the exceptions and privileges linked to the division of labour) to post-traditional law in which 'the expression of the universalisable interests of all members of society' (Ibid., p.110) has come to prominence. In this new universalised system of law, the exceptions and privileges once taken as given are deemed invalid and prohibited (Ibid.) while new legal norms are codified in agreement with 'free and equal beings' that reciprocally enter into a lawful rights-based relationship (Ibid.). Honneth views the historical development of the legal sphere as a process of deformalisation, i.e. a decoupling of legal recognition and social esteem alongside a process of universalisation, which involves the opening-up and democratisation of the legal sphere to include all persons based on their humanness. With the above in mind, it can be stated that legal recognition is moving away from a traditional form to one that reflects a post-traditional society that aspires to be more democratic and equal.

Self-respect

As with love recognition, Honneth determined that recognition and misrecognition both impact upon a person's relation-to-self. The bonds of love enable individuals to develop a relation-to-self that is viewed as basic self-confidence, thereby creating the motivation for an individual to act autonomously outside the comfort and security of small affective spheres. With regards to legal recognition, Honneth argues, with reference to the work of Joel Feinberg, that the granting of and obtaining of rights is intrinsically connected to 'the central psychological phenomenon' of self-respect (Honneth 1995, p.118). Feinberg connects the granting of legal rights to the attainment of self-respect by using the conceptual argument of 'Nowheresville', an imaginary town, whose inhabitants live a normal day-to-day life, apart from one crucial difference, in this town, individual rights do not exist. Feinberg's point is that due to the lack of rights, individuals lack the capacity to develop relations of self-respect towards themselves and to others (Feinberg 1980, pp.143–158). By being granted the same rights as others, an individual comes to learn that he or she is respected as an autonomous and morally responsible person and this mutual intersubjective recognition creates a sense of self-respect in which 'one is able to respect oneself, because one deserves the respect of everyone else' (Honneth 1995, p.118). This granting of rights by others enables a person to view themselves as morally responsible and gives the individual, as Honneth suggests, the 'possibility of seeing their actions as the universally respected expression of their own autonomy' (Ibid.). In the context of modern law, the argument is that dual processes of deformalisation and universalisation increased the number of once excluded individuals and groups, who can experience legal respect, and thereby, gain self-respect through reciprocal recognition. However, Honneth is adamant that the legal system should not recognise the social status (or the particular traits, abilities and achievements) of individuals but must view people uniformly in their humanness, i.e. as people and citizens, who are deserving of mutual rights towards one another. In Honneth's assessment, this condition is an important differentiation between traditional law and subsequent modern forms of legal recognition:

> What is required are conditions in which individual rights are no longer granted disparately to members of social status groups but are granted equally to all people as free beings, only then will the individual legal person be able to see in them an objectivated point of reference for the idea that he or she is recognised for having the capacity for autonomously forming judgements.
>
> (Ibid., p.119)

The statement above does not mean that individuals and groups are automatically conferred with legal recognition. As is well known, civic stratification has been a common tool used by nation states to regulate the rights and obligations of their respective populations by categorising people into a variety of legal statuses such as long-term residents or denizens, refugees and asylum-seekers (Carolan 2015). Thomas Hammer (1990) categorised resident third-country nationals, who enjoy civic and social rights yet limited political rights in a host country as a new form of social status known as denizenship. For an analysis of denizenship dilemmas in contemporary Europe and for a detailed discussion about this status and how it relates to exclusion, see the work of both Benhabib (2004) and Beckman (2009).

It is important to acknowledge that social struggle is an important process in the granting of recognition by others. The historical examples of this are many and varied. The most obvious example would be the American civil rights movement of the 1950s and 1960s, in which dark-skinned people, predominantly African-Americans, struggled to attain basic legal recognition, equality and self-respect on par with others in American society. This struggle became an example to others in America and beyond. For example, the civil rights movement that subsequently emerged in Northern Ireland involved Catholic nationalists publicly protesting against their unequal treatment in the predominantly Protestant-controlled province. Through these examples, it becomes apparent that social struggle, through actions of violent or non-violent protest and resistance, are important individual and collective tools used to counteract social shame. It is a struggle for recognition of one's right to be legally the same as others, i.e. an autonomous human being, who can partake in moral decision-making processes as others do. In relation to these struggles, Honneth states that

> In these exceptional historical situations – such as the one represented by discussions in the civil rights movement of the fifties and sixties in the US – the psychological significance of legal recognition for the self-respect of excluded collectivities breaks the linguistic surface ... one regularly finds talk of how the endurance of legal under-privileging necessarily leads to a crippling feeling of social shame, from which one can be liberated only through active protest and resistance.
> (Honneth 1995, p.121)

Universal value and its disrespect

The next form of disrespect identified by Honneth relates to social integrity in the legal sphere. This form of disrespect or misrecognition is intrinsically linked to the concept of equality in terms of the conferral of universal rights and being treated the same as others in society. Honneth roughly defines rights as

> ... referring to those individual claims that a person can legitimately expect to have socially met because he or she participates, with equal rights, in the institutional order as a full-fledged member of the community.
> (Honneth 1995, p.133)

For Honneth, an example of this form of disrespect is when an individual is 'structurally excluded from the possession of certain rights within a community' (Ibid.). In terms of a person's relation-to-self, such exclusion impacts upon a person's self-respect in that 'he or she is not being accorded the same degree of moral responsibility as other members of society' (Ibid.). When this occurs, the ostracised individual feels that he or she is 'not enjoying the status of a full-fledged partner to interaction, equally endowed with moral rights' (Ibid.). Such a denial of rights curtails a person's capacity to be autonomous in their actions and, in essence, violates that person's intersubjective expectations. (Ibid., p.134). The loss of such self-respect, by being denied universal rights, impedes the ability of an ostracised person to look upon themselves as a fully equipped legal being, who is equal to others they interact with on a daily basis. This is an issue of importance because it relates to the right to be recognised legally as human, being afforded the same rights and obligations as others and not being excluded or hampered in fully interacting and voicing one's opinion in a post-traditional democratic state.

Societal recognition

The third mode relates to wider societal recognition. Hegel and Mead viewed this sphere as a higher mode of recognition that rises above affections of love and universal legal identifications by the fact that people have a need for a 'form of social esteem that allows them to relate positively to their concrete traits and abilities' (Honneth 1995, p.121). Honneth develops on his predecessors by suggesting that a key component to social recognition is 'an intersubjective shared-value system' (Ibid.) in which individuals mutually esteem each other as unique persons by sharing 'an orientation to those values and goals that indicate to each other the significance or contribution of their qualities for the life of the other' (Ibid.). What differentiates societal from legal recognition is the fact that this form specifically relates to intersubjective recognition of concrete traits and abilities held by an individual in difference to others. There is an amendment here to be noted in relation to the term 'concrete traits and abilities'. In his work, Honneth has narrowly tied esteem recognition to the issue of contribution through work. However, like Zurn (2015, p.83), this study adopts a view of social esteem that broadly considers contributions to go beyond economic considerations in that esteem recognition can be related to the 'differential regard given to individuals based upon the degree to which their *traits, abilities,* and *achievements* are taken to make social contributions' (Ibid.). This stance keeps open the notion that morally admirable traits practised through overt religiosity may also provide the basis for recognitively claiming esteem.

Unlike the universal legal form, societal recognition is based on the recognition of difference, uniqueness and individuality. It is therefore inextricably linked to social esteem. Socially esteeming a person's traits, abilities and achievements is furthermore linked to the overall perception that such unique individual characteristics benefit society, i.e. they contribute to the value-horizon of a society. However, it must also be considered that dominant cultures may have *power-over* the form and the direction of a particular value-horizon and be in a domineering position to control what is deemed to be a contribution. With that said, for Honneth, relationships of recognition will be larger in scope and symmetrical if more plural value-horizons exist in society. On this point, Honneth suggests that:

> The cultural self-understanding of a society provides the criteria that orient the social esteem of persons, because their abilities and achievements are judged intersubjectively according to the degree to which they can help to realise culturally defined values. This form of mutual recognition is thus tied to the presupposition of a context of social life, whose members, though their orientation towards shared conceptions of their goals, form a community of value.
>
> (Honneth 1995, p.122)

58   Recognition and power

As with the two previous modes of recognition, Honneth advocates that the wider societal sphere is also an arena of conflict in which groups struggle for the dominance and hierarchical validity of their individual achievements and ways of being. This is a permanent arena of social struggle in which the worth of individuals and groups is incorporated (or not) into a society's value-horizon. On this point, Honneth states:

> In modern societies, relations to social esteem are subject to a permanent struggle, in which different groups attempt, by means of symbolic force and with reference to general goals, to raise the value of the abilities associated with their way of life ... the more successful social movements are at drawing the public sphere's attention to the neglected significance of the traits and abilities they collectively represent, the better their chances of raising the social worth or, indeed, the standing of their members.
>
> (Ibid., p.127)

The complexity of social recognition is emphasised by Honneth when he suggests that although such recognition should be an assessment of an individual's traits, abilities and achievements, it has been consumed into group-orientated status struggles. An individual's unique contributions are assimilated into a collective so as to advocate to the rest of society for the benefits of a particular way of life. This results in a person's individual form of honour or dignity, which comes to fruition by esteeming particular traits, abilities and achievements, being collectivised into a form of 'group-pride and collective honour' (Ibid., p.128). In general, such societal groups are cohesive and generate high levels of internal solidarity by the fact that the 'intersubjective value-horizon' (Ibid.) among individuals in these groups is mutually recognised. However, Honneth views esteem that is harnessed by collective lobbying as having a greater transformative potential when applied back to the individual. He states in this regard:

> The individual no longer has to attribute [to] an entire collective the respect that he or she receives for accomplishments that fit social standards but can refer them positively back to him or herself instead. Under these altered conditions, the experience of being socially esteemed is accompanied by a felt confidence that one's achievements or abilities will be recognised as 'valuable' by other members of society. We can meaningfully term this type of practical relation-to-self 'self-esteem'.
>
> (Ibid., p.129)

With the decoupling of legal recognition and social esteem in the system of modern law, a third form of recognition comes into view, which is social esteem through societal recognition. As with the spheres of love and legal relations, wider social recognition develops overtime through history. Honneth views the historical development of this sphere as a process of individualisation, which emphasises horizontal individual attainments of esteem against the esteem of hierarchical status groups as well as through a process of equalisation in which the scope of who can be esteemed is opened up to individuals in society based on merit and not due to asymmetrical social positions.

Self-esteem

Honneth argues that societal recognition gives an individual a sense of self-esteem through the process of recognising a person's particular traits, abilities and achievements 'above and beyond the experience of affectionate care and legal recognition' (Honneth 1995). However, realistically, societal goals can only be attained through group interaction. Therefore, a sense of esteem is attained by individuals through collective group membership, solidarity and action because 'only the group as a whole can feel itself to be the addressee of esteem' (Ibid., p.128). Collectives are composed of individuals, who stand in solidarity and symmetrically esteem each other (Ibid.). For Honneth, war is a good example of a symmetrical relationship of esteem in that it 'represents a collective event that is able to create spontaneous relationships of solidarity and sympathy across social boundaries' (Ibid.). However, with the individualisation of social esteem in post-traditional societies, individuals can associate accomplishments 'positively back to himself or herself' (Ibid.) instead of through a collective status. For Honneth, such developments ensure that 'the experience of being socially esteemed is accompanied by a felt confidence that one's achievements or abilities will be recognised as valuable by other members of society' (Ibid.). Honneth defines this feeling of self-worth as a 'parallel category to the concepts of basic self-confidence and self-respect' (Ibid., p.129). He refers to this form of relation-to-self as self-esteem and argues that

> the extent to which every member of society is [in] a position to esteem himself or herself, one can speak of a state of societal solidarity.
> (Ibid.)

With that said, it is important to clarify that societal recognition of an individual's traits, abilities and achievements is an unequal practice as unique individuals vary and cannot be accorded an equal level of esteem. Therefore, individuals do not have an immediate right to equal esteem, but more realistically, should be given an equal chance or opportunity to attain social esteem from others. Honneth comments on this difference between the principles of equality and achievement:

> The fact that 'symmetrical' cannot mean here that we esteem each other to the same degree is already clear from the essential openness to interpretation of every societal value-horizon ... 'symmetrical' must mean instead that every subject is free from being collectively denigrated, so

that one is given the chance to experience oneself to be recognised, in light of one's own accomplishments and abilities, as valuable for society.

(Ibid., p.130)

Particular value and its disrespect

The third type of disrespect identified in Honneth's theoretical model is related to the integrity of an individual's value, i.e. how individuals or members of groups are valued by society. Disrespect comes about when a way of life is denigrated by the cultural norms of a society. In other words, a particular way of living life is not valued by others. Numerous examples exist from the global historical record relating to denigrations of religion, gender, race or sexual identity. In other words, the misrecognition of minorities, who differ from the dominant ethno-cultural norms prevalent within a bounded nation state. Progressive countries have begun to recognise the value of these once ostracised groups. For an Irish example, the indifferent treatment of women, children and Traveller groups through the twentieth century are prime examples of maltreatment and ongoing reconciliation.

For Honneth, this 'form of behaviour [is] ordinarily labeled insulting or degrading today' (Honneth 1995, p.134). When a person is socially esteemed, it modifies a person's honour or dignity, today commonly called *status*, by the fact that the person's way of life or the person's manner of self-realisation is accorded value by a 'society's inherited cultural horizon' (Ibid.). However, the opposite is the case when a person's way of being is socially misrecognised. In this instance, the way of life of the person (or the associated collective) is not valued by individuals (and/or other collectives) in society due to the fact or perception that it is in opposition to the shared values and goals that constitute the continuing trajectory of that society's value-horizon. For Honneth, societal misrecognition has detrimental ramifications for a person by 'bringing with it a loss of personal self-esteem' (Ibid.) In such cases, an individual will feel that the worth of his or her particular traits, abilities and achievements is misrecognised and undervalued by society. Like the loss of self-confidence and self-respect, such devaluation of a person's self-esteem causes shame and anger that rebounds into a struggle for recognition to affirm one's identity and regain a positive relation-to-self.

Constructively criticising the theoretical frame

This research is positively inspired by Honneth's recognition theory in terms of its structured typology that distinguishes between respect and esteem, its multidimensional perspective on social life, and its ability to identify social pathologies through an exploration of everyday moral grammar. However, there have also been numerous critiques of Honneth's broad theoretical framework since its publication. This section will examine such criticisms, which is an important undertaking as it enables a positioning of this study.

Since the publication of SfR, Honneth's theory of recognition has been acclaimed but also criticised. These criticisms have come from outside sources but also from within the critical theory tradition itself. A detailed account of each substantial criticism will not be conducted here but merely listed for the sake of brevity. They relate to the questioning of whether the theory is anthropological and/or historical (Petherbridge 2013), the use of social psychology and the relationship between recognition and redistribution (Fraser and Honneth 2003), the scope of recognition (Laitinen 2010), a critique of the political focus of the theory (Deranty and Renault 2007), as well as Thompson's (2006) critique of the causal mechanism of the theory and of Honneth's teleological ideal of ethical life.

Of note is that many recognition theorists have claimed that Honneth's theoretical notions are too optimistically idealistic. A major criticism of Honneth's theory identified by numerous reviewers of his work relates to his conception of power. It must be stated that Honneth has always been open to debating with others and has remained flexible in terms of amendments to his theory that are deemed necessary (Honneth 2010, pp.499–520). The lack of a complex understanding of power is a recurring critique and has ramifications for this study that is inspired by Honneth's theoretical framework.

The complexity of power

Stephen Lukes (2005) gives a powerful account of the persistent problems and disagreements in academia in terms of how to view power. Inspired by broad yet refined Foucauldian insights, Lukes turns away from the view that power is specifically related to power-over others as coercive domination but that power can also be positively beneficial and involve agentic resistances. As McNay (1994) has cogently explained Michel Foucault 'was concerned to examine how power relations of inequality and oppression are created and maintained in more subtle and diffuse ways through ostensibly humane and freely adopted social practises' (p.5). As is well known, Foucault (2002) penetrated the micropractices of power-knowledge dynamics enabling his conceptual thinking to evolve over time from disciplinary power to biopolitical power and eventually to governmentality (McNay 1994, Hoffman 2013). He identified dual forms of power-over others in terms of negative *power as domination* and positive *power as constitution*. Examples of this dual power include the asymmetrical relationships between mother and child, teacher and student, as well as the legal system and its regulation of rights and obligations for citizens. In McNay's words, Foucault identified that 'power constrains individuals but it also constitutes the condition of possibility of their freedom' (McNay 1994, p.11). In other words, power can be domineering but it can also be productive in that it can constitutively shape an individual's identity and way of being as well as forming and driving capacities to resist.

As McNay and Hoffman have identified, even though in his personal life Foucault engaged and resisted forms of domineering power – by, for example, working with the Information Group on Prisons (GIP), enthusiastically supporting the Iranian revolution, and working on behalf of the Solidarity movement in Poland. However, paradoxically in his later works, he never fully sustains power as a positively productive force nor fully examines an agentic margin of freedom that enables an individual and/or collective to develop resistive practices. Instead, Foucault consistently slips back into an understanding of power-over in terms of domination by material or technical control.

The work of Philip Petit (1997, 2012, 2014) is important for understanding domination as *power-over* others. Petit defined domineering power as existing only to the extent that the domineering people have the (1) capacity to intentionally or unintentionally interfere negatively with others, (2) that the 'making of things worse' through interference is done on an arbitrary basis, and (3) that it is common knowledge that the above interference restricts certain choices the other is in a position to make (pp.52–61). Interference can be coercion against a body, a will or even manipulation that escapes common knowledge and productive powers (Ibid.). For Petit, laws and norms that constitute identity must be established to regulate relations and guard against forms of domination (Ibid.). Examples of regulatory power include a culture of legal rights that protects women and children from patriarchal abuse or employment regulations that guarantee appropriate labour conditions for workers (Ibid.). For Petit, non-domination is a 'gateway good' and for the realisation of social justice in the form of republican freedom what is needed is a mixed constitution and a communicative contestatory citizenship (Petit 2012, p.5). In terms of everyday interactions, he mentions that freedom from domination can be examined by the simple use of the user-friendly 'eyeball' test, which requires that

> ... people will be adequately resourced and protected in the exercise of their basic liberties to the extent that, absent excessive timidity or the like, they are enabled by the most demanding local standards to look one another in the eye without reason for fear or deference. They are able to walk tall [with confidence] ... enjoying a communal form of recognition that they are each more or less proof against the interference of others, in that sense, they command the respect of all.
>
> (Ibid., p.84)

Honneth on power

In terms of assessing Honneth's stance on power dynamics, since the publication of SfR, a number of criticisms have been presented that tackle the positioning of the concept of power in his theory of recognition (Van Den Brink and Owen 2007). One of the most succinct and in-depth investigations emanates from Danielle Petherbridge (2011, 2013). She criticises not only the accuracy of Honneth's reconstructive method but also his conception of power and how it developed in his work. She contends that his early work (Honneth 1991) had a much more nuanced understanding of power by reflecting on the work of Habermas (1984, 1987) and Foucault (2002). She determines that although Honneth did not share a systems-theoretic notion of power like Foucault, his action-theoretic notion of power was highly influenced by Foucault's claim that the social world is constituted as a field of intersubjective struggle (Petherbridge 2013).

Petherbridge suggests that, in his earlier work, Honneth is much more aware of social life revolving around action-theoretic forms of *micro-power*, i.e. an individual's capacity to agentically act against domination in an open field of social struggle and contestation. However, this perspective is diluted in SfR, when Honneth moves from the Habermasian notion of mutual understanding to the concept of mutual recognition and from the Foucauldian idea of *power/struggle* to the Hegelian concept of *recognition/struggle* (Ibid., p.36). In Petherbridge's opinion, a more nuanced conception of power is lost in the move from an action-theoretic perspective to the Hegelian notion of a struggle for recognition (Ibid.).

With that said, Petherbridge does take notice of Honneth's re-engagement with the 'problem of power' (Ibid., p.191) by acknowledging his reformed opinion 'that recognition can take ideological forms and that power can operate in ways that are productive of identity' (Ibid.). She views Honneth's article, *Recognition as Ideology* (Honneth 2012, pp.75–97), as a gesture 'towards Foucault' (Ibid.) in that it attempts to remedy the problem of power in Honnethian recognition theory and tackle pertinent questions as to what counts as a legitimate struggle for recognition and how power impinges upon recognitive relations?

In *Recognition as Ideology*, Honneth (2012) attempts to differentiate between legitimate and ideological forms of recognition. Like reification and invisibilisation, ideology is a second order social pathology in that its negative contents and ramifications are harder for ordinary citizens to reflect upon in the course of everyday life (Zurn 2015, p.99). In contrast, first order pathologies, such as patriarchy, insecure citizenship status and discrimination can be reflected upon and practically resisted.

Honneth characterises ideological recognition as having four prime characteristics: it must give affirmation to those it addresses, it must be credible, it must be contrastive in the sense of being an historical progression, and lastly, it must contain a degree of rationality to be believed (Honneth 2012, pp.78–85). However, although ideological recognition contains a degree of rationality, Honneth determines that it can be identified and separated from positive forms of recognition by acknowledging its irrational core and its inability to fulfil promises. This aspect of ideological recognition provides the solution for differentiating it from forms of recognition that are legitimate and ethically justified. As Honneth states, the irrationality found in ideological recognition is found in the 'discrepancy between evaluative promises and material fulfilment' (Ibid.), i.e. ideologies may rationally propagate potential benefit (whether that be internal and/or external), however, in reality, their inherent irrationality ensures that such promises never materialise. Ideologies do not have any substantive substance. For Honneth, the inability to materialise propagated promises is the solution to identifying the irrational core of ideological systems. For example, such forms of recognition include advertising and neoliberal working practices, in which the worker is transformed into an ultra-flexible and self-marketing entreployee (Ibid., p.92).

Despite Honneth's amendments and clarifications in relation to his thinking on power, Petherbridge (2013) remains critical of this revised formulation. She determines that Honneth's viewpoint of power lacks complexity by being overly focused on domineering power. Falling into the same thought pattern as Carr in Chapter 2, Honneth leaves unexplored how top-down constitutive power can be positively beneficial by productively shaping identities as well as how agentic forms of bottom-up resistive power relate and interact with the two forms of power-over in terms of the legitimation of authority. To support her critique, Petherbridge turns to the work of another critical theorist Amy Allen, who has in her work, explored the complex relationship between power and autonomy. Allen has researched the interactions between varying forms of *power-over* others (i.e. domineering and constitutive power) as well as agentic forms of power in terms of an individualised *power-to* act and collective *power-with* others to resist.

Variations of power

Amy Allen (1999, 2008, 2010) explores the dynamics of domination and productive power in the familial relationship between parents and their children. For Allen, Honneth's recognition theory cannot take account of 'modes of subordination that function without producing any struggle' (Allen 2010, pp.21–32). To illustrate her feminist critique, she uses the hypothetical example of a five-year-old girl, who due to her dependence in the familial sphere is exposed to domineering and constitutive power by growing up in a capitalist and hyper-consumerist society in which gender roles and norms are passed down from generation to generation. As Allen states in relation to this predicament:

> Elizabeth is receiving love and gender subordination in a single stroke for as long as she has been alive, and for all that time has been unable to assess that gender ideology critically because she has not yet fully developed the requisite capacity for autonomy, she is likely to form a psychic attachment to those subordinating modes of femininity that may prove, in adulthood, quite difficult to shake.
>
> (Ibid.)

In a group interview, Amy Allen, Maeve Cooke and Axel Honneth candidly discuss the disabling dynamic of domination alongside the ontologically enabling dynamic of constitutive power (Honneth, Allen and Cooke 2010, p.154). In relation to the illustrative scenario of Elizabeth, who symbolises Allen's argument that dependent children in the familial love sphere may be subject to domineering and constitutive forms of power without appeal, Honneth agrees that the transmission of such gender roles should be avoided because they persist today through parental transmission despite being the *cultural hangovers* of a past era:

these almost invisible processes of reproducing a certain picture of femininity by way of certain forms of care-giving are forms of recognition that are historically superseded. If one were to challenge the parents, they would say that they shouldn't be transmitting such norms of femininity. In other words, the parents' intentions would be to avoid doing so if they could. I would say, it's a hangover from a period of socio-cultural domination in which a certain picture of femininity prevailed. The parents are unable to avoid reproducing this picture even though they are consciously aware that it's a historically superseded form of recognition, of social evaluation and social esteem ... it is bad because it is historically superseded.

(Ibid., p.164)

Authority and social norms

With the limitations of Honneth's conception of power identified through the critiques of Petherbridge and Allen, the work of Cillian McBride (2013) comes into focus in terms of giving an informative account of the interaction between recognition, norms, authority and agentic resistance. In terms of struggles over the recognition of our identities and issues of power and authority, McBride puts into question whether recognition-sensitive individuals can transparently understand their identities and whether they are 'best placed to possess that knowledge' (Ibid., p.135). In contrast to Honneth's developmental account of recognition, McBride's interactionist approach determines that it is through intersubjective relations to others that our self-conceptions are adapted and revised 'in light of our encounters with others' (Ibid., p.140). Such everyday encounters lead to enlightening and/or disturbing revelations about who we really are (Ibid., pp.135–136). For McBride, recognitive relations play a pivotal role in the 'project of maintaining and realising oneself' (Ibid., p.141). In his opinion, struggles for recognition are essentially struggles over authority and the production of accepted norms. He states in this regard that they are

firstly, [struggles] over our self-interpretations, and secondly, [struggles] over the authority of the normative expectations which we have of others and of ourselves, and which others in turn, have of us.

(Ibid., p.136)

Put another way, recognition from B is valued by claimant A only if A recognises the judgemental authority of B and vice versa. McBride stresses the need to consider the 'role of objective social norms in our self-interpretations' (Ibid.). For him, social interaction is composed of informal social norms that guide our beliefs and actions about what is acceptable as normal behaviour. Such norms inform the variety of social roles people occupy and the normative expectations brought to bear by occupying such roles.

A key point made by McBride is that norms may be related to forms of domineering power. In his work, he highlights the issue of honour killings in ethno-Muslim communities as an example of how social norms acted-out to attain social esteem can be socially pathological and unreasonably legitimised by the authority of patriarchal power (Ibid., p.144). Another example utilised by McBride is the role of 'the good mother' and how women commonly find themselves dilemmatically subjected to competing demands from various authoritative sources – whether that be media experts, other mothers, family members, or employers. Such legitimised authorities determine how mothers ought to act in order to reach what is perceived to be the correct standard of what constitutes 'the good mother' (Ibid., p.161). As with McBride, Smyth (2012) highlights three roles that are adopted by mothers – expressivist, rationalist and pragmatist – that, as coping strategies, help mothers negotiate their actions and the social politics of motherhood that is regulated and controlled by the opinion of varying authorities.

McBride takes the stance that it is up to the agency of the individual woman to resolve such struggles by working out 'for herself how best to define and inhabit the role and cope with the inevitable mixture of recognition and misrecognition that must accompany her judgement' (2013, p.161). Such agency may involve 'an appeal to an alternative audience' (Ibid., p.156), which may legitimise the authority of one source over another with regards to 'good mothering'. Importantly for this study, McBride connects recognition struggles to authority dynamics as well as elaborating on the everyday pressures and contestations associated with social norms. As he states in this regard:

> … we must always attend to the way the social world is constituted by social norms, the informal rules which govern social interaction, from the ways we eat, dress and speak to one another, up to the roles we occupy and the constitution of social, economic and political institutions. These unwritten rules govern every aspect of our lives in ways we find so familiar that we often do not even notice that we are following these rules, applying them to ourselves and to others, and having them applied to ourselves in turn.
>
> (Ibid., p.141)

Table 3.2 below is an amendment to Honneth's recognition typology. It presents minor amendments made by Honneth over the years as well as amendments necessary for the context of this research. For example, in line with Honneth's revisions, this study focuses on traits, abilities and achievements. In the section related to forms of recognition, this research focuses on primary relationships in the family, friendships and the Muslim community. It also looks at rights and obligations in the legal sphere as well as solidarity, societal value and merit in the wider societal sphere. The revised table has two new rows, which indicate whether a mode of recognition is public or private and which principle of justice relates to each sphere of recognition. To better understand and visualise the *movement of recognition*, readers can operationalise each mode of recognition and their distinct characteristics in terms of respect, relation-to-self and disrespect by transposing Table 3.2 into Figure 3.1.

Table 3.2 The structure of relations of recognition (amended)

Recognitive aspect	Love	Legal	Societal
Mode of recognition	emotional support	cognitive respect	social esteem
Dimension of personality	needs and emotions	universal moral responsibility	particular traits and abilities
Forms of recognition	primary relationships (family, friends, lovers and community)	legal relations (rights and obligations)	societal relationship (solidarity, societal value and merit)
Developmental potential	—	generalisation, de-formalisation	individualisation, equalisation
Relation-to-self	basic self-confidence	self-respect	self-esteem
Forms of disrespect	abuse and rape, control	denial of rights, exclusion	denigration, insult
Personality threat	physical and psychological integrity	social integrity	'honour', dignity
Public or private	private	public	public
Principles of social justice	neediness (care/intimacy)	equality	achievement as contribution

Conclusion

This research, which aims to develop an understanding of the recognition experiences of Muslims in Europe, is inspired by the theory of recognition developed by critical social theorist Axel Honneth. Unlike Charles Taylor's theory of recognition, Honneth's theory is highly structured by differentiating between and within the spheres of love, legal respect and social esteem and by providing a unique insight into intersubjective relations, especially how misrecognition leads to a struggle for recognition to reclaim a positive relation-to-self and identity. From the standpoint of applicability, Honneth's philosophy is capable of facilitating and framing sociological empirical research into everyday intersubjective social dynamics and the conflicts that arise from such interactions. These characteristics justify why Honneth's theory has been used to frame this research project. This grounded theoretical framework enables a closer personal view of individual Muslim experiences of recognition in Europe. It can differentiate between experiences in multiple social spheres and decipher, through the use of everyday narrative, forms of positive and negative recognition as well as illuminate how the hurt of misrecognition leads to struggles for identities and ways of being.

Although Honneth's work is of the highest quality and carries with it the potential to be synthesised with sociological empirical research, deficiencies remain. As the above shows, Petherbridge identified a prime concern related to the treatment of power in Honneth's work. Although he has attempted to develop a capability of identifying ideological recognition, Petherbridge and Allen determine correctly that his formation of power is one-sided in that it can only identify ideological domination, i.e. domineering *power-over* others.

In contrast to the work of Allen, Honneth does not explore the more complex idea germinating in the work of Foucault (2002) that power can be both ontologically and productively constitutive of individuals and groups. Meaning that certain forms of top-down *power-over* others can be beneficially productive and constitutive in aiding individuals or groups to form and realise an identity and way of being in the world. Furthermore, Allen also clarifies the existence and importance of bottom-up resistive power that individuals and groups utilise to struggle against and circumvent the domineering and constitutive powers that impact them in everyday life. Thus, individuals possess the *power-to* act agentically by themselves and also have the potential to join their *power-with* others to form collective resistances against domination and constitutive control.

Alongside the critiques of Petherbridge and Allen, the work of McBride develops our understanding further on the issues of the recognition and legitimation of authority and how this relates to the maintenance and acting-out of societal norms. McBride's teasing out of the complex issues surrounding the recognition and power of authorities and social norms will be crucial later on when the book explores how young European Muslims attempt to find a recognition balance inside and outside of the Muslim family, located in European cultural life.

Taking as justified the critiques of Honneth's conception of power, this study aligns itself with the positions of Petherbridge, Allen and McBride and, through empirical research, aims to further knowledge and understandings about the interaction between recognition and power by focusing on Muslim narratives of everyday experience. With the scene set from background to theory, it is time to move to the empirical aspects of the study. This runs from Chapters 4 to 6 and presents *streams of narrative* to illustrate the everyday experiences of Muslim individuals and groups in the Irish-European context. In particular, these chapters focus in on the intersubjective recognition dynamics Muslims experience in the spheres of wider societal recognition, legal recognition, spiritual recognition, and in the affective sphere of love.

The next chapter, Chapter 4, is the first empirical chapter. It explores how Muslim individuals in the Irish-European context relate to non-Muslims in terms of receiving, or not, recognition and esteem for their traits, abilities and achievements in the wider societal sphere.

Bibliography

Allen, Amy. 1999. *The Power of Feminist Theory: Domination, Resistance, Solidarity.* Boulder, CO: Westview Press.

Allen, Amy. 2008. *The Politics of Our Selves: Power, Autonomy, and Gender in Contemporary Critical Theory.* New York: Columbia University Press.

Allen, Amy. 2010. Recognizing domination: Recognition and power in Honneth's critical theory. *Journal of Power*. 3(1), pp.21–32.
Anderson, Joel. Situating Axel Honneth in the Frankfurt School tradition, IN: Petherbridge, D. (ed.). 2011. *Axel Honneth: Critical Essays: With a Reply by Axel Honneth*. Leiden, Netherlands: Brill.
Beckman, Ludvig. 2009. *The Frontiers of Democracy: The Right to Vote and Its Limits*. London: Palgrave Macmillan.
Benjamin, Jessica. 1988. *The Bonds of Love: Psychoanalysis, Feminism, and the Problem of Domination*. New York: Pantheon Books.
Benhabib, Seyla. 2004. *The Rights of Others: Aliens, Residents and Citizens*. Cambridge: Cambridge University Press.
Caldwell, Lesley and Joyce, Angela. (eds.). 2011. *Reading Winnicott*. London: Routledge.
Carolan, Mary. 2015. Direct provision residents feel they 'belong to the last class'. *Irish Times*. 22 April.
Deranty, Jean-Philippe and Renault, Emmanuel. 2007. Politicizing Honneth's ethics of Recognition. *Thesis Eleven*. 88(1), pp.92–111.
Deranty, Jean-Philippe. 2009. *Beyond Communication: A Critical Study of Axel Honneth's Social Philosophy*. Leiden, Netherlands: Brill.
Feinberg, Joel. 1980. *The Nature and Value of Rights. Rights, Justice, and the Bounds of Liberty*. Princeton, NJ: Princeton University Press.
Foucault, Michel. 2002. *Power: The Essential Works of Michel Foucault 1954–1984. Volume 3*. London: Penguin.
Fraser, Nancy and Honneth, Axel. 2003. *Redistribution or Recognition? A Political-Philosophical Exchange*. London: Verso.
Habermas, Jürgen. 1984 [1981]. *The Theory of Communicative Action, Volume 1: Reason and Rationalisation of Society*. Boston, MA: Beacon Press.
Habermas, Jürgen. 1987 [1985]. *The Theory of Communicative Action, Volume 2: Lifeworld and System: A Critique of Functionalist Reason*. Boston, MA: Beacon Press.
Hammer, Thomas. 1990. *Democracy and the Nation State. Aliens, Denizens and Citizens in a World of International Migration*. Aldershot, UK: Ashgate.
Hoffman, Marcelo. 2013. *Foucault and Power: The Influence of Political Engagement on Theories of Power*. London: Bloomsbury.
Honneth, Axel. 1991. *The Critique of Power: Reflective Stages in a Critical Social Theory*. Cambridge, MA: MIT Press.
Honneth, Axel. 1995 [1992]. *The Struggle for Recognition: The Moral Grammar of Social Conflicts*. Cambridge: Polity Press.
Honneth, Axel. 2010. Grounding Recognition: A rejoinder to critical questions. *Inquiry: An Interdisciplinary Journal of Philosophy*. 45(4), pp.499–520.
Honneth, Axel, Allen, Amy and Cooke, Maeve. 2010. A conversation between Axel Honneth, Amy Allen and Maeve Cooke, Frankfurt-am-Main, 12 April 2010. *Journal of Power*. 3(2), pp.153–170.
Honneth, Axel. Recognition as ideology: The connection between morality and power. Chapter 5, pp.75–97, IN: Honneth, A. 2012. *The I in the We: Studies in the Theory of Recognition*. Cambridge: Polity Press.
Honneth, Axel. 2014 [2011]. *Freedom's Right: The Social Foundations of Democratic Life*. Cambridge: Polity Press.

Kuhn, Annette. (ed.). 2013. *Little Madnesses: Winnicott, Transitional Phenomena and Cultural Experience*. London: IB Tauris.
Laitinen, Arto. On the scope of 'Recognition': The role of adequate regard and mutuality. Chapter 14, pp.319–342, IN: Schmidt am Busch, H.C., and Zurn, C.F. (eds.). 2010. *Philosophy of Recognition: Historical and Contemporary Perspectives*. Lanham, MD: Lexington Books.
Lukes, Steven. 2005. *Power: A Radical View*. London: Palgrave Macmillan.
McBride, Cillian. 2013. *Recognition*. Cambridge: Polity Press.
McNay, Lois. 1994. *Foucault: A Critical Introduction*. Cambridge: Polity Press.
Mead, G.H. 1972 [1934]. *Mind. Self and Society: From the Standpoint of a Social Behaviorist*. Chicago, IL: Chicago University Press.
Neuhouser, Frederick. 2008. *Rousseau's Theodicy of Self-Love: Evil, Rationality, and the Drive for Recognition*. Oxford: Oxford University Press.
Parker, Stephen E. 2011. *Winnicott and Religion*. Lanham, MD: Aronson.
Petherbridge, Danielle. (ed.). 2011. *Axel Honneth: Critical Essays: With a Reply by Axel Honneth*. Leiden, Netherlands: Brill.
Petherbridge, Danielle. 2013. *The Critical Theory of Axel Honneth*. Lanham, MD: Lexington Books.
Petit, Philip. 1997. *Republicanism: A Theory of Freedom and Government*. Oxford: Oxford University Press.
Petit, Philip. 2012. *On the People's Terms: A Republican Theory and Model of Democracy*. Cambridge: Cambridge University Press.
Petit, Philip. 2014. *Just Freedom: A Moral Compass for a Complex World*. London: WW Norton & Company Ltd.
Rundell, John. 2001. Imaginary turns in critical theory: Imagining subjects in tension. *Critical Horizons*. 2(1), pp.61–92.
Rush, Fred. Conceptual foundations of early critical theory. Chapter 1, IN: Rush, F. (ed.). 2004. *The Cambridge Companion to Critical Theory*. Cambridge: Cambridge University Press.
Smyth, Lisa. 2012. *Demands of Motherhood: Agents, Roles and Recognition*. London: Palgrave Macmillan.
Spitz, Rene. 1965. *The First Year of Life: A Psychoanalytic Study of Normal and Deviant Development of Object Relations*. New York: International Universities Press.
Taylor, Charles. 1992. The politics of recognition, IN: Gutmann, A. (ed.). 1994. *Multiculturalism*. Princeton, NJ: Princeton University Press.
Thompson, Simon. 2006. *The Political Theory of Recognition: A Critical Introduction*. Cambridge: Polity Press.
Tyson, Lois. 1998. *Critical Theory Today: A User-Friendly Guide*. London: Routledge.
Van Den Brink, Bert, and Owen, David. (eds.). 2007. *Recognition and Power: Axel Honneth and the Tradition of Critical Social Theory*. Cambridge: Cambridge University Press.
Wiggershaus, Rolf. 1994. *The Frankfurt School: Its History, Theories and Political Significance*. Cambridge: Polity Press.
Williams, Robert R. 1992. *Recognition: Fichte and Hegel on the Other*. New York: State University of New York.
Williams, Robert R. 1997. *Hegel's Ethics of Recognition*. Oakland, CA: University of California Press.
Winnicott, Donald W. 1988. *Human Nature*. London: Free Association Books.

Winnicott, Donald W. 1991 [1964]. *The Child, The Family, and The Outside World*. London: Penguin.
Winnicott, Donald W. 2005 [1971]. *Playing and Reality*. London: Routledge.
Winnicott, Donald W. 2006 [1965]. *The Family and Individual Development*. London: Routledge.
Young, Robert M. 1994. *Mental Space*. London: Process Press.
Zurn, Christopher F. 2015. *Axel Honneth: A Critical Theory of the Social*. Cambridge: Polity Press.

4 Societal relations

Introduction

This chapter is the first of three empirical chapters. Through thematic and small story analysis of narrative data taken from semi-structured interviews and multiple focused discussion groups, this empirical chapter explores how first and second generation Muslims relate to the non-Muslim community they interact with daily in the Irish-European context. Attention is placed on themes and subthemes that specifically deal with perceived forms of misrecognition. In terms of wider societal misrecognition, the focus is on negative media stereotyping and various forms of everyday discrimination. In terms of legal misrecognition, the focus is on how denizenship status puts direct and indirect limitations on rights of residence and social opportunities. The last section explores identity issues in detail by focusing on narratives that provide an insight into how being different to the nationalised dominant identity standard supersedes universal sameness to others in terms of being recognised as a citizen and human being. It also gives a unique insight into how the research participants relate to being Irish as well as how Muslim youth struggle to have their multiple identities legitimately recognised by others in context.

Before beginning, it may be useful to briefly and concisely reiterate information about the methodology of this study, as outlined in the introduction to this book. The empirical data is qualitative and based on the collection and presentation of narrative. Firstly, sixteen pilot interviews were conducted, which helped focus the research on the relevant theme of recognition. Following on from the preliminary research, the empirical narratives presented in this study were attained through the conduct of twenty-five formal semi-structured interviews (SSI) followed by four focused discussion groups (FDG) comprising thirty-two participants. In total, the viewpoints of fifty-seven people have been used out of a total of seventy-three research participants Using NVivo qualitative data analysis software, all the narratives were thematised and relevant narratives and small stories identified and extracted. The most relevant of these are presented in the empirical chapters in the form of streams of narrative, which mixes similar viewpoints from both the interviews and focused discussion groups. The research narratives are presented verbatim and pseudonyms have

Societal relations 73

been used in place of the real names of the research participants to ensure privacy and confidentiality (see Appendix). Relevant attributes of each participant are stated in the main text. For example, Abdul (1st Gen, M, Cit, FDG) identifies a male, Irish citizen, who belongs to the first generation and participated in a focused discussion group. Likewise, Isra (2nd Gen, F, Den, SSI) identifies a female, denizen or long-term resident, who belongs to the second generation and conducted an individual semi-structured interview. Throughout the empirical chapters, participants from the semi-structured interviews are referred to as *interviewees* and focus group participants are referred as to as *discussants*.

Media misrepresentation

Through a diverse collection of interview and focused discussion group narratives, this section explores the pertinent issue of wider societal misrecognition in terms of media misrepresentation. This topic is examined in terms of how such representation is negatively viewed as sensationalist stereotyping in that it creates misunderstandings about Muslims and perpetuates discrimination. It negatively impacts upon an individual's positive relation-to-self and manifests a lack of trust between Muslim individuals and societal media. Lastly, narratives that normatively claim for more positive understanding, better representation and increased participation are presented.

Stereotyping, misunderstanding and discrimination

A large volume of the narratives from the interviews and focus groups relates to stereotyping, which is perceived as creating a negative perception of Islam and its followers. For example, a working journalist Akhtar, takes the view that if Muslims 'start practicing Islam properly' (Akhtar, 1st Generation, Male, Denizen, Semi-Structured Interview) then the 'stereotypes about Muslims' would 'prove to be false' (Ibid.). This statement indicates how this interviewee views personal action as a means to transform societal media representations. Akhtar continues by stating that 'there is a question of acceptability' in relation to whether Muslim youth in Ireland will be accepted for 'the way they are or cast aside as foreigners, as [the] children of foreigners' (Ibid.). This is echoed by Nazir, who states that some people in Irish society have 'a very negative picture of Muslim' (Nazir, 1st Gen, M, Cit, SSI). In his opinion, the media feeds such a perception by conveying a 'negative picture of Islam' (Ibid.). Saad (1st Gen, M, Cit, SSI) similarly states that 'sometimes we [the Muslim community] get bad publicity'.

Two females interviewed together, Dahlia and Safeerah, also do not feel represented by the media throughout Europe. For Safeerah (1st Gen, F, Cit, SSI), the Muslim name in Europe 'means bad things'. Dahlia (1st Gen, F, Cit, SSI) agrees and determines that this is because newspapers and other media 'back the stereotype again'. Saad determines that the media's job is to sensationalise information to sell media products and attract an audience. He refers to this by stating that 'the media is doing their job', which is to 'bring the stories that are sensational'. Unfortunately, the 'good news is no news' and 'only negative news can be sensational' (Ibid.). Sayyid (1st Gen, M, Cit, SSI) talks about Irish television when he states that the 'only time when the Muslims are featured there [on RTE, the Irish national broadcaster] is when there is some sensationalism going on, they want to paint him [the Muslim] bad or whatever'. This results in Muslim individuals making the decision to avoid Irish media and instead 'watch their own programs from their [home]countries' (Ibid.). Lastly, Firaq (1st Gen, M, Cit, SSI) states in relation to media sensationalism:

> They have to give you something that's kind of not boring in order for them to sell [their product] and for people [advertisers] to attract attention [to their products]. So media, being media, that's the way it's gonna be and we're not going to change [the nature of] it … the interesting news always when, you know, [the media] exaggerating something and unfortunately, in this era, which we are living in, is where [the media is] exaggerating things about Muslims.
> (Firaq)

Like their elders, the younger second generation interviewees have a similar opinion about media and its negative impact upon the small Muslim community in Ireland and in Europe more generally. They have a predominantly negative opinion towards media because it is perceived as the medium that facilitates stereotyping and has thus manifested a lack of trust. Speaking generally, Ayyub (2nd Gen, M, Cit, SSI) states that there are many Muslims, who do not trust the media as 'they believe the media is saying hateful things'. Nurdeen (2nd Gen, M, Cit, SSI) states in relation to international news that 'you just have to look at SKY and Murdoch. It's not really news' while Adam (2nd Gen, M, Cit, SSI) similarly opines about SKY News that such media corporations 'exaggerate everything'. A young female interviewee, Isra (2nd Gen, F, Den, SSI), comments on the link media constantly makes between Islam and terrorism and how this impacts Muslims in the West. She states the 'the media publicises all these kinds of problems' related to Islamic terrorism, however, this in itself 'will also probably bring a problem' (Ibid.) in that Muslims feel this is stereotyping and disrespectful. In other words, the media is presenting or possessing you 'for something you haven't done' (Ibid.). In the interviews, substantial criticisms exist in terms of negative media portrayals of Muslims and Islam in Irish and international media. In academia, research on the topic of media misrepresentation is extensive (Poole and Richardson 2006, Shaheen 2009, Knott, Poole and Taira 2013).

Similar negative opinions related to misrecognition emanate from discussions that took place within the young male focus group. Notably, the theme of media misrepresentation was prominent and many discussants felt that the media tarnished the name of Islam in Europe and across the globe. Masud (2nd Gen, M, Cit, FDG) latches on to the word 'tarnish' and clarifies that he would 'use that one word' to describe how the media views Islam and Muslims in general. Aban (2nd Gen, M, Cit, FDG) enters the conversation to opine that the media have latched onto Islam because they are afraid of the rising Muslim population growth in Europe. He asks the moderator to 'think about it', especially emphasising the point that the media know 'the religion [of Islam] is growing' (Ibid.). He refers to the example in the UK where 'every week Islam is growing by three per cent' (Ibid.). In a comment that indicates a transnational reflection, Aban criticises the media's attention on terrorism and acts of violence against Western countries, such as the US and UK, when similar acts are occurring in countries like Burma, in which Muslims are 'dying' (Ibid.). In this discussant's opinion, the media 'don't care about them at all' (Ibid.), i.e. the suffering of Muslims in less developed non-Western countries around the world. In Aban's opinion, the media looks at news from only 'one side' when it 'should just look at both sides' (Ibid.).

At this point, Masud re-enters the conversation and emphasises the point that Muslims are treated in a particular way by Western media. To state his point, he uses 'the example of what happened in America' by explaining that the actions of a mentally ill individual involved in a high school shooting will not be perceived by the media as an act of terrorism as the 'guy was sick' yet hypothetically, if that individual was Muslim or looks foreign, 'the word "terrorist" is used' (Masud). For this discussant, this indicates that the word terrorist is 'reserved just for us' and 'that's where the media comes in' (Ibid.). This perception of media impacts Masud's feelings in that when he sees or hears such news items it 'really does annoy' him as he takes the view that 'it's not the truth' (Ibid.).

Another theme related to negative stereotyping is how such media creates misunderstandings about Islam and Muslims generally. In the interview narratives, Nazir has the view that misunderstanding is exacerbated by journalists who 'don't know about Islam' and 'don't sit down with Muslim people', particularly the grassroots of the community. The two female interviewees from the first generation, Dahlia and Safeerah, are concerned that such media misrepresentation has a negative impact on non-Muslims and their perceptions of Islam. As Dahlia states on this point:

> They [the media] are always talking about the bad side, [the] burka. Prophet Muhammad married how many women? What else? [voicing the media] 'Many wives, many wives, you [Muslims] have'. That's always [the story], I never saw [anything different], where's [the good stories]? Islam is a big, huge [religion], just only these two points and you [the non-Muslim] are left with all this [just two points].
>
> (Dahlia)

For Akhtar, the large gap between negative media representation and positive everyday action must be bridged by actively participating in media and by speaking to and convincing others, who are 'far removed from Islam and Muslims', of the positive contribution Muslims make to Irish-European society in their everyday lives. Nabeel (1st Gen, M, Den, SSI) makes a concise statement that emphasises the pervasive role that the media has in disseminating knowledge about Islam to the wider public. This interviewee agrees that there is a lack of ethical recognition of Islam in Western society and that this has caused a lack of understanding about the Islamic religion (Ibid.). He goes on to say: 'because our [society's] understanding of Islam, in general, is what the media talks about [in terms of] the problems' (Ibid.). The female interviewees narrate that the media does not understand Islam or Muslims. Dahlia opines that there is a 'deep meaning of Islam' that advocates civic participation but the 'media will never cover it, unfortunately' and Safeerah states that the media has 'wrong ideas' about Islam and it is hard for Muslim individuals to 'change it and say, "this has nothing to do with Islam"'. Kaleem, a convert to Islam who adheres to political Islam (1st Gen, M, Cit, SSI), does not trust journalists. In his opinion, 'most journalists, they have no idea of Islam' and are just interested in a 'media sound bite' (Ibid.). He narrates a small story about the problems he faced when the Garda Special Branch interrogated him about opinions he expressed to a journalist:

> They [the special branch Gardaí] stopped me for two hours and questioned me about newspaper articles. This is very interesting thing that, after this [incident], I was speaking to my family about it and I was just saying the way, the whole media thing, they [the Gardaí] were holding up newspapers they brought, they didn't have anything like proof that I'd done anything or been anywhere, except for newspaper articles and it just hit home to me the fact that, 'hold on here', the first time that I've seen anyway, 'they're taking newspaper articles, what a journalist wrote whether it's true or not, to be true'.
>
> (Kaleem)

For the young interviewees, the second generation, the propagation of media stereotypes is connected to the continuing misunderstanding of Islam generally by wider society. Ayyub strongly criticises the media for having 'a superficial understanding of Islam' and proclaims that Islam and its followers have become a profit-making product for capitalist media organisations in the West. Aziz (2nd Gen, M, Den, SSI) states that the 'biggest problem is that people misunderstand Islam, especially with the media'. He continues by emphasising the key role and responsibility the media has as the main medium 'where people get information' to allow them to better understand what Islam is (Ibid.).

In the narratives, several interviewees link negative media portrayals to the perpetuation of everyday discrimination. Certainly, most interviewees perceive everyday discrimination to be significantly caused by societal media, which manifests misunderstandings and stereotypes about Islam, thereby, negatively impacting Muslim people in their everyday interactions. Indeed, a significant proportion of the interviewees mention the impact of stereotypes on everyday people. Ayyub states that the media 'categorises people' and that the vast

Societal relations 77

majority of people in Irish society 'see stereotypes that have been implanted in them'. Hakim states that the media is 'planting racism in the minds of Irish citizens' (1st Gen, M, Cit, SSI) and Sayyid states something similar by referring to Irish media as a 'racist media'. In this interviewee's opinion, Irish television media is 'too white' (Sayyid) even though it is financed through a general license fee and is supposed to represent a pluralistic democratic society. In his opinion, Irish media is 'ignoring completely the immigrant community as if they are non-existent' (Ibid.). Sayyid states strongly that:

> if you look from RTE to RTE2 to TG4 to TV3, all the radio [stations in Ireland], do you hear any immigrants, do you see any immigrants? Television's too white, it's too white, it's too white ... we are all paying license [fee], we are paying taxes, we are paying television licences and there's nothing, as if the immigrant community was non-existent and that does not all go well, not for the immigrant community, who's going to suffer [and] their own [wider] community is going to suffer.
>
> (Ibid.)

The above is echoed by Daleela (2nd Gen, F, Cit, SSI), who asks the question: 'when was the last time you saw a Muslim on a television programme that wasn't a terrorist'. Isra, another young female interviewee, comments about the negative impact the media has on Muslims in the West in terms of their interactions with others in the wider social realm. She advocates strongly that 'it was wrong to blame all Muslims' for the terrorist actions of a few and adds that media representations do have a causal connection to everyday discrimination:

> those people who attack you on the street, they've seen what they've seen on the news, they heard what they heard on the news and they tell you those things they heard, and they judge you, but they don't charge you as a person, they charge you with your [head]scarf and that's a huge problem.
>
> (Isra)

Another young woman, Furat (2nd Gen, F, Cit, SSI), is deeply annoyed by the gap that exists between media representations and the everyday life lived by the grassroots of Muslim communities. She is adamant that the media never shows Muslim individuals like her 'walking down the street ever, a normal, dual citizen, Irish brought up Muslim girl that has a very open mind' (Furat). Instead, she perceives that the Irish media uses its persuasive power to show only the stereotypical image of the Muslim as terrorist. Such representations annoy Furat:

> It annoys me a lot is that once they are doing a programme about that [Muslims], for some reason the producer has to include 9/11, you know, the twin towers being knocked down, and so instantly they're trying to prove to everybody, they're trying to persuade [voice lowers], persuade them [the

viewers] into thinking Muslims are this type, terrorists or what not and I haven't yet seen a programme were it kinda shows Muslims in a good kinda light.

(Ibid.)

Impact on relation-to-self

Such negative media stereotyping, general misunderstandings of Islam and the everyday experience of being Muslim in Ireland has had vast repercussions in relation to the issue of trust between Muslims and the media. The statements from first generation interviewees, Akhtar, Kaleem and Nabeel, agree with each other that there is a lack of trust generally between members of the Muslim community and the media. Akhtar states that a lack of trust has developed after journalists have taken the words of Muslim individuals and 'twist it, turn it, fry it, boil it'. For this interviewee, the lack of trust between Muslim communities and the media 'is a big thing' (Ibid.). He narrates a small story related to the Jihad Jane case in Waterford to illustrate how important responsible media reporting is to the Muslim community, and how irresponsible reporting impacts the community in terms of its interaction with wider society:

> I told them [broadsheet journalists] straight forwardly, 'look, if you sensationalise this [news story], the Muslim community is just going to distance itself from the media altogether, they're just going to go into a closed closet and they will go back in'. I felt that they [the journalists] understood this situation.
> (Akhtar)

Kaleem opines that the media 'basically lie', particularly print media, which for him is 'very dangerous, completely negative'. Although he has actively participated in several media productions, he continues to view media with distrust and as a hard-to-control communicative medium. He doesn't 'believe the media will ever really say what [it should]' and it won't 'ever put me on a show and announce exactly what I believe' (Ibid.). Nabeel defines the relationship between the Muslim community and the media as 'not that healthy'. Negative experiences related to media production processes are perceived as not conducive to developing trust. For example, Nazir describes his experience of speaking to a journalist about Afghanistan, his home country. The term 'home country' is used consistently in participant narratives. Home country is a common term in the Muslim community, for both first and second generations, to denote the country of origin, i.e. a country or region that the first generation immigrated from and where family connections or roots remain. Nazir states the following:

> As a journalist, [she] doesn't know what is in Afghanistan, what is going [on] in Afghanistan, how ordinary people knows about that. So, this is important. So journalists, most of them, are bringing negative picture of Islam and they don't know about Islam and they don't sit down with Muslim people.
> (Nazir)

Societal relations

In the interviews, there are various narratives that explicate how media affects an individual's relation-to-self. Most of these references point to how media stereotypes negatively impact an individual's feelings. Saad reflects on how media misrecognition makes individuals in the Muslim community 'feel bad'. This feeling is connected to the disconnection between how Muslims are living their everyday lives and how such lives are reflected upon by the media. For this interviewee, negative media stories connecting Muslims to terrorism 'actually disturbs' (Saad) people in the Muslim community. As he states in relation to living a good contributory life in Europe versus the negative global media image of the Muslim as terrorist:

> We feel bad that we are living in this country and we are doing quite well, we have quite positive image [in Ireland] and then when something happens maybe in Europe or in America and we say 'oh, thank God, this is not again another Muslim' because anything will, anything, bomb explosion or anything happens like in Norway (i.e. the 2011 Utøya massacre) this is what happened, we were all praying that hopefully it is nothing to do with Muslims.
>
> (Saad)

Furat, a young female interviewee, elaborates further on media misrepresentation and how it has personally affected her own relation-to-self. She narrates a small story that conveys how the media can impact the everyday lives of Muslims in Ireland in terms of perception and misrecognition. In this narrative, she is embarrassed in front of her friends by a media programme that she feels misrepresents Muslims, and thereby herself, as terroristic. She is frustrated by the ability of media to denigrate her identity in front of her friends, disrupting how she feels about herself and how she feels others perceive her to be. Her small story is as follows:

> It's really, really frustrating because then like I remember one day I was sitting down and they had this program with Muslims and with all my friends there [at her house], half being Irish, half being different ethnicities and they (the program) were talking [about] 9/11 and how bad it was, and I was really embarrassed sitting there because, you know, it kinda showed me like, you know, I didn't know where to look. My friends felt nervous themselves because they didn't know whether to look at me or not to look at me.
>
> (Furat)

Of interest is the way in which many young Muslims negotiate their feelings and actions towards media. One interviewee is of particular interest in this regard. Azad (2nd Gen, M, Cit, SSI) states in his interview that he does not follow Irish media anymore. He clarifies that he 'barely even reads [print media] because, most of the time, [when] I open something it will be like "a Muslim something, a Muslim fundamentalist, a Muslim this"' (Azad). Further on in the interview, it becomes apparent that his agentic action to isolate himself from particular media is related to a perceived personal experience of media discrimination. He confides that: 'something happened to me once' (Ibid.). The situation being referred to has to do with the publication (in a well-known Irish tabloid) of online racist comments directed towards the interviewee. He states about this incident:

> it was years ago but maybe that kind of bad experience just put me off from the media at all, to the extent that I never bothered following what the media [report], what's up in the media and stuff like that. So, in a way like [I] kinda lost faith in it.
>
> (Azad)

The need for understanding, representation and participation

Although many narratives are negative in terms of criticising the media and its perceived impact on everyday life, other narratives are critical in terms of proclaiming a normative stance, a hope, that media should play a more positive civic role in Irish society by showing Muslims in their everyday contributory capacity benefitting European life.

For example, Nazir takes such a position and advocates that the media should play a more 'positive role' in society. Dahlia states concisely that there is a 'deep meaning of Islam' and the 'media will never cover it, unfortunately'. For this interviewee, the deep meaning of Islam relates to the advocacy of civic participation. This form of critique is also expressed by young female interviewees. Daleela asserts that the media, particularly Irish media, could do more to 'portray Muslims a bit more positively'. In a similar reference to responsibility but with more inference to reciprocal action, Isra expresses the need for the Muslim community and European society to mutually 'show the good way that the Muslim community are doing [contributing], rather than just focusing on terrorism, terrorism, terrorism'.

Interestingly, criticism is also reflected towards the Muslim community itself in that the interviewees advocate for more media interaction and more proactiveness by Muslims in Irish and European media to rectify the perceived negative image of Islam and to create more positive representations, which are closer to the lived experience of the Muslim grassroots. Hakim strongly advocates for the Muslim community to be 'more proactive' in Irish and European media, which he views as a 'subjective' medium of communication.

Such statements that promote participation in media also indicate the existence of the opposite, i.e. there is a tendency in the Muslim community to be inactive towards media forms and hence be removed from the representation of their own lives. Ubaid (1st Gen, M, Den, SSI) discusses this issue. He states categorically that Muslims in Ireland and throughout Europe need to try to participate in the local, national and pan-European media because the 'only way we can change that [media] is to be part of it' (Ibid.). This interviewee, who was born in Europe and lived his whole life in various European cities, is critical of the tendency of individuals in the Muslim community to consume

Societal relations 81

'Arabic newspapers' (Ibid.) and other media content from their home country. In his opinion, such actions are 'isolating' and are 'creating a bigger issue' in terms of integration and participation (Ibid.). He then goes on to strongly advocate for Muslims to contribute to their community by participating in and utilising various media. Importantly, Ubaid advocates for Muslims to civically act as democratic citizens in the communicative public sphere:

> What is your contribution as a community to the media, as an individual, to the media? Could you write an article? Did you, on a collective level, organise an event, conference where you invited the media and told them about your reservation? Did anything like that happen? It hasn't [happened in the Muslim community]. So, since we [the Muslim community] are living in a democratic country and Islam is also a democratic religion. Islam is for democracy. So, you can react to that democratically. Why not write articles? Why not become involved?
>
> (Ubaid)

As has become apparent through the above statements, many first generation interviewees are critical of how their own generation relate to media in the Irish and European context. Mazhab (1st Gen, M, Cit, SSI) states something extremely important in relation to how the first generation perceive the future role of the second generation, particularly in relation to public participation and media involvement. He views Muslim youth, who have grown up in the European sphere, as having the potential to enact better communication with the wider social sphere. Due to the younger generation's language, education and cultural competencies, i.e. through their social capital, they have a stronger capacity to represent Muslim concerns and problematic issues to the wider society. In other words, the younger generation can 'react with the media' (Ibid.) in a more productive way. As Mazhab states about the potential of the second generation to create more mutual understanding:

> We [the Islamic community] are hoping that the new generation can involve more with the media, they can speak up and they [in Ireland] are a lot of college graduated.
>
> (Ibid.)

However, it must be noted that action related to social struggle takes many forms. It can involve action to isolate oneself or action to participate. In contrast to Azad's experience (see pp.79–80) who took cognitive action to avoid Irish media, which he felt disrespected him as a citizen, Aamil (2nd Gen, M, Cit, SSI) actively decided to take part in a television documentary that focused on the Muslim community in Ireland to publicly defend his community, culture and Islamic religion. It is therefore a very good example of how individuals use their agency to struggle against forms of power and to regain positive recognition. Aamil's small story clearly outlines the causal mechanism of a struggle for recognition. In the story, he hears about the denigration of Muslim women by a well-known right-wing journalist. Such disrespect creates anger in Aamil, which leads to action in the form of deciding to actively participate in the television programme so as to struggle against denigration and regain positive recognition and relation-to-self. Aamil's small story is as follows:

> I'll tell you what happened. There was Stefan, the director of that show. He actually came into X [my workplace] with his crew. I do know what he was looking for. He said to me, this was the first time meeting [him], he said to me 'there's a guy [a journalist], Alex, he's against the Muslims', so I go 'in what way is he against the Muslims' because I'm not a, I'm not a faithful Muslim, you know what I mean, but I still, if somebody's going to say 'I'm against the Irish', I'm gonna say 'what way are you against the Irish, you tell me' … He actually said a lot of different things but one of the things that really peed-me off, is it okay [to say peed-me off] yeah, he peed-me off because he actually said that the women that wear the niqab are like the characters in Pac Man or like, the men are insulting the women by telling them to dress up like that or whatever but no, that's not reality, the reality is, if the woman is comfortable in it … You have to go with the generations growing, growing, growing, growing, you know, I'm not going to tell my wife 'go out and wear niqab'. My wife has her own will.
>
> (Aamil)

For male discussant Azaan (2nd Gen, M, Cit, FDG), there is a need in Irish society for equal interaction but also an understanding and appreciation of difference and diversity in everyday life. In relation to pluralism in media, i.e. the issue of employing presenters and newscasters from different religious and ethnic backgrounds to reflect modern day diversity in Irish-European society, he states that such symbolic gestures will not 'really matter' (Ibid.). This narrative negates symbolic recognition in favour of more concrete recognition in everyday life, which will increase understanding between diverse people. Essentially, Azaan is advocating that all people, whether Muslim or non-Muslim, must try to learn to understand other cultures and not stand in isolation to each other. On this point, he states the following:

> It's just the very basis of understanding different people, different ethnic minorities and understanding of people's different cultures because we can't really be very narrow minded or seclude yourself to your own culture because there's hundreds of different countries all over the world.
>
> (Azaan)

Discrimination

The following section examines the narrative perceptions of societal misrecognition in terms of structural and everyday discrimination. The interview and focus group narratives delve into this topic under the following sub-themes related firstly to a general identification of perceptions of institutional social exclusion and how the social pathology of discrimination manifests itself in everyday interaction as the *prejudice of first impressions,* particularly in relation to the female Muslim experience of wearing the hijab in the public sphere. Then the chapter focuses on how discrimination affects an individual's relation-to-self, especially in terms of self-esteem. In the last section, two small stories about the cultural phenomena of art and sport are utilised to identify the interactive common ground that recognises ability and has the capacity to overcome pathologies of discrimination.

Structural exclusion and everyday discrimination

Firstly, in terms of discrimination, the theme of structural exclusion from institutions and social norms did arise within the interviews and focused discussion groups. Despite Safeerah insisting that discrimination against Muslims in Ireland is 'not systematic or it doesn't happen every day', several narratives relate to such forms of perceived systematic exclusion.

In terms of sporting culture, Yaseen (1st Gen, M, Cit, SSI), an older Muslim who had arrived in Ireland in the 1950s, references the lack of Muslims in the field of professional sport in Ireland. He states that at present 'you don't find a single one in athletics, a single one in rugby, nothing' (Ibid.). Four interviewees, Akhtar, Hakim, Ubaid and Adeeb (1st Gen, M, Cit, SSI), mention the difficulties Muslims have in relation to the Irish educational system, especially how young Muslims find it difficult to gain access to Catholic schools that give priority placement to baptised Christian children, thereby ensuring that Muslim children are further down on the list of potential students to gain entry to a local school. As interviewee Hakim states in relation to educational discrimination:

> In particular access to secondary schools. The Republic of Ireland still has a hierarchy policy that goes back to the eighteenth century. Muslim entry into schools is a secondary choice. Muslims are ninth on the list to be accepted.
> (Hakim)

It must be acknowledged that not all Muslim interviewees agree with the promotion of denominational schooling but see the school as a common area that should be separated from the influence of religious institutions. Firaq clarifies his position about how the problem is actually the continuation of the denominational educational system in Ireland. He is against the control of any school system by one religious tradition and calls for the separation of education from religious control so as to aid the integration of all people into Irish society. He states in this regard:

84   *Societal relations*

> I think the education system will be sorted out eventually. I think, not because of the Muslim community, but because of the normal progress [of the separation of Church and State] what will happen here is that religion will be separated from schools and that will be, in my view, will offer a better school to everybody. Not just Muslims, but Protestants, Presbyterians, Jews, everybody. There's no [reason for it], it's not right, it's not moderate to have Catholic schools in Ireland running the educational system and ignoring everybody else, you know, Protestants [and Muslims and those who are secular] … Many other countries, advanced countries have already, like in Canada since the 1980s, they've got rid of religion of school.
>
> (Firaq)

On top of Firaq's critique of the education system and its denominational character, he also criticises policing in the Irish state, particularly the Gardaí and their uniform policy in relation to wearing the hijab:

> There's very few Mu[slims in the Gardaí] … I don't know of any Muslims who have joined the Gardaí … first because with Gardaí women they would not [accept the hijab], a Muslim woman would need to wear [the] headscarf and the Gardaí here they say 'sorry', you know. They won't allow that [the hijab] in the Gardaí and as long as the Gards want to keep that attitude then they are not going to be representative of those minority communities who are around [Ireland].
>
> (Ibid.)

As well as criticising the Irish police force in terms of exclusionary behaviour towards the hijab, interviewees Firaq and Kaleem – in opposition to the vast majority of interviewees and discussants, who generally had very positive opinions of the Irish police and security services – strongly criticise special units of the Gardaí and the Army for their rough-handed approach to Muslim individuals detained and under interrogation. Firaq claims that individuals have had their legal rights disrespected by security forces. For example, Kaleem, a convert to Islam, who adheres to a form of political Islam and has extreme geopolitical views about Islam's place in the global order, makes strong narrative statements indicating that he has experienced severe physical disrespect from the state security forces for vocalising subjective opinions. From his perspective, the following interaction that occurred with the security forces caused him significant physical and psychological distress:

> The people who came to the door, the first time they were somebody else [not the Gardaí]. They were plain clothes [officers], they had machine guns. I think one or two had masks over their faces, they were something, they smelled of army, I think that's the reason why I got bounced from wall-to-wall and kicked up and down, even when they had handcuffs on, which is really bad, they broke my nose. I start[ed] reciting the Qur'an,

which [indicated this] is really bad because, you know, I was afraid what was going to happen, I'd always [thought about being] kidnapped or something, you hear about stories, you know, Shannon [and rendition flights] is only down the road.

(Kaleem)

In terms of exclusion from social norms, there are narratives that emphasise the difficulties in being different to the dominant identity standard, which is firmly rooted in Irish societal culture. This is generally referred to by Daleela, who states that she has a strong Islamic religious identity, however, she adds the caveat that such a Muslim identity, which differs from the dominant standard of Irish identity, 'is not that compatible with [Irish] society' (Ibid.). This dominant Irish identity standard refers to being a light-skinned Catholic male with nationalist tendencies. Such a domineering and pervasive identity standard that constitutes the legitimised social norm of Irishness is a particular mixture of ethnic, religious and nationalist attributes.

Being different to cultural norms and the dominant identity standard has implications for the everyday experiences of Muslim youth. This is indicated by discussant Maja's (1st Gen, F, Cit, FDG) small story about her children's experience of discrimination at school. She focuses on the problems that her children encounter in school from other children, due to their difference from the identity standard and social norms of the majority. She mentions children questioning her son as to why he is not allowed to eat ham. She recounts that discussions can turn nasty between her sons and other non-Muslim children. Maja states that 'sometimes if they're [the other boys are] angry', they say to her son 'go home. Don't stay. Go home'. (Maja). Such comments have forced her children to defend themselves and by doing so reply: 'No! My dad, he's a doctor here, he's paying tax. We are working here. It's not your right to say to me "go home"' (Ibid.). Hurriyah (1st Gen, F, Cit, FDG) echoes Maja's narrative by restating the words 'go home to your country'. Elmira (1st Gen, F, Cit, FDG) clarifies that these words do not suggest going home to your house but return to your home country, the place where your parents originated from. She clarifies: 'Homeland! Your roots, your roots' (Elmira). Dahlia, who took part in the focus groups as well as giving an interview with Safeerah, enters the conversation to support the reality that some children are 'forcing them [Muslim children] to this kind of initiation, this kind of argument'. Dahlia and the other discussants are not happy for their children to partake in such discussions. She also states that, although rare in primary school, such interaction becomes more common in secondary school, a time of adolescence, which represents the 'very critical years' of identity formation (Dahlia).

Despite the above references to structural exclusion, the overall majority of narratives relate to everyday discrimination. Such negative experiences revolve around the discrimination of what makes Muslims different to the dominant identity standard of Irishness. Such differences relate to individual traits that differ from traditionally legitimised social norms, which are accepted as normal in Ireland's cultural matrix. The misrecognition of surface-level traits, in contrast to normatively recognising the underlying abilities and achievements of individuals, has been referred to by numerous interviewees and discussants, particularly females, as the *prejudice of first impressions*.

Such examples of everyday discrimination within the interviews include Mazhab stating clearly that 'there is incidents' of discrimination, which have been exacerbated by the 'economic situation'. Similarly, Iqbal (1st Gen, M, Den, SSI) states that 'there's many incidents' and the frequency has 'gone up'. This interviewee declares that discrimination is definitely 'on the rise' (Iqbal). Nabeel takes a realistic and practical stance by stating that the expectation of discrimination is 'something natural' for minority groups, i.e. individuals belonging to a minority religious group have an expectation that they will suffer discrimination because their way of life and spiritual recognition is different to majoritarian social norms and the culturally established identity standard. Adeeb emphasises how societal injustice is referred to in the Muslim community as religious intolerance and that there is a need to struggle against such forms of discrimination. He comments on how perceptions of injustice filter down through the generations in the Muslim community:

> The mentality of the Muslims, they relate that [social injustice] to the religious problem and they said 'because you're Catholic and not Muslim, you're treating me like this, then you will see, then I'm delivering and passing this message to my kids', and 'my kids, those guys they treating us, they don't want us to be with them, but we are here, we don't have any chance [opportunity]'.
>
> (Adeeb)

In terms of references to on street discrimination, Sayyid states that he personally knows about 'incidents of racism', while Iqbal states that Muslims on their way to the mosque were 'pelted with stones and rocks'. Yaseen makes an interesting comment about a friend of his, a powerful and well-known Islamist leader, who walked anonymously around Dublin but felt out of place:

> While he was here [in Dublin], he comes on business, he said it, you know, 'that everybody looked at him as a vendor, a fruit vendor', because he doesn't fit our community here.
>
> (Yaseen)

The younger second generation interviewees primarily discussed experiences of being discriminated against on the streets of Dublin. Generally, this misrecognition takes the form of verbal abuse, which aims to denigrate and insult, and therefore, it has the potential to create feelings of shame and to affect a person's relation-to-self. For example, Adam, a convert of Irish ethnicity states that 'absolutely you get a lot of "go back to your own country"' and Isra recounts her 'first time wearing the scarf [hijab] and walking down the street, [and] people said, "go back to where you come from"'. Furat, a

Muslim of Libyan ethnicity, remembers how she was called a 'Paki' on the street. She clarifies: 'I'm not a Paki, I'm Libyan' (Furat).

Although most of the discrimination is verbal, sometimes it does break out into acts of physical abuse that humiliate and damage a person's sense-of-self. Nurdeen speaks of the time he was attacked 'down the road from the mosque' when 'three teenagers popped [hit] me in the nose'. Furat describes how her friend, who was walking down the street, had her hijab ripped off her head. She clarifies that the reason for such action was to 'humiliate her [friend] in front of everybody.' Azad, a young dark-skinned Muslim male of African descent, narrates how he experienced physical discrimination when walking around his local area. He states that 'when walking the streets, you have to be prepared, like [possibly] someone's going to throw a comment or something' (Ibid.). To avoid this 'antisocial behaviour', he will 'try as much as possible to avoid walking down that side [of the street]' (Ibid.). Interestingly, he finds not only the acts of discrimination and of avoiding it difficult but also trying to assess the reasons behind such public abuse. Was he discriminated against because he is Muslim or because of his skin colour or is it general antisocial behaviour that he happened to fall victim to? By questioning the act of discrimination, he is reflecting on its complexity and is reporting that it does psychologically impact the victim, who attempts to understand the reasoning behind such abuse:

> Sometimes you be like 'okay he did that, the only way he did that is because I'm different or because of my skin colour or because of this, and this and this.' So, it's difficult to say, it could be antisocial behaviour or it could be racial because, I don't see it, but I do experience [it], like I do experience it from time to time along those sides [areas of Dublin].
> (Azad)

Similarly to Azad, Daleela also recounts her experience of trying to assess the probable cause for the discrimination she suffered. She states that she experienced a few incidents 'where you get called names or you clearly see that someone has a problem with you because of your religious and cultural background' (Daleela). For this female interviewee, it does create paranoia. She questioningly states that 'sometimes you never know if it's your own paranoia or not' (Ibid.). Another Muslim youth, Aziz is one of two interviewees, who mentions the issue of 'name-calling'. He talks about the 'joking about' and 'slagging' that occurred in his secondary school (Aziz) and Nurdeen succinctly reflects on past childhood experiences by stating: 'I grew up being called names'.

Such abuse does not stop when one reaches adulthood, as Nurdeen continues to state in relation to his public activities of conducting da'wa (calling people to Islam via the act of public preaching) in Dublin city centre. This interviewee comments on a guy, who regularly comes by the da'wa table 'every two or three weeks and gives out' (Nurdeen). This man publicly calls Muslims such things as 'suicide bombers' (Ibid.). When asked about the frequency of discrimination at the da'wa table, Nurdeen states that 'out of three days [of doing da'wa] you get it once or twice' (Ibid.). Adam discusses his acts of da'wa and experiences of discrimination, which constantly link Islam and being Muslim with terrorism and particular acts of violence. He states that 'we've been made to feel guilty' and 'there's not one day I stand over there at the da'wa table that I don't hear "oh, September 11 …"'. He stresses that discrimination is to be expected when publicly preaching on the main thoroughfare in the city of Dublin. As this convert to Islam states, 'absolutely, like you get a lot of "go back to your own country"' (Adam). In terms of relations with the Gardaí, he states that overall relations are positive. However, he experienced one incident that made him realise the precariousness of his position as a young convert propagating a minority religion to a majority, who are either predominantly secular or Christian:

> There was one incident where, a female Garda and a guy came up and he was so 'Muslims are terrorists, the Prophet Muhammad was a paedophile' and he made this cutting action with his [finger], across his neck and, [he said] 'these Muslims will kill you!'. Now I was twenty-feet away, I could hear this man shouting this and there was a Garda standing beside him and when I asked the Garda to remove him because he was inciting hatred, she said she 'didn't hear a thing?'.
>
> (Adam)

Within the second generation male discussion group, Azaan explains how discrimination is very much a present-day struggle for Muslims in the Irish-European context. As an example, he talks about an anonymous letter received by all mosques and Muslim restaurants, the day before the discussion took place, which stated that 'Irish people want Muslims out' (Azaan). The discussant clarifies that 'obviously it was written by some[one] not representing Irish people, of course' (Ibid.). Yusuf (2nd Gen, M, Cit, FDG) states that he had 'seen the letter', which was being talked about in the mosque on the night of the discussion group. He states that the anonymous letter writer is 'a really stupid person' and provides evidence for this by stating that the letter had contained 'basic vocabulary mistakes'. This statement creates laughter among the other discussants. For Yusuf, the perceived stupidity of the letter writer ensures that he is 'not the scariest scumbag' (Yusuf) or somebody to be taken seriously. He states loudly to the other discussants: 'I was looking at it [the letter] and started laughing' (Ibid.). Despite Yusuf's claim that the letter is a joke, Azaan interjects into the conversation to explain the contents of the letter and how such threats relate back to the influence of the media:

> He [the letter writer] was telling everyone, he was writing and he was saying that 'everyone that is Irish, true Irish people' something like that 'want all the Muslims out and they're going to attack Muslim people on the street and they're going to get their kids to attack Muslim kids in schools and they're going to do this and that' and whatever, 'until

Muslims are out [of Ireland]' and they said that 'if any Muslim people die in the process, we hope you burn in hell'. So obviously, well I'm not 100 per cent sure, but well like I'm pretty sure, that some of it would have to be done through media and stuff ... so people, whether they are extreme or hate Muslims or not, they will have that fear like put into them because of the media.

(Azaan)

The most insightful narratives about discrimination as the *prejudice of first impressions* emanates from female narratives, particularly in relation to wearing the hijab and being publicly identified by others as Muslim in the public sphere. Interviewee Safeerah insists that discrimination against Muslims in Ireland is 'not systematic or it doesn't happen every day', however, as Dahlia explains, 'some kinda incidents' have happened that are related 'about hijab'. Overall, when reflecting on her life and position in Irish society, Dahlia finds herself to be 'lucky' to be a full citizen and legally recognised in comparison to the isolation experienced by asylum-seekers in Ireland and across Europe. Safeerah and Dahlia narrate an enlightening small story that illuminates how difficult it can be for Muslim women to be in the Irish public sphere, particularly when that being goes against social norms and the dominant cultural identity standard.

For Dahlia, a positive relation-to-self, particularly self-confidence, is intrinsic to wearing the hijab and being different to the normalised identity standard. However, trying to be Muslim in the wider public sphere can be a difficult everyday intersubjective struggle that is also dependent on one's relation-to-self. Dahlia narrates a small story about a Filipino friend, who did not have the confidence to wear the hijab in public and be seen as different to others in everyday life:

DAHLIA: I think it depends on how you are confident and some, like I have a friend, she was a Filipino Christian and she converted to Islam, she wear the hijab immediately, she enjoyed [it] but she find herself like 'I'm a stranger, [yet] everyone look at me'. I said, 'You think this. They are not looking at you [they are looking at the hijab, what you represent], if they look at you, it's okay.'
SAFEERAH: She wanted to feel, you know, [spiritually] affected.
DAHLIA: She said, 'I want to feel [that] I'm normal.'
SAFEERAH: The same as everybody else, yeah.
DAHLIA: I said, 'and what's normal?'
SAFEERAH: Some of them does though, some of them does [stare].
DAHLIA: But that not affect me, to be honest, I am proud of what I have [the hijab covering my head and the religion that prescribes it] and then at the end [of the story about the Filipino woman], she decided to take the hijab and she took it [off], because why? The [social] pressure.

(Dahlia and Safeerah)

90 *Societal relations*

Some first generation males indicate their awareness of the issues that their female loved ones encounter in everyday interaction. For example, Firaq discusses the position of the hijab in Irish society. First, he states that 'equality and discrimination is a big issue' and that 'women are more affected by it [discrimination] than [Muslim] men' (Firaq). He continues by narrating how his wife has experienced discrimination more often than himself. He reasons why this is the case by referring to the visibility of Muslim women in that their difference is 'more obvious with their headscarf … and that makes [them] some kind of clear targets for discrimination' (Ibid.).

Such an experience is expressed by second generation interviewee Furat, who mentions her friend's hijab being 'ripped off her'. She also comments that the hijab carries with it the generalised perception and connotation that Muslim women lack agency and are forced to wear the headscarf by male patriarchal powers. As she states about this: 'the first thing that people think when they see the headscarf is "she [is] made wear it, I betcha that's against her will, I betcha her father or her husband [made her wear it]"' (Furat). Daleela states her opinion that the hijab and prejudice are linked and that by the simple act of wearing the hijab a Muslim woman is placing herself in the aim of discriminatory acts. She states that 'you're the one who's wearing it [the hijab], you're the one who's facing the prejudices' (Ibid.). Another female interviewee, Isra, states that in her own experience 'you hear people saying, "all Muslims are terrorists, you shouldn't be bombing everywhere, why are you killing [people]?"'. This interviewee is adamant in her claim that Irish people 'just do discriminate with the scarf and they have [a] problem [with it]' (Isra). This has impacted the everyday lives of many Muslim women. Isra describes her interactions with other Muslim women and how discrimination consumes their daily lives:

> I have met with a lot of young [Muslim] women, who are facing [discrimination] every day, almost [all] their life, on the bus, on the street, in the shops, everywhere.
>
> (Ibid.).

On the link between discrimination as the *prejudice of first impressions* and the sphere of work, once again the three young female interviewees above, Daleela, Furat and Isra, narrate their negative work experiences and connect it to wearing the hijab publicly. Two respondents, Daleela and Furat, discuss problems of wearing the hijab when attempting to attain employment and Isra gives an example of the difficulties she has faced when wearing the hijab in a public work space. Daleela once again expresses her feelings of paranoia but this time in relation to attaining work. She states that 'you can never know why you didn't get the job, it could be you or it could be the first impression they are going to get of your [religious or ethnic] culture' (Daleela). Furat states something similar by commenting that 'another thing about the headscarf is that at work, sometimes you don't know whether you're kinda getting declined for a job' because of it. To highlight the problems associated with the hijab and employment opportunities, Furat narrates a small story about a girlfriend, who always wore the headscarf but could not attain a job interview. In this story, the female friend 'decided that it [the hijab] wasn't for her, [so] she took it off' (Furat). Due to this decision, 'as soon as she started applying for this job, she was getting call backs left, right and centre and they were trying to woo her' (Ibid.). Consequently, Furat's friend began 'kind of thinking "was it really that [the hijab] was kind of stopping me from getting a job?"' (Ibid.).

Also, the following small story narrated by Isra is a good example of the recognitive-power dilemmas faced by young Muslims in Irish-European context who encounter, in the work place, challenges to their religious identity from others in positions of authority. The small story below shows that Muslim youth do struggle against forms of power that attempt to limit their freedom to express an Islamic identity in public. As shown in the narrative below, Isra successfully struggles for the recognition of her most salient identity and the freedom to express it by wearing the hijab in a public workspace. Of note is that Isra is willing to sacrifice monetary employment than give up the most salient part of her identity:

> I remember one day I was [working at Dublin] airport. I was wearing my [head]scarf and the woman [a security woman in the airport] told me to remove my scarf [hijab], I look at her and say 'listen, you cannot tell me some things, I'm not going to remove my scarf'. I showed her and said 'listen, this is my scarf, I'm not going to remove it'. If you want to sack me, you can sack me, but I'm not going to remove it … So, the woman did understand what I'm saying and where I'm coming from and then she let me go. If that day I didn't say 'I'm not going to do it', she will keep on doing it to any other Muslim woman, who was passing the airport, but I said 'no' and then she agreed, and she say 'okay' and she let me go. So, that's why I said one person cannot spoil a whole thing.
>
> (Isra)

Within the first generation female discussion group, Meera (1st Gen, F, Cit, FDG) reasons that such societal misrecognition against the hijab is caused by a lack of knowledge and understanding of difference. She states that, in her everyday life, she is constantly talking about Islam to other people and has come to realise that 'some people don't really know why I wear scarf [the hijab]' (Meera). In her opinion, there is a deep misunderstanding about Islam and Muslims in Irish-European society. Hurriyah enters the discussion with a narrative that explores how knowledge is related to the themes of recognition and respect:

> With knowledge, they [non-Muslims] can change recognition to us [Muslims] more. With my eyes, the recognition from the respect. If you respect yourself, people will respect you. If you yourself respect others, people will respect you, it's reciprocal. Like you cannot be recognised

until when you to yourself acknowledge other people's differences, not criticising them, you understand me, because we are very easy to judge people, you know, even within myself as Muslim, we judge each other 'oh, she's not wearing the hijab, she's not doing this'. Leave that to Allah to judge. So within ourselves, I would say 'we have to search inside ourselves' you understand ... so, in so many ways as well, recognition comes within yourself, respecting the other people and ready to work with people, without discriminating them. Then, there will be unity.

(Hurriyah)

In the above statement, Hurriyah is emphasising the core importance and connection between knowledge, recognition and respect. In the first line, she emphasises that a greater degree of societal knowledge about Islam will change the recognition that Muslims receive from others. She then succinctly connects recognition to respect and positions it as important to the self and others in that it is a reciprocal exchange. For Hurriyah, respect and recognition are first performed by the need to respect and recognise oneself, and then a person can tolerate the differences of others instead of being judgemental. This discussant acknowledges human fallibility and the tendency to judge each other. She states that Muslims also judge other Muslims, especially in relation to the hijab. She advocates for humans to stop judging each other. In her opinion, people must use their spiritual recognition to leave judging to God, an abstract phenomenon. Hurriyah stresses how recognition is a self-relation in that 'recognition comes from within yourself' (Ibid.) but that it also has an external aspect, which involves recognition of and co-operation with others 'without discriminating [against] them' (Ibid.). For this discussant, the acting out of this internal and external knowledge will create unity and solidarity in society.

Transitional phenomena as common ground

With forms of discrimination identified, a pertinent question comes to the foreground: is there a common ground between Muslims and non-Muslims in Irish-European society? A place where discrimination as the *prejudice of first impressions* can be overcome and people can be recognised equally as human, as citizens, and respected for their individual traits, abilities and achievements. Two small stories, by Fusaila and Masud within the youth discussion groups, provide a reflective insight on the above integration question. Both small stories emphasise the importance of cultural transitional phenomena, a Winnicottian concept, as a reciprocal common ground that aids interaction between people.

Isha (2nd Gen, F, Cit, FDG) is cognisant that when two different people meet there can initially be a *prejudice of first impressions*. Although this is a negative aspect of the human condition, this discussant is also adamant that such discrimination can be overcome. Through communication, people 'start to get to know you' and in a small timeframe, 'like just five minutes', when they hear you speak English with an Irish accent 'then they might actually see

Societal relations

you as a person instead of as a Muslim' (Isha). Isha's sister, Fusaila (2nd Gen, F, Cit, FDG) adds a small story that elaborates on how she feels recognised in an artistic social setting. She positions this in relation to the prejudice that manifests around first impressions and how this can be overcome. Her small story is as follows:

> It depends on what you associate yourself with as well because me, Isha and Rifa, we are artists, we do art. Like in our classes as well we'd be like the only [artistic] Muslims because Muslims don't tend to do that thing. We [Muslims generally] go more into like [being] doctors and law and all that but we're more in the creative side. So, we associate ourselves with that kind of thing and when we like, when we go to like exhibitions and stuff like that people will, the first thing always they'll see, 'Muslim', because we're wearing our scarves but then they'll be like 'an artist', I feel like we all understand each other, we're all creative so I feel like I'm really accepted in the art world because we all have a creative understanding.
> (Fusaila)

In the above narrative, Fusaila clarifies that she, her sister and their friend Rifa (2nd Gen, F, Cit, FDG) are not the same as other young Muslims because they have a 'creative side' (Ibid.), i.e. they are artists. The choice of such a profession is unusual for Muslims in that many young European Muslims, under parental influence, enter the medical, legal or financial professions. Fusaila speaks of her experience of going to art exhibitions and how she is immediately seen through her particular race and Muslim traits, i.e. wearing the hijab. However, in terms of abilities as an artist, she believes that in time she will be understood and accepted by her artistic peers, who share the same professional skills and creative occupation. At the end of this statement, she confides that she generally suffers two prejudices to do with first impressions: 'me personally, I get two prejudices when you first see me, I'm Muslim and I'm black and then later I'm Irish and I'm this and I'm that but yeah, that's me' (Ibid.).

The second small story relates to Masud's experience of being recognised as an accomplished soccer player and how such recognition of his meritocratic abilities on the pitch overcomes the *prejudice of first impressions* off the pitch. Masud states that he has received recognition for his abilities as a soccer player from various people. Although traits do come into it, he stresses that in relation to the game of soccer, ability is most important. On this point, he differentiates between the recognition of traits versus that of abilities:

> All over the place, people that you wouldn't know that I've never seen, and they do recognise you [when you play soccer at a prominent level] and you are different because you stand out, like the different name, you look different, everything about you is different. So definitely ability is one thing for me. It's always stood out, it's always been there for me.
> (Masud)

94 Societal relations

Masud distinguishes between recognition on the pitch for his abilities and the prejudice received off the pitch in his everyday life. He states concisely that 'no', he never received discrimination 'on the soccer pitch' because in such transitional arenas 'there is that respect' (Ibid.). He acknowledges his varying experiences on the pitch with those off the pitch, i.e. on the street, where 'out of nowhere someone could come up to you and be like "ah, you're this, you're that". I've had that a few times' (Ibid.). Overall, this discussant feels that the recognition he receives on the pitch is good for him personally but is also generally beneficial for Islamic identity in that other people get the opportunity to see a Muslim in a positive contributory light. On this point, Masud states his feelings about being recognised for his abilities and relates this back to his Muslim identity traits:

> it feels good to be recognised for what you're doing and then people know you're Muslim. Like my name is Masud … but they still know [I'm Muslim]. So, it is something good. So, they do know you're Muslim and there's respect and [the] coaches and all respect me for doing Ramadan and playing at the same time. So, it is good.
>
> (Ibid.)

Impact on relation-to-self

In terms of discrimination's affect on an individual's relation-to-self, first generation female discussant, Hurriyah, determines that societal misrecognition has a negative all-encompassing impact on maintaining a positive relation-to-self. She states about the impact of misrecognition on the self: 'Yes it [discrimination] does [affect relation-to-self], mentally, physically, socially it would, it will do' (Hurriyah). This discussant has an advanced understanding of the dynamics of recognitive relations. Her remark invokes Maja to enter the discussion and narrate a small story about her personal experience of perceived misrecognition. This story relates to her attending a fitness centre, located in a plush hotel in Dublin. Maja narrates her small story in Arabic and Dahlia translates it to English:

> It's a small story happened to my friend Maja. She felt disrespect from a female receptionist at a hotel fitness centre … Maja said she 'felt this lady doesn't respect me. She looks at me in a very bad way'. This make her at the end, 'I don't want to go back' and she paid the full fee for the year and she said, 'I don't want to go back there' and I [Dahlia] said, 'Why? She's just a receptionist. Just go, speak with the manager, say something, why you stopping?' She [Maja] say 'I don't want to go there, I'm not happy. Her eyes, her way she talking to me, you know that smallest thing'.
>
> (Maja)

Societal relations 95

Maja's small story is an example of how she perceived an everyday experience of disrespect from a receptionist. Such perceptions are highly influenced by her feelings in that she felt the receptionist did not respect her. This perception, backed by a cognitive-emotional reflection, is corroborated by how the receptionist looks and communicates to her. Through such communicative gestures, Maja perceives that the receptionist does not respect her. The feeling that her visible surface-level traits are not respected has an impact upon Maja. Although she has paid the yearly fees to use the fitness facilities in the hotel, she is certain that she will not return and be subject to disrespect. For this discussant, respect comes before monetary considerations. In a further conversation with Dahlia, Maja explicates further reasons why she perceived herself to be disrespected. She states that when she tried to speak to the receptionist, she was not given any attention, i.e. she was made invisible. Dahlia confirms the importance of being recognised by stating 'I respect attention'. Maja felt that her enquiries were not given sufficient attention: 'she [the receptionist] said [towards] any question, she said abruptly "I don't know, I don't know", like that'. In terms of the annual fees, Maja states: 'I don't like war [fighting about it] anymore, I don't care [about losing money]'. Dahlia confirms that Maja has lost money, but due to suffering disrespect, she has lost something more important and harder to replenish, her self-confidence. As Dahlia states: 'I think she don't care about that [losing money] but she lost her confidence because [of] that way'.

In relation to Masud's small story above about being recognised for his abilities on the soccer pitch, when probed as to whether such recognition positively affects his relation-to-self in terms of self-esteem, he responds by stating that it is good to receive recognition for his abilities, even though he is different to the other players on his team in terms of traits such as skin colour, ethnicity and religion. He confidently states that on the soccer pitch, he is given respect and his abilities are recognised. Masud thus differentiates between the respect and recognition he receives on the pitch for his abilities and the misrecognition he receives on the street, where his surface-level traits are discriminated against by others. He states the following narrative about being 'in-between' in terms of identity and how the transitional phenomenon of soccer provides the meritocratic common ground, where individuals, despite their differences from each other, can be recognised for their particular meritocratic traits, abilities and achievements. For Masud, playing with others in a cultural transitional space overcomes the *prejudice of first impressions* that impedes everyday life off the pitch:

> It's good. It's good, yeah, it's good to feel recognised in a place like this [Ireland] where you're different, especially at the [high] levels maybe I've played at and I feel like I am being recognised ... I was the only different one in that changing room. Like everyone else was pure Irish, like a hundred per cent Irish and I'm there. I've lived in Ireland my whole life but, you don't feel a hundred per cent Irish and you don't feel a hundred

96 *Societal relations*

per cent Libyan because it's the same thing [issue]. You feel a bit excluded in a way but yet you're still living a fifty-fifty kind of thing. So, it does feel good to be recognised for your ability and yeah, people do know me and that's something I like. It's good to know that wherever I go, because they know me, you're not going to get stick for it, so I've some sort of respect because of soccer.

(Masud)

Limitations of rights of residence

This section focuses on aspects of legal misrecognition, particularly on the uncertain civic status of denizenship and how such categorisation impacts negatively upon the familial sphere.

The uncertainty of denizenship status

In the first generation interviews, Saad refers to the negative experiences that denizens encounter in Irish society and vocalises what he perceives to be an issue in the Muslim community in relation to the status uncertainty experienced by denizens, who may do something 'right or wrong to obtain [a full legal] status'. For example, there is evidence that denizens have married Eastern European women in Ireland to gain secure Irish and European citizenship (Cahill 2013, Brady 2014). Such actions illustrate the status uncertainty faced by various groups, i.e. asylum-seekers, refugees, illegal immigrants and denizens and how these experiences may lead to extreme actions to attain a more secure and beneficial legal position in society. Saad narrates a small story that elaborates on how such forms of status uncertainty negatively impact individuals and the society enforcing forms of civic stratification:

> Somebody who is here only a short time, four years or five years and they don't have any resident status or permanent resident status [denizenship] or some other status, they will be very uncertain and those are the people who will actually try to do something right or wrong to obtain that status so then you will see some negative stories [in the media] and then you will see that some people come in [to the country] and they try to make a business of different things and all this so there is some negativity surrounding those things.

(Saad)

Another first generation male interviewee, Ubaid, stresses that the reason why multiculturalism is failing is because immigrants to Europe have not been accorded secure legal recognition from host states because immigrants are still viewed as temporary workers, i.e. only working for a period then returning to their home country. Nation states do not 'recognise them as citizens' or even as 'members of the society', which has led to the formation of denizenship, a status that limits social and political rights in democracies (Ubaid). In Ubaid's opinion, denizens are 'not recognised the same. They're in-between' (Ibid.). They are not asylum-seekers, who depend on the state but also, they are not full citizens, who are recognised by other citizens as being independent and capable of making political and moral decisions. It is important to clarify that although the common argument against the status of denizenship relates to the unfair asymmetrical distribution of rights to third-country nationals, De Schutter and Ypi (2015) convincingly argue for mandatory citizenship because the asymmetrical distribution of obligations solely to citizens is also an unequal and unfair burden to carry. Ubaid stresses the need for the younger generation of Muslims to be conferred with citizenship to prevent isolation and promote a positive feeling of belonging. On this point, he states that:

> if these [citizenship] issues are addressed, and Muslims are seen as [who they are] and they are appreciated as citizens of Ireland, from grassroots level up to the top, then I think there will be some little bit of confusion, but at least, the youth will not feel that they are isolated and not citizens of Ireland, [by addressing such issues] they [the youth] will still feel citizens of Ireland.
>
> (Ubaid)

The youth also discuss issues related to the uncertain status of denizenship. Interviewee Nurdeen states concisely that 'in terms of legal recognition, if you're an Irish citizen you can't be kicked-out of the country'. Aziz gives a critical account of his denizenship experience in relation to the application process that is information deficient and drawn-out in terms of time. For Aziz, this bureaucratic process adds a great deal of uncertainty to everyday life and to the possibility of fulfilling future hopes. In his interview, he states the following:

AZIZ: In terms of legal recognition, I have been here for ten years and I still have not gotten citizenship. My flatmate [who is also Muslim] and his whole family have been here for eleven years, and they have the same problems as us. The thing is you can't follow up on the application, which is annoying.
INTERVIEWER: Why do you think you have had to wait this long to receive citizenship?
AZIZ: I've no idea, [I] can't follow up on it. I really have no idea.

(Aziz)

Civic stratification and familial disruptions

A number of narratives give an insight into how the uncertainty inherent to denizenship status has a detrimental impact upon familial relations. Such a connection is strongly emphasised through narrative small stories. For example, second generation female Furat narrates a story about a close female friend, who has been 'living here [in Ireland] all her life' but who applied too late for full citizenship status, i.e. her father applied after she had turned eighteen years of age. However, by the time her application was submitted, the immigration authorities 'were looking for different criteria' (Furat) in particular the need for adults to have worked several years in the Irish state. Lacking such experience, Furat's friend did not meet the necessary requirements and had to leave Ireland and move to Libya, her father's home country. The following small story narrated by Furat recounts how legal misrecognition negatively impacted her friend's personal circumstances and familial relations:

> It [legal recognition] definitely does affect her [the narrator's friend] because she is studying in Libya at the moment and because she is studying there, she can't come [to Ireland] whenever she wants to visit her parents, like her brothers, sisters, mother, father, all have citizenship except her. So, she has to apply for the visa, if it's a visiting visa, a study visa, or whatever it is, she has to go through that process just to see her mother, her father, or they [the parents] would have to go down there [to Libya], you know. It's made it very difficult [for] her, made it very difficult for her.
>
> (Ibid.)

The second generation male discussion group also gives an insight into the varying experiences of friends, who are legally stratified and categorised into citizens and denizens. During the discussion, Yusuf states confidently on this topic: 'I was born here so it doesn't make a difference'. He clarifies that he and his whole family have passports 'so it wasn't really an issue' (Yusuf). He then compares his positive experience of being a citizen to the negative experience of denizenship. As a citizen, Yusuf states that he didn't have to wait long for a passport, and unlike denizens, have 'his hopes up' in terms of attaining a passport and being legally recognised by the Irish state. This discussant is critical and cynical about the power the state has over the conferral of citizenship and is glad that he did not have to 'beg for the red [Irish] passport to come so that I can be free' (Ibid.). He comments that not only does he have one passport, he also has dual citizenship with his Libyan home country. Masud identifies with the statement relating to dual citizenship and comments correspondingly 'that's the same here for me' (Masud). Yusuf re-enters the conversation and looking to Aban states: 'but you're different' (Yusuf).

The recognition of a different status by Yusuf marks the point at which Aban enters the conversation to talk about his denizen experience. In his narrative, he elaborates on his parents' experience of coming to Ireland and waiting a long time, approximately ten years, to attain Irish citizenship. He comments how, as a child, he was unaware of the difference between himself as a passport-holding citizen and his parents, who had not attained legal recognition and had to use new visas each time they travelled outside Ireland. For Aban, the family structure was stratified between those members conferred with citizenship and those with the lesser denizenship status. Reflecting

Societal relations 99

upon the impact of this stratification, he clarifies that applying for travel documents was stressful and time-consuming. Prayer gave his parents comfort and consolation through the stress and uncertainty of this situation:

> It took them a while to get it [citizenship], like ten years to get it but as I was growing up, I didn't know what difference it made. Like I had the Irish passport, they just had a few travel documents. Whenever we went away, we were going away with something different ... like a visa to where you're going. It was stressful and took ages for everything to get done but for the past two years like, you know, they just thank God, you know, my parents made the prayers and all. The whole family has it (citizenship) at the moment so everything's good.
>
> (Aban)

Limiting access to opportunities

While the status of denizenship curtails political participation, particularly voting in national elections, the narratives give an insight into how a lesser legal civic status also puts limits on the attainment of basic opportunities that are commonly afforded to people who have attained full citizenship.

Education and freedom of movement

The narratives in this section identify the basic good of education as a major concern for denizens, who have not attained full citizenship, and the recognition that they have the capacity to make moral decisions that impact upon the political community. This is exemplified by first generation interviewee Adeeb, who states the following small story illustrating how an uncertain civic status impacts the younger generation in terms of the financial capacity to gain entry to education and how such limitations impede the ability to be in society and progress towards new forms of being. Adeeb's critical narrative on this topic is as follows:

> he [the young Muslim] can't get [a student] grant, so he stop, he [the person in authority] can't allow him [the young Muslim] to be, 'you should pay the full [student tuition] amount [for a third-country national]' and that affect him [the young Muslim] but mean exactly because he had been here for ages [many years] and he's not recognised even as [a] citizen, [he is recognised] as nothing, like his father and his father is all the time complaining about this country [Ireland], he hate roses. This is such a problem, big problems of conflict for the community.
>
> (Adeeb)

From a youth perspective, Aziz discusses his denizenship experience and strongly criticises how his lesser civic status brings hardship and stress upon his parents' lives and finances in that his university enrolment fees are high because he is categorised as a third-country national, despite having lived most of his life in Ireland. For Aziz, legal misrecognition has put a significant burden upon his parents, even more so considering his younger brother is coming of age and intends to go to university. His narrative on this matter is as follows:

> Interviewer: Do you feel that you want to have Irish citizenship?
> Aziz: Yes, it makes things a lot easier. For example, when going through security at airports and when I travel, I have to sort out a visa, which is a hassle. I also have to pay ten thousand in university fees each year and my brother is coming through to university and he will have to pay the same, which is a big burden on my parents.
> (Aziz)

The above narrative highlights the criticism directed towards legal misrecognition by a denizen, who feels burdened by not being recognised as having the same legal rights as the majority. This interviewee states that he has been in Ireland for ten years yet has not received full citizenship status. He knows of other families, who have the same problem and that there is an increase in Muslim denizens attending third-level educational institutions in Ireland. Interestingly, Aziz claims that legal misrecognition has negatively impacted upon his familial sphere in that his parents have had to pay expensive educational fees, which is a significant financial burden (Faller 2012). This narrative emphasises that spheres of recognitive interaction can influence each other in detrimental ways, i.e. legal misrecognition not only impacts the individual but also other social spheres such as the family.

Within the first generation female discussion group, Hurriyah also mentions how, by their legal status, denizens are limited in the possibility of accessing education. On the topic of denizens paying high university fees due to being categorised as third-country nationals, she comments that she does 'know people' (Hurriyah) who have experienced this situation. She states that these denizens 'have to wait another couple of years before they can get themselves nationality then they can go back to school because of the red tape [bureaucracy]' (Ibid.). Here she is making the point that some denizens co-ordinate their educational attainment with the conferral of citizenship. Hurriyah views this half-status as 'absolutely' a limitation (Ibid.). It is an impediment that has a negative practical impact upon people's lives and being. She explains that by suffering such a financial block to education, denizens 'can get frustrated' (Ibid.). She then stresses the point that these people 'want to exercise their human right' to unfettered access to education (Ibid.).

A similar narrative about educational fees for denizens is discussed in the young male discussion group. The comments are made predominantly by Aswad (2nd Gen, M, Cit, FDG), who makes the point that denizenship can impact on the ability of a person to attend third-level education by the fact that a denizen's recognised status means that they must pay higher educational fees. For this discussant, the main practical issue surrounding legal misrecognition is 'college fees' (Aswad). He comments on his own experience of having to pay expensive fees when he first attended college and reflects that he only received citizenship three years later. Like Aban, Aswad thanks God that his financial burden was eased by attaining 'a scholarship before [receiving citizenship] that covered most of the cost' (Ibid.). Of note is that through a campaign by denizen students to highlight their difficulties, the Irish government and the Department of Education has acted to ensure that the ever-increasing number of denizens, who have lived the majority of their lives in Ireland, will not have to pay high third-level educational fees. Albeit a fix to an unfair situation and easing a financial burden, it does not correct the primary problem of civic stratification, which continues to this day.

As well as limitations on educational access, impediments to freedom of movement were also mentioned by a selection of interviewees and discussants, who view legal misrecognition as practically impacting on their ability to move freely, whether to a home country or through Europe. Reflecting on Aziz's comments (see p.100), when asked about his feelings towards attaining citizenship, he confirms that he would like full citizenship status for practical reasons, such as cheaper access to university education but also for going through security at airports and for ease of travel out of Ireland without the need to obtain a visa.

The most interesting narrative about this issue comes from Abdul (1st Gen, M, Cit, FDG), who took part in the first generation discussion group. His comments focus on his experience as a denizen and how his life in Europe changed for the better by receiving Irish citizenship. He narrates a small story about his experience of planning to drive through Europe, back to his home country, to see his family in the Russian caucus. In the past, as a secular denizen, he recounts that he had no problems travelling through France. However, upon becoming more visibly religious, he perceives a distinct change in how he is treated when applying for a transit visa:

> A couple of years ago, I want to travel home by car and in order to do that, I have to go through France and I have to do like a transit visa for French embassy. But eh, I did it second time. First time, I didn't have the beard. I looks normal. They give me visa in 2005. But last time, I had a beard, at this time and they refuse me. I think because of that, because I'm Muslim like, you know and I feel very bad because [my] parents were waiting for me. I want to go home, and they refuse the visa without any reason. They don't say any reason, but I thought that the reason was because I am Muslim.
>
> (Abdul)

The above small story illustrates how Abdul perceives that his change from being a non-practising to a practising Muslim had ramifications for his plan to drive back to his homeland through France. For the second trip, he has the expectation that he will obtain the travel visa. However, this time, he is visibly identified as Muslim. He perceives that this difference is the reason for being refused a transit visa. He feels 'very bad' that he has been blocked by the French authorities and unable to see his family (Ibid.). Rashid (1st Gen, M, Den, FDG), a quiet discussant, whose contribution to the focus group is minimal, states that 'they', i.e. the immigration services or police, 'do that for jilbab [long coat worn by Muslims]' (Ibid.). This comment emphasises that Muslims have the perception that immigration services, in France and other countries, do visibly identify and carry out religious profiling of Muslims based on surface-level traits.

Impact on relation-to-self

A variety of narratives give an insight into how legal misrecognition affects an individual's relation-to-self, particularly in terms of self-respect. Labeeb (1st Gen, M, Den, FDG) vocalises how he has applied for citizenship three times but failed in all attempts. He also mentions that he has been refused the right to work and that his marriage ended in divorce, which led to being separated from his children. Labeeb blames the governmental and legal bureaucratic systems for his misfortune and determines that prejudice against his Muslim-ness is the prime reason for his difficulties. In terms of feeling, Labeeb agrees that he felt angry against such treatment by the state. He lost self-respect in terms of how he was treated and how, as he perceives it, his religious difference as a Muslim impeded his ability to acquire legal recognition. On the topic of losing self-respect, he states:

> Of course [I feel like I lost some self-respect], I [was] treat[ed], I [was] treat[ed] very, very badly. I [was] treat[ed badly but] I have no criminal record. I never been fighting or arguing with anyone here.
>
> (Labeeb)

In relation to Abdul's small story about being refused a visa to travel through France to see his family in the Russian caucus, he recounts how such misrecognition made him feel. He states that 'after [my visa application was rejected], I feel very like stressed because, you know, I want to go home, and I can't'. In contrast to his denizen experience, Abdul recounts his experience after receiving Irish citizenship, which overall is much more positive. In terms of his travels as an Irish-European citizen, he states:

> since I received Irish citizenship, like you know, I feel free like you know, I don't have to go and ask somebody for visa or something like that, I free to go wherever I want … I think it's a very good right for me, like you know. I feel very happy with that.
>
> (Abdul)

In terms of how legal recognition relates to self-respect, Idris (1st Gen, M, Cit, FDG) adds to the conversation by returning to his own experience of travelling the world with an Irish company. He describes being a citizen as a positive feeling and is proud to represent Ireland as an Irish citizen. This discussant makes a distinction between his sense of being simultaneously an Irish citizen and an Egyptian national:

> I felt that not only I'm recognised in this country [Ireland], but you know, I feel inside me that I am Irish, and I feel proud of representing the country. I mean I'm still maintaining that they know I'm Egyptian origin because of the name and as I said you can never change that, but you know, it is a good feeling to be able to have an adopted country and to be able to say 'yeah, I have [citizenship], I'm an Irish citizen but I'm an Egyptian national.'
>
> (Idris)

For Idris, positive feelings are connected to the process of attaining a nation's citizenship. He received an Irish passport in the early 1980s and states about receiving such recognition that 'it is great because it allowed me a lot of freedom' as compared to his experience in Muslim-majority countries. For this discussant, in 'our [home] countries', legal recognition 'as a human' and 'as an individual' is not forthcoming (Ibid.). He strongly criticises Muslim-majority countries for being 'about the appearance of the religion' rather than implementing 'what it says' (Ibid.). Practically, with the Egyptian passport 'I go nowhere', which he views as 'a shame' (Ibid.). For a long time, the Egyptian passport did not represent civicness and human freedom and that is why, in Idris' opinion, Egypt has experienced bouts of revolution. On the other hand, when he received the Irish passport, he was 'delighted' because, as he says, 'now, I'm human' and can travel freely with dignity (Ibid.). He also states that when he travels, even to his home country, 'I go with the Irish passport' (Ibid.). When asked if receiving an Irish passport affected his sense of self and whether he would define it as self-respect, he confidently responds 'absolutely' (Ibid.). However, alongside such positive feelings is 'sorrow at the same time for my own background' (Ibid.).

The need for civic participation and contribution

The discussion group narratives highlight how gaining full legal recognition enables an individual to venture further into society to participate and contribute to the value-horizon of their social and political community. For example, Labeeb supports Idris' comment that Irish citizenship (with its corresponding rights and obligations) gives an individual freedom and opportunity, which is not readily available in some African and Middle Eastern home countries (Labeeb). This statement is striking in that Labeeb does not have full citizenship himself but is a denizen, whose citizenship application has been rejected several times.

Labeeb goes on to state a positive view of universal civicness that transcends religious particularness and gives an indication of how he lives his everyday life as a denizen. He states that he is unemployed and is 'receiving help from the

104 Societal relations

government' (Ibid.), most probably in the form of unemployment benefit. He seems to correlate social welfare payments not to the state, who distribute such payments, but to other citizens in Irish society, who pay and contribute via taxation. He vocalises his appreciation to Irish society for coming to his aid in terms of providing him with social welfare while unemployed: 'who paying this tax, who paying this money, [it's] from the Irish society and the majority is Catholic or Christian' (Ibid.). He adds that he reciprocates the aid he receives by civically volunteering 'to work for my community through St. Vincent de Paul' (Ibid.), a Catholic charitable organisation. Labeeb recognises the reciprocal nature of being a citizen, which involves the moral responsibility to enact rights but also obligations. Alongside receiving social welfare payments, his civic identity is active in reciprocating back to his community, thereby proving that he is not a burden but a contributing member of society. This is reflected in the following statement:

> I'm not working at the moment. I volunteer to work for my community through St. Vincent de Paul but some people [in the Muslim community] might have problem with that [working for a Christian charity] but I'm going to volunteer to work for St. Vincent de Paul to prove to my [wider] community, to provide for my [wider] community because I don't want to sit back in the room where [I am] watching television. Why the government giving me money and there is some way that I can contribute.
>
> (Labeeb)

In this statement, Labeeb suggests that some members of the Muslim community may have an issue with his decision to volunteer for a Christian charity. Idris asks a question of Labeeb: 'and do you think there is a problem in doing that'? (Idris). Labeeb responds 'no' and then reflects that 'some people might have problem with that' (Labeeb). Overall, he is happy to be civically active and participating in the wider community. When asked about making civic contributions to his community, he responds:

> I'm three-years doing that [volunteering]. So, I mean, the understanding between the religion and stuff like that [civic participation], I think some people [in the Muslim community] find it difficult. It might be based on their background from back home or whatever, religion, but we live together in our [home] country, Christian and Muslim, peacefully, there's no difference.
>
> (Ibid.)

The most concise statement about the confidence to participate and contribute in wider society emanates from first generation discussant Abdul, who opens-up about his feelings in terms of receiving Irish citizenship and how it transformed his levels of participation. As a denizen, he tried to be generally 'good with people' (Abdul), however, he admits that most of his socialising was contained in the confines of his Islamic community in that he mostly 'dealt with [the local] mosque' (Ibid.). However, upon receiving Irish citizenship, Abdul remarks that he 'thinks more responsible like other people'. This is an indication that his self-respect increased and that his confidence to stand up for himself is buttressed by legal recognition. By being fully legal, he can view himself as a responsible citizen, who has rights but also obligations to others in society. Abdul makes the following remark about this change in identity status:

> If somebody say to me [when I was a denizen] 'aah, you foreigner like', I take it like, you know, but now [as a citizen] like, even if they say that, I don't care about what they say like. I feel like I have some responsibility for this society like, you know. Even people if they don't like me it's up to them like. It's their business like. Anyway, I feel like I have to do something to bring some good stuff to this society. It doesn't matter like what people think about me, you know. I feel more responsible when [I] received the citizenship.
>
> (Abdul)

The above stance is also confirmed by Sadiyya (1st Gen, F, Cit, FDG), who states that legal recognition, in her opinion, implies that 'you can say what you want to do and go out and start relationship'. Likewise, a young female second generation discussant, Saiba (2nd Gen, F, Cit, FDG) views full citizenship as obliging an individual to civically participate and contribute beyond their ethnic or religious community for the benefit of wider society. On this point, Saiba narrates a conversation she had with her mother that went as follows: 'I want to do stuff for the Irish community [but] she'd be like "oh, but why?"'(Saiba). This statement implies that Saiba understands the participatory obligations of being a citizen and struggles to justify such actions to other familial members, particularly those from the first generation. Fusaila adds to Saiba's conversation by jokingly voicing a hypothetical response from Saiba's mum: 'you're not Irish!' (Fusaila).

Saiba keeps the conversation going by explaining what citizenship means to her. She explains that she sees herself as a citizen and feels she has to 'contribute to my community' (Saiba). It must be questioned, which community she is referring to? She clarifies this point by stating that as a citizen she feels the need to contribute to all communities, i.e. to her Islamic community, to her ethnic community but also to the wider societal community. She states on this point: 'not only my Islamic community but also like the Irish community' (Ibid.). Interestingly, she confirms that her mother questions her actions. Saiba voices her mother: 'but why are you doing it?' (Ibid.). Once again, her mother's question is not left unanswered. Saiba responds: 'I'm not only those things' (Ibid.). This statement indicates that she has an Islamic and ethnocultural identity but also, she acknowledges other identities, one of those being a civic identity. This is exemplified in the statement: 'I'm also Irish, in a sense' (Ibid.). Such a narrative gives an indication of how she views being Irish. She acknowledges that she is Irish but with the caveat, 'in a sense'

106 *Societal relations*

(Ibid.). It could be argued here that this discussant is referring to herself as Irish in terms of being an Irish citizen and differentiates such Irishness from its nationalist and ethno-cultural forms.

Perceptions of identity

The above focus on societal and legal misrecognition inevitably redirects this study to the salient issue of identity. In this section, narrative data gives a vivid insight into how the recognition of difference supersedes the recognition of sameness, i.e. visible difference takes precedence over being recognised as a universal citizen with equal rights and obligations to other human beings. Then the viewpoints of Muslim youth are explored in relation to how they relate to an Irish identity, particularly in terms of 'being different Irish'. These narratives give an insight into how Muslim youth accept, maintain and utilise their multiple identities but how problematic issues persist in terms of how other people perceive such identifications.

The supersession of sameness by difference

The narratives give a valuable insight into how Muslim individuals in the Irish-European sphere perceive difference to others, especially in terms of how the recognition of surface-level traits negatively supersedes the sameness that legal recognition universally and equally offers to citizens.

For example, second generation female interviewee, Furat, makes an interesting statement related to the tension that exists between sameness and difference in everyday interaction. Her statement refers to how citizenship's universal sameness has been tied to nationalistic ethno-cultural attributes, which come into conflict with difference formed through an individual's particular traits and unique way of life. She states the following in relation to how a person's particularness is recognised before a universal civic status:

> Legal recognition ... myself, personal opinion, is that you always have to think twice about what you are doing legally because you always feel like as if because I'm a foreigner how will they treat me you know. For example, I was in a situation where somebody else was in the wrong but I'd feel like I wouldn't be able to bring [it] up because it's not going to be dealt with that way, that person's the Irish person, I'm the Muslim, you know, the foreigner, which side will they take, so you'll always have that fear, the constant background fear of 'is there a point or is there not a point to speaking out?'.
>
> (Furat)

Through this narrative, the interviewee, who is an Irish citizen, states that in everyday interaction she must 'think twice' about her legal recognition (Ibid.). She feels that what makes her different to other citizens, i.e. her foreignness determines how she will be treated by others in the first instance. She gives an example of a situation in which an ethnic Irish person is acting wrongfully, however, she feels that she cannot speak out about such action because she feels that her moral claim will not be dealt with appropriately because 'that person's the Irish person, I'm the Muslim' (Ibid.). It is this 'constant background fear' (Ibid.), which prevents her from speaking out against wrongful acts committed by others. This statement is interesting as it delineates how citizenship in the Irish nation state has been attached to ethno-nationalist attributes and conceptions of identity. Even though, the interviewee is an Irish citizen with the same rights and obligations to other citizens, she has a fearful feeling that her ethnic and religious difference supersedes the civic sameness she attained through legal recognition. Her abstract universalism as a citizen, which is filtered of particularisms, cannot compete with the recognition of surface-level differences that constitutes the individual in terms of race, ethnicity and religion. Tensions arise when such differences diverge from the dominant norm of what is perceived to constitute the identity standard of Irishness.

Within the first generation female discussion group, Ghazalah (1st Gen, F, Den, FDG) reflects on how abstract the status of citizenship can be when applied in everyday life. Her statement gives a very good insight into the dynamics differentiating recognition as an abstract universal form and being recognised for one's differences to others in everyday life. She states that legal recognition as 'just on paper' is practically useful when one is 'in civic places' interacting with state bureaucracies such as immigration services, passport offices and hospitals (Ghazalah). In this discussant's viewpoint, legal recognition is symbolised by 'documents [or] papers' that generally are 'working fine' (Ibid.). In this regard, the state recognises rights and obligations based on the stratified civic status it assigns to everyone.

Ghazalah then moves the discussion from the legal sphere to the wider sphere of societal recognition. She exclaims: 'now, go to the practical life, go to the reality, no difference. I'm still the Egyptian, or the Sudanese, it's no different.' (Ibid.). This statement brings to the conversation the point that abstract universal citizenship loses its strength in everyday interaction because in the wider societal sphere, particularness or different traits are more visible while the abstract status of being a citizen is harder to detect and cannot be recognised by others during initial interaction. Her narrative makes a clear distinction between the benefits that universal legal recognition has in state institutions, but that such a status is weak to be practically recognised in wider everyday life. In terms of the supersession of legal sameness by the prejudice towards surface-level difference, Hurriyah makes the following statement:

> and you always remain like that. America, UK, it's like that. It will always be there. You will always be a second-class citizen. You will never be a first-class citizen because of your colour.
>
> (Hurriyah)

108 *Societal relations*

Through this statement, Hurriyah as a dark-skinned woman, is confirming that injustice is inextricably linked to the interaction between being a full citizen (with universal rights and obligations in relation to others) versus being a person of difference by having a particular religious, racial or ethnic identity in opposition to the majoritarian identity standard and legitimised social norms. For this discussant, even though she is a citizen of Ireland, a human being, who has universal rights similar to others, she understands that some of her particular identities and norms devalue her being in the eyes of others (Hurriyah). In response, Dahlia narrates a small story about her own experience of misrecognition by others in an Irish airport. She states the following:

> In the airports, actually the red passport, the Irish passport, working perfectly but I saw something, I'm kind of like observ[ing] a little bit around me. I saw, even if I'm holding the Irish passport and I have Irish [citizenship] and you read [it when] you're in front of me, someone told me, 'no, no, this is the EU queue'. [The person says] 'look it's that way' and I say, 'thank you and continue [my own way]'.
>
> (Dahlia)

The above story is interesting as it gives an indication of the divergence between reality and perception in an act of interaction. Dahlia queues in the EU line because she has been given legal recognition by a European state. She is a citizen and holds in her hand the 'red passport' (Ibid.). However, other people in the passport control line view her as not being an Irish or European citizen but a foreigner, a Muslim, who has mistakenly joined the wrong queue and should move to the designated area for third-country nationals, i.e. the denizen line. It can be said that the someone who conversed with Dahlia does not initially perceive her to be a citizen of Ireland or Europe but recognises her firstly in her particularity and difference, as a Muslim woman wearing the hijab, and thereby, negates the possibility that Dahlia could be a citizen.

Within the second generation female discussion group, Saiba and the sisters have received Irish citizenship. Saiba narrates her own experience of being a citizen in Ireland. She states that she has been one since her family came to Ireland in 1997. She then tells a small story about attending secondary school. Many people didn't think she spoke English because she was 'very quiet' (Saiba). She distinctly remembers a teacher asking her if she had a red (Irish) passport to which Saiba replied affirmatively. She then questions how she is recognised in the societal sphere. Despite being an Irish citizen all her life and having the same universal rights and obligations as other citizens, she criticises people who only see her particular different traits and treat her like a foreigner. She states concisely about this form of misrecognition:

> I've had one [Irish] passport all my life and people walking around me like 'you're a foreigner' and I'm like 'but I'm a citizen, I live here all my life, I went to school here, come on'. I just take it in my stride and move

on, but I mean people obviously, of course, automatically they'd be like 'you're a foreigner, like your different'.

(Saiba)

In Saiba's discussion group, multiple discussants feel and vocalise that a universal abstract legal identity is superseded by a person's more recognisable particular traits, whether to do with religion, skin colour or ethnicity. Isha and Rifa respond together with an affirmative 'yeah' with Fusaila declaring 'totally'. Isha interjects with a balancing view by stating 'up to a point, up to a point but not always'. She continues by stating that 'it won't be forever' (Isha), indicating that the recognition of particular traits over an abstract legal identity will not last indefinitely. However, at the moment, the recognitive power lies with 'first impressions most of the time' (Ibid.). In response to her sister's more optimistic assessment, Fusaila narrates a criticism against nationalistic identities and people who hold ethnocentric views. She criticises such people who are 'real patriotic' and who, even if they know you're a legal citizen, will say 'this is my country' (Fusaila). Rifa agrees. Fusaila then imitates these ultra-nationalist views by voicing how such people talk: 'you're taking our jobs, you're doing this, you're doing that' (Ibid.).

Being 'different Irish'

The following section narratively highlights the crucial point that the research participants do not negate being Irish but alternatively view such an identity in a more civic sense compared to the dominant and socially normalised ethno-cultural and nationalistic perspective of Irishness.

To start, Farid (1st Gen, M, Cit, FDG) stresses the complementarity between Islam and civicness in relation to how a national identity interacts with Islam. He uses the example of war. He states that if Ireland was to go to war tomorrow, Muslims 'don't go [and] fight for Ireland' (Farid). In his opinion, only those who have a nationalist Irish identity would fight and die for their country. This discussant states that 'only Irish people fight for Ireland. You know, so that is a national thing. That's a national identity' (Ibid.). For Farid, many Muslims 'don't believe in something like a national identity' (Ibid.). He also associates cultural behaviour such as drinking alcohol and paying interest as being closely linked to such an identity. Importantly, Farid stresses the lack of connection between being Muslim and a national yet strongly emphasises the complementary relationship between being Muslim and civic. The clearest indication of this opinion, or 'feeling' as he calls it, is the following statement:

we [Muslims] don't feel like we're national, Irish national. Probably, we feel more civil. Like, vote civil rather than Irish.

(Ibid.)

110   *Societal relations*

The topic of Irish identity and how to conceive it pertains most strongly to the second generation, who are actively questioning their identities and attempting to resolve dilemmas that arise. Similarly to Saiba's statement above that she is 'also Irish' but with the caveat 'in a sense', female discussant Fusaila defiantly talks about her personal identity struggle and how it is integrally related to how she is perceived by others.

> I didn't consider myself Irish for a long time because people didn't accept it, so I didn't accept it but like, if they don't want me to be Irish, I'm not going to be Irish. So, it's only like about, just last year, I realised that I grew up with these people, you know what I mean, I'm just as Irish as they are.
>
> (Fusaila)

Isha comments specifically on the relationship between having an Islamic and Irish identity and how she came to understand her difference to other Irish people at an early age. She claims that Muslim identity 'is installed in you from a really young age' (Isha). Such identity configurations, 'that you are Muslim' (Ibid.), are most likely socialised through parental initiatives, which is a process facilitated and supported by the wider Islamic community. Fusaila then states that when she was young, 'I knew that I was kinda different to everyone else' (Fusaila). This difference becomes visible when she states: 'I was Irish, but I knew that I was different' (Ibid.). The term *different Irish* is mentioned. Isha replies 'yeah' in agreement with the term and then states that being Irish yet different means that you must 'have [a] thick skin' because you face discrimination due to your difference to others and will inevitably meet 'people that are prejudice towards you' (Isha). Although these negative aspects exist, Isha still has a positive and optimistic reflection in relation to this identity because she 'grew up that way' (Ibid.) and has come to be confident in her difference to others. She states about this outlook: 'I really appreciate that I can go out different. I feel confident to go out in anything' (Ibid.).

Within the second generation male discussion group, Azaan states that he personally lived the 'whole Irish life' because of the influence of his Mum who 'is Irish'. His mother was born and raised an Irish Catholic and converted to the Islamic religion upon marrying a Muslim man. Azaan lived many years with his grandparents, whose house was a place where normalised Irish behaviour was part of everyday life:

> uncles and aunts came by and they drank [alcohol] and they smoked. So, I kind of lived through the whole 'this is Ireland, this is what Irish people do'.
>
> (Azaan).

Azaan does not view Irishness as related to a particular way a person looks, i.e. that they should be 'Caucasian, freckles or ginger hair' (Ibid.). For this discussant, Irishness has more to do with 'the way you act in the country'

(Ibid.). He describes how he celebrated family occasions socially in pubs, which is a common norm practised in Irish cultural life:

> it was a 21st birthday party and we went to the pub for it and we were all partying and music and it's just the Irish life, so we all did that and for my grandparent's 60th and their anniversaries, we'd go out for parties and all that. So, it's the Irish [life], we lived as Irish people. My grandparents were Irish, and they lived their whole lives like that. So, you know, I think it's not really how you look but more how you've been living here.
> (Azaan)

From the above statement, it can be stated that Azaan does perceive himself as Irish through how he acts rather than how he fits the visual stereotype or norm of what an Irish person should look like. The above comment spurs Siddiq (2nd Gen, M, Cit, FDG) to enter the conversation to clarify his opinion that the 'perception of Irish people is changing'. He mentions the impact foreigners, i.e. people of difference are having in Ireland in that they are changing the social dynamic of the country. For this discussant, Irishness is becoming like 'being American' in that differing people in a pluralistic society identify with the meritocratic nature and openness of a modern way of life. Thus, being different to the majoritarian identity standard is losing significance. For Siddiq, Ireland is going in a similar direction to America, where merits and abilities are gaining more societal esteem and particular traits are not discriminated against but respected in their difference (Siddiq).

Conclusion

This empirical chapter shows that by examining narratives thematically and through relevant small stories, it is possible to discover and unearth new sociological knowledge about Muslim everyday life in the wider Irish-European societal sphere. Through the streams of narrative above, we learned that media misrepresentation is a significant concern for first and second generation Muslims. They feel that national and international media does not show the true picture of their lives but instead feeds into the securitised perception of Muslims as isolated and posing a security threat. The narratives also highlight that perceptions of misrecognition do negatively impact individuals in that it impedes the maintenance and growth of their self-esteem and positive relation-to-self of themselves as contributors to society. Resisting passivity, Muslims are struggling against such forms of misrecognition. There is narrative evidence that calls for media to better understand and represent Muslim life and action as well as showing that the first generation deposit their hope of a more interactive future in the participatory potential of the younger second generation.

Alongside the perceived media misrecognition is the concern about structural exclusion and everyday discrimination. As detailed in Chapter 2, there is no evidence to support Carr's unsubstantiated claims that the Irish government and

112 *Societal relations*

its institutions are racist. In fact, the vast majority of research participants in this study held very positive viewpoints of the Irish government, its institutions and policies. With that said, there are institutional policies in operation that require updating. For example, in accommodating non-Catholics and the non-religious in relation to educational access. Out of a total of seventy-three research participants, only two first generation male interviewees stated negative viewpoints against policing and the Irish security services. The empirical data did identify that the primary concern for Muslims remains everyday discrimination from individuals. For the research participants, the perpetuation and fuelling of such individualised discrimination can be traced back to the influence of the media. This discrimination permeates everyday life from the working sphere, to the weekly household shop, to interactions on the street. As with media misrepresentation, there is evidence that it does negatively affect an individual's positive relation-to-self by decreasing levels of self-esteem. Importantly, it has been identified that transitional phenomena in cultural life, such as art and sport, act as safe arenas where Muslims are respected for who they are and for their skills, abilities and achievements that contribute to their community and wider society. Such cultural transitional phenomena provide common ground upon which integration processes between Muslim and non-Muslim youth can be intersubjectively initiated, maintained and developed.

In terms of the legal sphere, Muslims have been civically stratified into different status groups such as citizens, denizens and refugees. The narrative statements and small stories outline how denizenship creates stressful uncertainty in the lives of Muslims and even stratifies families. This legal misrecognition creates further issues by limiting denizens in terms of access to education and freedom of movement. Despite paying taxes, denizens are limited in terms of acting as moral responsible agents with the same rights and obligations as others in society. This civic stratification also overburdens citizens with obligations. As the narratives show, such legal misrecognition does have negative implications by affecting a person's positive relation-to-self in terms of reducing their capacity to harness and develop self-respect as a contributor to the shared value-horizon of society. In the streams of narrative, a struggle for recognition is identified relating to the need for the acknowledgement of the complementary relationship that exists between Muslimness and civicness.

By asking the research participants about their experience of societal and legal recognition in everyday life, identity issues come to the fore. Many second generation narratives highlight the viewpoint that in everyday life sameness in terms of being an equal citizen to others is superseded by a person's differential traits. This leads to a feeling among Muslim youth that despite being Irish and European citizens, their traits in terms of religion, race and ethnicity take precedence over their civic identity. The narratives also show that Muslim youth feel like outsiders because they differ in identity terms from the dominant Irish identity standard, which ensures that they will always be perceived as 'different Irish'. In other words, although they are citizens, they will never be perceived by others in society as truly Irish or

European. This is a dilemmatic situation for Muslim youth, who feel that they are and should be recognised varyingly according to their multiple identities. However, the dominant nationalistic identity standard impedes the recognition of being, leaving Muslim youth in-between, misrecognised and lacking intersubjective legitimation.

With societal and legal recognition explored, this study moves onto the issue of spiritual recognition, which is a key form of recognition for Muslims, whose primary identity is based on religion and fulfilling daily recognition to God. Chapter 5 explores the coping mechanism and comfort offered by spiritual recognition.

References

Brady, Tom. 2014. Hundreds of Portuguese women fly in for 'sham marriages'. *Irish Independent*. 24 April.
Cahill, Ann. 2013. 400 a year trafficked for sham marriages. *Irish Examiner*. 1 February.
De Schutter, Helder and Ypi, Lea. 2015. Mandatory Citizenship for Immigrants. *British Journal of Political Science*. 45(2), pp.235–251.
Faller, Grainne. 2012. Children of non-EU nationals facing huge college fees. *Irish Times*. 17 August.
Knott, Kim, Poole, Elizabeth and Taira, Teemu. 2013. *Media Portrayals of Religion and the Secular Sacred: Representation and Change*. Farnham, UK: Ashgate Publishing.
Poole, Elizabeth and Richardson, John E. (eds.). 2006. *Muslims and the News Media*. London: IB Tauris.
Shaheen, Jack G. 2009. *Reel Bad Arabs: How Hollywood vilifies a people*. New York: Olive Branch Press.

5 Spiritual relations

Introduction

Axel Honneth's (1995) theory of recognition does not focus on the theme of spiritual recognition. However, in terms of this research, the absence of a discussion about spiritual recognition cannot be justified, particularly as this study focuses on individuals, who identify themselves as having a salient spiritual identity and belong to a religious community (Modood 1998). With that said, it must be stated that in line with sociology's standards of methodological agnosticism, this study remains silent on the issue of divine existence.

The classical sociological view of religion has been and remains highly influenced by the grand theories of Emile Durkheim and Max Weber. On one hand, Durkheim (2001) viewed religion positively as the site where collective consciousness raised its normative hopes and ideals. In Durkheim's opinion, religion has 'obscure aspirations towards the good, the beautiful and the ideal' (2001, p.315) above and beyond the reality of everyday life. On the other hand, despite his orientalist view of Islam as a militaristic warrior religion, Weber (2001) presented a famous differentiation between the social strata of elite institutional virtuosi, who generate legitimation for themselves by controlling and conserving religious meaning versus the religion of the suffering and struggling deprivileged strata, who rely on a salutary religion as a form of justified compensatory esteem to facilitate access to resources, physical well-being and psychic comfort (Weber 1966, 1978). While the grand theories remain influential, contemporary sociology of religion is primarily guided by an interpretation of empirical data, particularly in relation to everyday experiences of religiosity.

To answer the question, why do people become religious, Furseth and Repstad (2006) explain that contemporary sociologists of religion utilise four theoretical frames. Firstly, in line with Weber's idea of religion as a coping mechanism and facilitator of comfort from suffering and everyday struggle, *deprivation theory* determines that 'religious commitment is a result of compensation' from various forms of disadvantage in everyday life, whether that be economic, social, organismic, ethical, psychic or existential (Ibid., pp.111–114). Secondly, *socialisation theory* determines that we think and act in certain ways due to our upbringing or socialisation into a contextual world. This relates to the dynamics of intergenerational relationships. The third is *rational-choice theory* that determines that self-interested individuals make rational and calculated choices in relation to religious commitment and behaviour (Ibid., pp.114–117). And lastly is the *theory of seeking*, which determines that individuals are on a life quest and seek the goal of meaning and belonging (Ibid., pp.120–122).

Connecting this research to the above, it can be stated that the narratives in this study firmly connect to all of the above theories. Certainly, the majority of the research participants have been socialised into the Islamic religion by the culture of their family, community and home country yet there is also evidence of Muslim youth utilising agency to search the internet and rationally select fatwa rulings that match and suit their everyday lives in the Irish-European context. Alongside this, they also seek meaning and belonging through the practice of their religion as individuals and as part of a religious community.

The link between deprivation theory and spiritual recognition is significant in this study. Many narratives emanating from the first and second generations confirm the positivity of religious observance as a form of compensatory esteem that provides protection from the pain of pathological intersubjective interaction in everyday life. In other words, religion provides the individual with tangible benefits and resources and also acts as a comfort and coping mechanism from physical and psychic ill-health.

The relationship between religion, disrespect and the reinvigoration of a positive relation-to-self has been studied by Melvin L. Rogers (2009) in relation to the African-American experience of slavery. Rogers, who disapproves of how secular critical theorists commonly dismiss religion as ideological, investigates how individuals rebound from disrespect to 'generate the motivation necessary to prompt social conflict and transformation' (Ibid., p.184). In his opinion, Honneth overly favours secularised 'formal' systematic spheres of recognition to develop 'psychological and moral autonomy' and 'obscures' alternative systematic ways in which individuals create integrity and 'affirm their normative self-understanding' (Ibid.). For Rogers, the over-reliance on legal recognition ensures that individuals are dependent on modes of recognition that cause suffering in the first instance, creating a paradoxical situation. An alternative view would be to give forms of abstract recognition, i.e. cultural transitional phenomena, more sway in the theory of recognition. For example, he views the ability of African-American slaves to hold social death 'at bay' – as explained by the utilisation of religion – as an alternative form of recognition to the formal structures situated in everyday life. To create a positive self-understanding, slaves 'employed religious imagination' (Ibid., p.185). By being creative with their spirituality, particularly the Story of Exodus, slaves could 'address [the] existential threat of slavery' (Ibid.). This is a strong argument for the fact that spiritual recognition has a positively productive and constitutive impact upon an individual's struggle for recognition and identity formation. Rogers explains his viewpoint as follows:

>The practical result of the locution [utilising the Story of Exodus] was to remove from view, among other things, the obstacle of racial discrimination that prevented the acknowledgement of one's particularity and its place in the larger well-being of the community. More immediately, however, if the Story of Exodus worked as historians and others have described, then the corresponding sense of peoplehood provided precisely the vision of worth that each individual searched for. It indicated their importance by virtue of the similar journey they shared. They were esteemed in light of their struggle and allegiance to God.
>
>(Ibid.)

Through the presentation of streams of narrative, this chapter delves into the everyday Muslim experience of spiritual recognition. The narrative data is divided into themes relating to how spiritual recognition creates religious support and solidarity, as well as how Muslim youth are creatively utilising this recognition to search for a common ground in authentic Islam, which stresses the importance of practicing a civic identity in the Irish-European context.

Religious support

This section explores narratives relating to spiritual recognition, particularly in terms of how such an abstract form has practical benefits by acting as a comfort and coping mechanism against the harsh reality of everyday life inherently constituted by intersubjective struggle. In addition, the narratives also explore how spiritual recognition relates to feeling and self-confidence.

A comfort and coping mechanism

In line with deprivation theory in the sociology of religion, many of the empirical narratives in this study suggest strongly that spiritual recognition supports the individual by acting as a valuable coping mechanism that provides comfort against a range of pathologies that permeate everyday interactive life with others. The majority of such narratives emanate from the focused discussion groups. For example, Idris opines that Islam 'soothes' and is for all of 'humanity'. It is a universal human coping mechanism by the fact that prayer is an attempt to gain recognition despite 'all the troubles that you have in the worldly day' (Idris). This point is expanded further by Dahlia, who expresses her viewpoint that reading the Qur'an collectively with other community members helps psychologically with everyday struggles and ills, in terms of living in a foreign land and homesickness. She states about the positivity and rewards of religious study:

>It's to help our inside, to build our inside. In this country, especially we are living abroad, we are away from home, that's a really tough position

for us. We find here to sit and read Qur'an together that's a kind of recognition between ourselves and Allah.

(Dahlia)

Another first generation female discussant, Ayan (1st Gen, F, Cit, FDG), strongly emphasises how her spiritual belief and recognition gives her strength, power and confidence to tackle everyday struggles, in the family as well as in wider interactive spheres. She states that having 'belief' in God and following the prescriptions of Islam is positive for the self in that it '[makes] us strong' (Ayan). In other words, recognition to God beneficially aids the person in their struggles through everyday life. As Ayan states in this regard: 'Our belief is that Islam make me strong, I can fight, I can do anything' (Ibid.). This comment suggests that spiritual belief gives a person internal strength and the self-confidence to partake in life, despite the struggles that may arise. Dahlia translates Ayan's comments in terms of the attainment of power by stating 'yes, to give us power!', thus, linking recognition to God with the attainment of personal power and autonomy. Ayan makes connections to the familial sphere, by mentioning that she is the power dynamic of this social arena. She emphasises that matriarchal power is created by God and she 'can be the dynamo of the family' but that such a position 'comes from our beliefs inside the heart from God' (Ayan). Dahlia emphasises the practical health benefits that spiritual recognition has for tackling everyday struggles. She agrees with Ayan and adds 'exactly, we fight depression. We fight feeling homesickness' (Dahlia). For this discussant, spiritual recognition is related to two essential aspects: 'Power and secondly, prayer' (Ibid.).

Echoing Dahlia's comments about how spiritual recognition has positive health benefits, Sadiyya returns to how recognition to God through prayer can help with practical struggles in life. What is interesting about her comments is that she specifically mentions psychological struggles related to depressive conditions. She mentions the uplifting aspects of spiritual reflection by stating that 'sometimes if you feel depressed just read, open [the] Qur'an and after that you really feel [better]' (Sadiyya). Dahlia supports this comment by stating in response 'open the Qur'an, that's the hope!'. Through their comments, Sadiyya and Dahlia are emphasising the psychological benefits that spiritual recognition gives to people struggling with the realities of everyday life. It can give hope and can also make 'the depression less' (Sadiyya). Once again, Ayan returns to the theme that spiritual recognition is a battery, i.e. a rechargeable form of empowerment. She states that when you are 'travelling to God' (Ayan) you specifically make this journey to feel internally empowered and ready to tackle the everyday trials of life. In line with socialisation theory, this is one of the major reasons to ensure that the younger generation recognise God and attain a way to be empowered. On this point, Ayan states:

[When] you travelling to God, you come for more power inside yourself that what give our beliefs in God. Give us the power to, in our life, to do with the children, everything. So, we can convince our children when you have beliefs you can prepare them and let them, give them this way for them, this power.

(Ibid.)

The above statements are also reflected within the second generation discussion groups, Azaan states that he went through 'a phase' at the beginning of his teens that was marked by isolation and depression. He 'left the mosque' and 'kept to himself' (Azaan). He describes this period as a time that he went 'all hardcore' (Ibid.). This phase was reflected in the music he listened to, a form of rock music called emotional hardcore. He openly states that his psychological health was not good, and on reflection, he was 'real depressed' (Ibid.). Azaan emphasises that this period of his life was 'tough' (Ibid.) but he also reflects on how reforming friendships with other young Muslims brought him back to conducting prayer, which alleviated his depressive symptoms. He associates prayer as an act of recognition to God with a confessional function that has similar qualities to counselling and forms of talk therapy. To communicate his point, he aligns Islam and Christianity through the idea that prayer is an act of confession, which can relieve the psychological tension associated with 'bottling up' everyday worries and concerns (Ibid.). He acknowledges that people who keep worries and problems to themselves can be deeply disturbed in that their negative thoughts can 'kind of break them' and they might 'crack up eventually and just go crazy like, especially if it was something bad' (Ibid.). In Azaan's opinion, the confessional in Christianity provides a means for transacting everyday problems to another person without the fear of being judged, just as in the playfulness associated with psychoanalytic therapy. After the act of confession, the person will 'feel somewhat relieved because you'd let it out and told someone' (Ibid.). He then compares this to his own religion, Islam, in which the act of prayer is viewed as a private form of confessional between the individual and God:

> When you're bowing and stuff you can let everything out and ask for forgiveness and tell God everything you've done and whatever and you wouldn't have to have told the priest. No one in the world could know or has to know what you've done and you can still feel that release because you've told or you've asked for forgiveness and you've let it out like, you know and no one can hear you, no one has to hear you.
>
> (Azaan)

After these comments about confessional prayer, Yusuf, another second generation male discussant, clarifies that the act of prayer as confession is only used when you're 'wronging yourself' and does not exempt an individual from wronging or misrecognising another person. As he states, in this situation, 'if you are wronging someone else, you have to go apologise to them, so you can't just go and kill someone and just be like "God forgive me"' (Yusuf).

Yusuf continues his narrative into how praying to God alleviates the negative aspects of worldly life. He states that for him spiritual recognition as recognition to God is beneficial in that it enables a person to learn how to cope with the stresses and hardships presented by everyday life. For Yusuf, spiritual recognition is a coping mechanism. He mentions the relief and satisfaction he feels when conducting prayer:

> if I'm going through stress throughout the day, if I'm like sick of studying, if I'm having troubles and I put my forehead to the ground, I feel such a sense of relief, you know. Such a sense of satisfaction like, I can make [it], I can, for me I'm there and I'm facing God, you know, and I can just say anything I want and that just makes me feel so good.
>
> (Ibid.)

Masud identifies with Yusuf's narrative. He also states that praying to God 'feels good' and this feeling is especially heightened 'when you are going through tough times'. Aban enters the conversation acknowledging that as a believer, he is aware that secular people 'don't believe' because they 'say "God is not there"'. He opposes this position, which views life as solely created so that people can 'have fun, to do whatever you want and then you just die and you're gone?' (Aban). He does not agree with this assessment of what life is about. However, he is open to differentiating between recognising God and the institution of religion. He acknowledges that 'every religion has its own theory' (Ibid.). At this point, just like Azaan and Yusuf, Aban moves to the practical application of his religion as a coping mechanism for everyday life. He narrates a small story about the stress of undertaking examinations and how his mother advised him to say a prayer beforehand to calm his nerves and clear his mind. However, he states that sometimes he forgets to pray, which causes him to 'feel like I'm struggling, struggling and everything. When I say it [to God], it comes better, so that's how I know' (Ibid.). For Aban, spiritual recognition is a mechanism to ease the struggles of everyday life.

Yusuf adds that the perceived existence of God not only eases everyday suffering and struggle but is aesthetically evident in the beautiful complexity of the world. As he states: 'the skies, the mountains, you look around, you know there's a creator' (Yusuf). Through such worldly evidence, Yusuf believes that this work of creation should be recognised and acknowledged by those who benefit and are conscious of its existence. He clarifies that he recognises God and his work:

> by going every single day, putting your forehead to the ground, you speak to him, you know that at the end of the day, death is not the end, you know there's a hereafter and that is what you work towards.
>
> (Ibid.)

For Yusuf, recognition to God goes hand in hand with the evidence that there is an afterlife, which is free of suffering and struggle. The afterlife is paradise and

120 *Spiritual relations*

motivates behaviour in this worldly life. Reaching such paradise becomes a reason to 'work hard' in all spheres of life (Ibid.). For Yusuf, it [spiritual recognition as evidence of an afterlife] acts as 'a kind of motivator' in that it 'pushes you' towards the goal of attaining entry into a sphere of existence that is devoid of hardship, suffering and struggle (Ibid.). At the same time, in his opinion, 'any problems you have in life, any difficulties, it [spiritual recognition] just eases everything off, you know' (Ibid.). Once again, aligning with Winnicott's thinking on cultural transitional phenomena, Yusuf returns to the point that recognition to an abstract phenomenon, to a higher entity, is a coping mechanism against the difficulties inherent to a socially intersubjective form of existence. Although such forms of recognition may seem irrational and a trap set by institutional ideology, as Winnicott shows, cultural transitional phenomena in the form of art, religion and science provide a playful space for adults and children to attain comfort through various obsessional practices, or 'little madnesses', which practically help in negotiating everyday binaries such as dependency/independency, illusion/reality, subject/object (Kuhn 2013).

Impact on relation-to-self

The following section presents narratives that give an indication how spiritual recognition affects an individual's relation-to-self, particularly in terms of feeling and self-confidence. A revert to Islam, Kaleem has much to say about spiritual recognition, which he refers to as a natural 'referential instinct'. For this interviewee, spiritual recognition aids success and happiness in life by providing comfort and purifying an individual's heart. For Kaleem, spiritual recognition to God provides a unique 'inner cleanliness' of the heart (Kaleem).

Idris, within the first generation discussion group, echoes Kaleem's statement above, by internally positioning the impact of spiritual recognition as being located 'in the heart'. Furthermore, he states that the 'heart can't see' but that the 'heart can feel' (Idris). Importantly in Idris' opinion, spiritual recognition is not devoid of reason. For this discussant, it is cognitively rational in that the heart is connected to mental processes. He uses a common saying to emphasise this point: 'we say "the heart is the heart of the mind"' (Ibid.). For this discussant, spiritual recognition is fundamentally about feeling and belief and 'that's the recognition to God' (Ibid.). He highlights how prayer is a repetitive act of recognition to God that provides comfort and reflection away from 'all the troubles that you have in the worldly day' (Ibid.). Therefore, Idris is equating spiritual recognition with feeling and belief and as a form of human coping mechanism:

> Feeling and belief, feeling and belief and that's the recognition [to God] and every time you watch and stand in front of God, you are standing in front of God, and you try with all the troubles that you have in the worldly day, you know, people can lose sight of what they are doing but,

Spiritual relations 121

you know, the repetition maybe one day will get you to recognise and to recognise and to be recognised.

(Ibid.)

When asked about what specific feelings emanate from recognising God, Idris clarifies that such recognitional acts give a feeling of 'cleansing', 'cleaning' and 'purity' (Ibid.). He stresses that such recognition is also beneficial for one's self and well-being in that it creates a system of life that makes you a better person-to-self and to others.

> You know, the benefit is also for you. I mean it's like a system of life. It's not just a belief, it's a system of life. You follow this and you are a better person. Not because it organises your day, simple thing [like] prayer organises your day. You take a break at certain times. Everything you do is [for your well-being], and there is also a hadith, 'everything people do, Muslims do, it's for themselves' ... for your own well-being except fasting. Fasting is for God because you do it, and you know that he is watching you too ... It's teaching you to stop having what is permitted.
>
> (Idris)

In terms of whether spiritual recognition relates to self-confidence, a second generation female discussant, Isha, affirmatively agrees by stating concisely: 'yeah, it does do that'. In terms of communal support promoting self-confidence, Nejeed (2nd Gen, M, Cit, FDG) opines strongly in relation to community relations that 'you're not just an isolated person here'. By this he means that people in their Muslim communities are not isolated from each other but are members of a social community that are all connected and know each other. Therefore, as he states, 'you're known by your name, you're known for who you are' (Nejeed). As to whether community support gives self-confidence to an individual, Nejeed responds 'of course, yeah' (Ibid.).

Saiba, a young female discussant, makes an important statement that links utilising autonomous choice in religious practice to ensuring the development and maintenance of self-confidence. She criticises any form of religiosity that is forced upon people. She directly criticises the patriarchal powers in her community that force Muslim women to wear body coverings against their will. For this discussant, submission to such force means that Muslim women, who wear these coverings against their will, are not autonomous individuals and such actions destroy self-confidence. On the point of connecting autonomous action to self-confidence, Saiba states:

> Once you not doing it because other people expect you to do it, or because it's the norm and you accept it within yourself, I think you'll find it much easier to answer questions of like oppression and do you feel oppressed? You just say 'no' or other times where I think people that are, have to wear the hijab or have to practise certain ways, they'd be like 'I'm

122 *Spiritual relations*

not oppressed but like why?' and they wouldn't have reasons because technically they are, they're being forced to wear it and if you believe in it [Islam] yourself, I think you'll feel a lot more confident in yourself.

(Saiba)

Religious solidarity

This section explores religious solidarity in terms of how a collective bond through adherence to a religion has a regulative function by perfecting and maintaining individual religious practice.

Regulating the religious collective

Alongside narratives that stress Islamic spiritual recognition as an individual action and relation-to-self, the narratives also emphasise how a strong collective bond regulates an individual's everyday religious practice. Idris comments on the Hajj pilgrimage by emphasising his viewpoint about the collective solidarity and equality that is symbolised and embedded in Islamic theology and practice. For this discussant, the pilgrimage represents the Day of Judgement in which all people become one and the same under the umbrella of Islam. Similar to the secular concept of citizenship, he views this Islamic symbolism as a means of making particular people 'the same' (Idris), i.e. universal to each other. Idris states the following about the Hajj pilgrimage:

> The Day of Judgement is when you go to Hajj and you are doing that walk and people are pushing and shoving and people, some people are annoyed when they see people [being aggressive] and they say 'ignorant' and this and that but this is an example of the Day of Judgement, where everybody is there. Where everybody is the same, where there's no difference between a president and a sweeper so that kind of thing. You're all the same. No matter who you are, or what your background, rich, poor whatever, and that is the way when all is up on the last day. This [pilgrimage] is a microcosm of that day. So, everything in [Islam], within our religion has a symbolism.
>
> (Ibid.)

The first generation female discussion group offers an insight into how collective religious solidarity can also act as a beneficial regulatory mechanism over the struggle individual members have with the norms prescribed by the religion. For example, Meera openly clarifies that she believes 'God [is] here' (Meera) but that in terms of her everyday actions in relation to prescribed norms, she confides: 'I'm not following everything, you know, no, I try!' (Ibid.). A fellow discussant, Sadiyya, consoles Meera by replying to this statement with a reason for her not following Islamic norms to the letter: 'because you are human, human being' (Sadiyya). Meera agrees. Ayan follows by also emphasising the fallibility of the human condition: 'because we are [human], we are who [make] mistakes' (Ayan). Dahlia provides narrative evidence of how a female communal study group provides a regulative mechanism to individually recognise God but in a synchronised manner. As she states, about such collective solidarity and how it regulates correct religious adherence and provides a coping mechanism against everyday struggle:

> I find our meeting here every Wednesday that's a kind of very spiritual recognition between this team [the female study group] and God. We came here just sitting, reading Qur'an, that's the main thing, to learn how we can live Qur'an [in] the correct way and learn some spiritual things. It's to help our inside, to build our inside. In this country, especially we are living abroad, we are away from home, that's a really tough position for us. We find here to sit and read Qur'an together that's a kind of recognition between ourselves and Allah.
>
> (Dahlia)

Dahlia's statement emphasises how the Muslim women's study group meets regularly to promote and regulate their individual spiritual recognition in a collective manner. They come together one day per week as a supportive 'team' (Ibid.) and read the Qur'an to collectively learn how to correctly act-out spiritual recognition in line with Islamic sources. As Meera's statement proves, an individual may find it difficult to live correctly as a Muslim in a non-Muslim country, therefore, collective support and communal interaction provides a support system enabling Muslim women to spiritually 'build their inside' (Meera). The group also provides a mechanism to provide support, care and remedy isolationism. As Dahlia states, it's a 'tough position for us' to be Muslim immigrants in a non-Muslim country (Dahlia). She views reading the Qur'an communally as 'a kind of recognition between ourselves and Allah' (Ibid.).

Authentic Islam and the youth's search for common ground

This section aims to show how second generation youth are actively differentiating between what is perceived as Islamic versus what is perceived as cultural. This ongoing debate among Muslim youth illustrates how everyday dilemmatic issues are alleviated by gaining flexibility through the process of searching for, rationally selecting, and utilising online rulings (fatwa) that emanate from alternative Islamic sources. This section also explores how Muslim youth in the Irish-European context are agentically filtering out perceived forms of negative Irish and home country culture to attain a purer, more authentic interpretation and practice of Islam. It is perceived that such a process brings one closer to being a 'good Muslim'.

Due to increased globalisation, growing individualism and spiritual consumerism, Volpi and Turner (2007) have determined that traditional Islamic authorities at the local level, such as parents, Imams and traditional scholars, are less in demand and are being challenged by a 'multiplication of authorities'

124 Spiritual relations

in Islamic jurisprudence. Such authorities are also confronted by the reactivation within Islamic thought of critical reasoning or *ijtihad*, which enables a more precise and flexible contextualised interpretation of the Islamic sources, particularly for Muslims in Europe. In sociological terms, Turner (2010, p.534) states that such spiritual consumerism is fed by online fatwa markets offering a plurality of Islamic rulings that are democratically delivered and individually accessed through new technologies.

The bypassing traditional centres of authority and power coupled with the flexibility offered by online fatwa markets, young second generation Western Muslims have been able to use their individual and collective agency to recognise and legitimise alternative sources of authority. The choice involved in choosing Islamic rulings from online markets can be linked to rational choice theory, which determines that individuals rationally assess situations based on self-interest in terms of potential rewards. Linking this back to the theme of resistance in socialisation theory, although parents certainly have significant constitutive power to shape their offspring's actions and identities, Furseth and Repstad (2006) emphasise the commonly negated reality that children also have the capacity to influence their parent's identity by negotiating and transmitting their 'individual religiosity as a form of adaptation and learning' (pp.115–116). Muslim youth in the Irish-European context are searching for the normativity of Islam, i.e. for an authentic interpretation and practice of Islam that challenges the ethno-cultural version traditionally and habitually followed and brought to Europe in the *cultural baggage* of the first generation. Such challenges and criticisms of traditional authority and power have been spurred on by feminist critiques (Marranci 2010) and have centred on an attempt to:

> discriminate between the central and unchanging aspects of religious teachings and what has been incorporated as a result of cultural impact. In other words, there is a search for an authentic form of religion, where the cultural aspects are sifted away. For a sociological perspective, one may say that the attempt is being made to reinterpret the religious tradition in a new cultural context.
> (Furseth and Repstad 2006, p.195)

Differentiating between Islam and culture

The second generation male and female discussion groups give a narrative insight into how Muslim youth, in contrast to the immigrant first generation, view and differentiate the relationship between Islam and culture. For example, for Azaan, Islam provides the common ground for Muslims of diverse ethnic and national backgrounds to associate with each other on the same level. This discussant stresses the potential of spiritual recognition to traverse particularity by directing attention to the universal message of an abstract transitional phenomenon, i.e. the word of God. To support this statement, he specifically refers to the example of the Hajj pilgrimage to Mecca, where large numbers of

Muslims from different ethnic and racial backgrounds come together under the banner of Islam to worship God and the prophet Muhammad (Azaan).

Aswad joins the discussion to add some complexity to the above point by stating his opinion about how ethnic and national groups mix in the Muslim community. He gives a much more realistic picture as compared to Azaan's ideal by differentiating between the experiences of the second generation as compared to the first generation. Aswad opines that it is 'an advantage being youth' because as he states 'you have no problems' with particular ethnic and/or national differences. For this discussant, the youth look beyond particular differences when living in the European context, which is exemplified by 'kids out playing with each other there' (Aswad). Although his viewpoints are positive about second generation interaction, he is critical of the older generation, who have problems with ethno-national differences between them. As he states on this matter: 'but actually the older generation have this problem. It's a big thing in the old generation and you can see parents not talking [to each other]' (Ibid.). In contrast to Aswad, Aban explains that ethno-cultural similarities between Muslim youth can also provide positive grounds upon which relationships can be built and maintained. He states the following about his everyday experience in Dublin city centre:

> Say like I'm in the middle of the city and I see a group of Arabic speaking people, they're speaking Arabic like, I'll probably walk up. Like they see me, if I'm talking on the phone in Arabic, they'll all approach me and say 'oh, you speak Arabic' and I'll be like 'yeah' and they'll ask what country you are from and introduce ourselves to each other, and we'll just talk for a little bit. Most of these Arabic lads, I didn't even know them and all of a sudden, I'm like their friend.
>
> (Aban)

In relation to the tension that exists between Islamic and ethno-cultural identities and how some of the younger generation are actively avoiding certain forms of ethno-cultural practice, perceived as having a negative impact on Islamic identity, Azaan clarifies that 'a lot of it [Islam and culture] intertwines at some stage'. For this discussant, Islamic identity is specifically related to living by 'the rules of the Qur'an and the Sunna' while culture is 'a completely different thing' (Azaan). He then asserts that 'every country' has its 'own set of culture and living' and that the children of immigrants are 'going to sort of have that culture, whether you like it or not' (Ibid.).

In relation to being influenced by parental *cultural baggage,* Hussein (2nd Gen, M, Den, FDG) states that 'you just kind of grow up with it'. Azaan agrees that immigrants usually do have such baggage because they are themselves socialised by the fact of having once 'lived in an Arab country'. However, not all culture is seen negatively by the discussants. Yusuf opens up about his experience of 'speaking Arabic like just from the second you're born' and Masud refers to the fact that culture 'starts off at home' through

126 *Spiritual relations*

certain actions like 'eating your home food, you do this, and you do that'. Yusuf agrees with Masud and also views food as a positive item to be taken from the cultural bag brought from the home country: 'yeah, home food exactly'. Masud reflects on how culture is passed from one generation to the next in the following narrative. He does not equate power and domination with the passing of cultural traditions from one generation to the next but as socialised habits, formed through living in a specific contextual environment:

> Our parents were raised in Libya or their home countries and they obviously have that culture and it's only natural for us to develop that from them. It's not like they force feed that into us, it's just [how] they were grown. They pass it on, it's something that continues.
> (Masud)

In terms of the differentiation between Islam and culture within the second generation female discussion group, Fusaila exclaims that 'it's really hard to see the difference' between an Islamic and an ethno-cultural identity. Saiba continues the discussion by giving her personal opinion, which is that she would 'see Islam [as taking] precedence over culture'. She explains her familial situation where her parents would agree that Islamic identity takes precedence, but in reality, 'they don't practise it' (Saiba). As to whether her parents still have cultural traits, she agrees that her parents are 'really cultural' (Ibid.) and then gives an interesting narrative that offers an insight into how ethno-cultural and Islamic identities are both used to enforce parental control in the familial sphere. This narrative gives a good differentiation of how the Muslim youth view the relationship to parental power as well as the relationship between Islam and culture. Saiba states the following:

> They [the parents] wouldn't really understand the pure like, the actual [authentic] Islam, so when they've lost all the [argumentative] resources in [their] cultural reasons, they'd be like 'oh, but Islamically as well' because my parents would know that I'd listen to anything they'd say because I wasn't allowed to do it Islamically. Culturally, I'd just be like 'that makes no sense, I don't care' but then they'd be like 'Islamically' and then I'm like 'you can't just pick and choose' when you want to use Islam or culture.
> (Ibid.)

This narrative illustrates how Saiba's parents use their constitutive power with reference to ethno-cultural traditions and then move onto a more Islamic reasoning. This confirms the notion that the first generation link culture and Islam together. Saiba is keen to avoid culturalised Islam, which developed in the home country and practise the pure and authentic form of Islam. She clearly states that the first generation 'wouldn't really understand the pure like, the actual Islam' (Ibid.). For this discussant, her parent's cultural argument does not convince her, but an Islamic argumentation is acknowledged as important. Notably, she criticises her parents for deploying and selectively mixing cultural and Islamic arguments.

In relation to young Muslim adults conducting their own research about Islam to justify and legitimate their everyday actions, Saiba explains that as a child, she never differentiated or 'saw the difference between the two' (Ibid.), i.e. between Islam and culture. However, upon growing up, she states that she would see 'different contradictions' between what 'culture would do and then things Islam says' (Ibid.). She then gives an example of such contradictions with reference to the example of a 'big wedding':

> My parents would always be a fan of the big wedding, the big white wedding and everything and then researching it Islamically in Islam that's a contradiction to Islam and it's like you don't know which one to believe in like.
> (Saiba)

At this point, the sisters, Isha and Fusaila, enter the conversation to discuss their familial situation in relation to Islam and culture. Unlike Saiba, their parents are presented as Muslims, who differentiate between Islam and culture. Isha states that her father used his own agency and 'tried his best not to get us into the [home country] culture'. Thus, the sisters grew up speaking an Irish dialect of English and not their home country language. Isha also recounts that the communication between herself and her parents was good in that 'my Dad, he always talked, sat us down and explained everything to us' (Isha).

Fusaila then brings up the issue of *filtering out* cultural traditions, which are negatively perceived as inhibiting the proper practice of Islam. In terms of this filtration, she states directly that 'I find that most of my friends do that [filter out negative culture]' (Fusaila). She continues her narrative by explaining how these actions involve a learning process in which young Muslims intersubjectively interact with each other and identify which ethno-cultural traditions complement or go against the teachings of Islam. In this regard, she states the importance of social interaction and how, in the Irish-European context, Islam has become the common ground for Muslim youth, who emanate from families with diverse ethno-cultural traditions.

> We mix the cultures like, we don't hang around with our own [home country] people so we really notice our cultures and Islam when we're together [with other young Muslims], 'oh, we don't do that, this is Islamic' so we notice that. So, I find that Muslim is our overall identity and that's where we find ourselves most accepted.
> (Fusaila)

As has been stated above, globalisation and the evolution of digital interactive technologies have enabled Muslim youth in Europe to challenge social norms and local authority figures, i.e. parents, Imams and traditional Islamic scholars. Through the focus group narratives, it has come to light that such challenges

128 *Spiritual relations*

relate back to everyday social dilemmas encountered by Muslims in a liberal context. In his work, Ramadan (1999) outlines the everyday dilemmas encountered by young Muslims and critically argues that traditional Islamic jurisprudence is not practically reflective of Muslim life in modern Europe. Instead, he argues that Islamic scholars and the jurisprudence they interpret from the Islamic sources is mentally stuck in time and place, i.e. in the era of the Prophet Muhammad. Ramadan advocates for the reapplication of critical reasoning (*ijtihad*) in Islamic jurisprudence and for young Muslims to accentuate an Islamic-civic conception of Muslim identity in the European context to resolve everyday dilemmas between prescribed Islamic action and the social norms of everyday life (Ibid.).

This debate about the practical application of traditional versus reformed-contexualised Islam is present in a long discussion between participants in the second generation female focus group. The debate is too long to reproduce in full here but centres around two everyday actions, handshaking and travelling with a mahram, that consistently create intersubjective dilemmas for Muslim youth in the European context. By attempting to resolve such issues, a debate is opened up relating to whether traditional Islamic jurisprudence is practically suitable and actionable in the European context or whether Tariq Ramadan is correct in advocating for Islamic scholars to use critical reasoning in their work so that their rulings are contextually applicable to modern life in a liberal European environment.

Handshaking is an issue because in formal and informal social contexts, for example at job interviews, young Muslim women are prohibited from shaking hands with males. The other issue, travelling with a mahram, involves the need for Muslim women to be chaperoned by a male family member for their protection when travelling. Within the second generation female focus group, Saiba and Fusaila take different sides in this debate. Saiba argues that Islamic jurisprudence should change over time depending on context so that Muslim women can shake hands with males in certain contexts and that modern travel, for example by aeroplane, does not require a male chaperone. For Saiba, Islamic jurisprudence is static and must change to accommodate modern times and its everyday practices. Of note is that Saiba confirms that she has searched many online Islamic fatwa sites looking for rulings to resolve such dilemmas but with no success. On the other hand, Fusaila is adamant that traditional Islamic rulings should remain immutable and fixed in time. In her opinion, any contextual change to such rulings to accommodate everyday action is innovation and prohibited. Fusaila believes that women are prohibited from shaking a man's hand in an interview and that women require a mahram for protection when travelling.

The above debate highlights that interaction between Islam and culture is an important issue for young Muslims living in the European context, especially when such interaction creates everyday social dilemmas. While some young Muslims are satisfied with the status quo and feel that traditional scholarly rulings are correct and should be followed without question, other youth feel that Islamic rulings need to reflect the context of modern-day European life so that intersubjective social dilemmas between Muslims and non-Muslims can be resolved.

Filtering negative culture and searching for authentic Islam

The following section presents narratives that highlight the process by which second generation Muslim youth are filtering negative ethno-cultural traditions and searching for a perceived to be authentic Islam. Such a process challenges and influences traditional authorities and is perceived as providing the solution as to how Muslims can live an Islamic life in an Irish-European environment.

Within the second generation male discussion group, Yusuf discusses the mix of cultures that the youth are exposed to from their familial and community environments and from the wider context. He gives his personal experience about how he negotiates his home-country culture and the culture he is exposed to in his everyday life in Ireland. Such a cultural negotiation is regulated through the remit of an Islamic identity. He clarifies that Muslim youth have a 'cultural mixture' between 'this [Irish culture] and whatever you had at home' (Yusuf). His practical way of negotiating both cultures is to 'just kind of take the best of everything' (Ibid.). This is important because by stating that he takes what he perceives to be good or positive from both cultures, it implies that there must be forms of ethnic-culture that are perceived as negative and this also implies that this discussant has some means by which to assess the character of cultural norms and practice. Yusuf further explains what he does with the perceived to be negative parts of Irish and home country culture. He confidently states: 'I just neglect it. You just leave it' (Ibid.). Masud supports this comment by narrating his personal experience: 'I avoid it [negative culture]'. Yusuf concurs and uses Masud's terminology to restate his point in relation to alcohol consumption in Irish culture: '[you] avoid it exactly. Just like drinking [alcohol], you just avoid it' (Yusuf).

The above comments about avoiding the Irish cultural habit of drinking alcohol refocuses the discussion towards forms of ethno-cultural tradition that are identified and bypassed by young Muslims. In terms of Irish culture, Hussein clarifies that '[drinking is] not in our [Islamic] culture' while Siddiq refers to the Arab cultural practice of smoking 'shisha' as an action also to be avoided. On hearing these two examples, Yusuf clarifies that ethno-cultural actions to be avoided relate to both 'Irish culture or Arabic culture'. Yusuf relates a high or low degree of religiosity with the propensity of a family to either avoid or act-out the negative aspects of culture. On this point, he states that:

> My parents didn't really teach me anything that's bad in my [Arab] culture because they are very religious, but you know, with other parents because they neglect that [religion] as well. They [my parents] don't look to it [negative culture] because they think it's very ignorant but, with

other people if their parents are not really religious they would have that [negative Arab culture] at home.

(Yusuf)

Siddiq clarifies his position against the negative Arab cultural trait of smoking shisha. This discussant clarifies that, as a Muslim, he views shisha as haram (forbidden) for the reason that it damages bodily health and 'harms you' (Siddiq). He then narrates how Islam views this negative act as associated with the ideology of culture:

> so when it comes to a cultural thing like smoking shisha, Islam would say 'no' to that. So that's where you'd see this conflict between the two ideologies.
>
> (Ibid.)

Aswad swings the discussion over to identifying the positive aspects of Irish culture. In this discussant's opinion, there are distinct cultural traits that differentiate Ireland from Arab countries and that is the act of trust. For this discussant, Irish people 'have a really great trust' in others that comes easily and is 'something great in the culture' (Aswad). However, in the Arab world, 'sometimes that trust is not there' (Ibid.). Nejeed enters the conversation and redirects the conversation back to a discussion of positive Arab culture in relation to the transitional phenomenon of sport, particularly soccer. He points out that Algerians 'love soccer' (Nejeed). Yusuf, a Libyan, shouts 'they [Algerians] would not shut up about soccer.' Aban, differentiating himself as an Algerian, states in reply that 'that's the difference, like Libyans they don't really think about what it [soccer] is'. Aban mentions 'the shock' when his home country, Algeria, won a soccer match against Germany during the 1982 World Cup in Spain. Although he brought up the narrative about the Algerian obsession with soccer, he adds the caveat that such an intense passion for the game creates arguments and divisions between Algerians and other groups. For Aban, this implies that soccer may sometimes supersede a universal Islamic identity that views all Muslims, despite ethnic and national affiliation, as the same in their recognition to God.

> They [other Arabs] they don't really go more to soccer than us [Algerians]. We like soccer, like we think it's a part of us. We love playing soccer. So then when we talk about it, we get into like arguments and then that starts, we start hating each other and start not talking to each other because of our soccer, some stupid things. We keep forget[ing] that we're Muslim and start going to what we were born and raised looking at.
>
> (Aban)

Similarly, the second generation female discussants narrate their experiences of actively filtering out what they perceive to be negative culture to attain a

Spiritual relations 131

purer and more authentic form of Islam. For example, Saiba states that 'there's a lot of negative culture'. She and multiple other discussants agree that young Muslims are purposively recognising that some ethno-cultural traditions are not Islamic, therefore, such actions should be avoided through inaction. Isha enters the discussion and links her Islamic identity to this act of filtering out negative culture and how this differentiates herself from others. She states in this regard: 'That's why we, in our cultures, in our own separate cultures, we would be seen as different' (Isha). Saiba agrees that such a relationship to ethno-cultural traditions defines and distinguishes the new generation of Muslims. However, Isha clarifies that such an identity is not always favourably looked upon by other members of the Muslim community. In terms of how the youth are recognised, she claims that ethno-cultural Muslims 'think we're better than them' (Ibid.). However, as Isha states, Muslim youth are performing such actions so as to 'follow the real Islam' (Ibid.). She continues by stating that such action by Muslim youth 'leads to many arguments with our parents, our uncles or aunties and all that because they don't agree, and they laugh at us' (Ibid.). Fusaila adds a point that 'you also get called "extreme"'. Saiba and Fusaila are in agreement. Saiba responds to Fusaila: 'Exactly, exactly. My parents think I'm like a fundamentalist'.

In terms of whether the above filtering creates a better recognition to God, Saiba says 'yeah definitely', Fusaila replies 'yes', and Isha responds clarifying that the youth are trying to act in 'the right way' and attain the identity of a 'good Muslim'. In terms of whether such filtering actions and the movement toward a purer form of Islam creates a common ground in which young Muslims of all ethnic-traditions can come together in a unified way, Saiba responds affirmatively: 'I agree, everybody did definitely get along'. Isha states positively, 'I definitely agree with that' and explains her agreement by comparing her experience of living in Ireland versus the UK. Unlike in Dublin, she states that in London, Muslims interact in relation to their ethno-cultural traits to the point where whole areas of the city are split up into cultural neighbourhoods. The discussants then talk about how London is ethnically differentiated, unlike Ireland. Saiba states that when in London 'we wouldn't hang with the other community'. Fusaila agrees that in London there are 'whole areas full of my people, Tanzanians and whole areas [to Arabs]'. Isha gives an example of when she and her sister went to London with Rifa, who is Algerian. It ended up that 'she [Rifa] would go to the south, we'd go to the east [of London]' (Ibid.) because that is how the city is divided. Saiba agrees with the above statements and, with Mahala (2nd Gen, F, Den, FDG), adds that segregated districts lead to mosques catering to a specific ethnic group that follow a particular sect of Islam.

Fusaila contrasts the London experience to Dublin and positively states that 'in Ireland', she realised that people in the community 'hang onto' their Islamic identity because there are 'so few of us'. Rifa agrees that the small size of the Muslim community in Ireland means that Islamic identity is struggled for and maintained. Fusaila returns to her opinion that Muslims in

Ireland 'hang onto the real Islam' because it joins everyone together despite there being 'so many of us, different cultures, different cultures'. Saiba agrees that Islam has become the common ground enabling the heterogeneous Muslim youth to come together. Fusaila agrees 'definitely' and explains why mixing with other cultures is positive for Islam in that it can aid a person in how they subjectively practise their religiosity:

> I want to have like different cultures in my life because I feel like my friends keep me grounded. When I'm straying too much in my culture, they're like 'you know, that's not Islam'. If you hang around with different cultures, you realise that you need to find a common ground somewhere and Islam is that common ground.
>
> (Fusaila)

Returning to the filtering of ethnic-culture and whether all young Muslims are filtering out what is perceived to be negative ethnic culture or whether some young Muslims aim to keep and maintain such traditions, Saiba reflects on a group in school, who were 'very cultural'. Both Rifa and Fusaila confirm that 'they were cultural'. Rifa then adds that this group were not only cultural but that they were also 'fresh' arrivals from their home country. Saiba confirms that this group had not 'been here [in Ireland] that long'. Fusaila calmly states: 'give them time'. Saiba explains that this group 'held onto their culture'. She then goes on to state an insight into how time and interaction constructs identity and how she herself filtered out negative ethnic culture, rebelled against tribal culture, and forged what she believed to be a purer form of authentic Islamic identity:

> I've been here [in Ireland] longer than she [Bisma] has but we're from the same place [in Somalia] but people would see her more as Somali than me because she practises more Somali traditions than I do but basically, it's just because I'm here longer and I kind of like dropped a lot and I was raised like in Ireland and where she was like, she was new to it. Maybe in about ten years she'd be a different person. We grew up all our lives and we were told like 'tribe is like a big thing' and then researching it Islamically and it's like one of the worse things to do ever and we try to filter that out.
>
> (Saiba)

On reflection, Saiba clarifies that such an identity transformation has been 'so hard' because 'in our families' ethno-cultural identity is still given a prominent and important role. Isha agrees and adds that it is even harder 'especially when you are the first generation to do that'. This statement is claiming that the second generation is the initial generation to actively resist and filter out negative culture in an attempt to construct a pure and authentic form of Islamic identity. Saiba agrees with Isha's statement and supports it by stating the following:

Exactly, [we are] the first generation to kind of like rebel out from the whole traditions and cultures and they'd [the first generation] be like 'but what's wrong with you?' and they're [the first generation are] like 'I know Islam doesn't teach it but still it's culture'.

(Ibid.)

Fusaila opines that the second generation are questioning and challenging the mix of ethno-cultural and Islamic traditions espoused and practised by the older immigrant generation. She states that the young generation are asking the question 'why?'. Rifa provides the answer: 'yeah, it's culture'. In terms of whether the youth are changing and socialising the opinions and practices of the first generation, Fusaila replies: 'yeah, some do'. She then makes an important statement about how the second generation can productively influence and constitute their parents' behaviour and identity:

My Dad says that 'me and Isha changed our whole family' because we used to practise like them and then it came a time when we started hanging out with all my friends, me and Isha [were] like 'we're all doing something different here'. So, then when me and Isha changed ourselves, it changed the whole family and then it kind of created a domino effect, kind of changing the community little by little.

(Fusaila)

Fusaila credits her sister and herself for changing familial action and identity. Through social interaction with ethnically diverse friends, they identified differences in how various friends (with different ethno-cultural traditions) practise Islam. This made the sisters change how they practised their traditions and identities, which then influenced members of their family and, according to Fusaila, slowly changed and resocialised practices in their Muslim community. Isha confirms that such a transformation is a slow process.

The above narrative also resembles the opinion of young male interviewee Nurdeen, who comments upon how he, as a Western Muslim, has been able to influence and socialise his mother and wife, who have both retained home country culture in their identities and everyday practices. On this point Nurdeen states the following:

My mum has changed quite a lot [of cultural baggage]. She came here [to Ireland] when she was quite young and she had some cultural baggage, she is slowly losing it. I would not want my son to grow up in Pakistan because there's a lot of cultural baggage there. My wife comes from Pakistan and she had a lot of cultural baggage. She has seen [how to find a pure authentic Islam] through me, my sisters and friends in the mosque. She is losing some of the [cultural] baggage.

(Nurdeen)

For Nurdeen, it is also important for the upcoming second generation, who are agentically locating a space for a revitalised Islamic identity in the Irish-European context, to pass such practical knowledge to future generations. In this regard, he is adamant that 'the third generation will follow the second generation' (Ibid.). Similarly, Fusaila also emphasises that the more senior Muslim youth are 'always trying to educate the younger' Muslims in terms of being able to differentiate and filter-out negative culture, thereby enabling them to gain a closer proximity to a more real, purer and authentic Islamic practice and identity. Such identity positioning acts as a common ground for a diverse range of Muslim youth living together in an Irish-European context. It also enables a strong perception of attaining a better recognition to God, to the familial and community spheres in terms of religious adherence and practice, and to the wider societal sphere in terms of promoting Islamic civicness as positive participation and contribution.

Islam's civic component

This section explores the narratives that give an insight into how the research participants view the relationship between Islamic and civic identities. Particular attention is paid to narratives that emphasise the civicality of Islam, i.e. narratives indicating the existence of an Islamic-civic component of identity. Secondly, narratives are used to explore how the life story of the Prophet Muhammad, particularly in terms of his time spent in exile in Medina, constitutes a key example and influence upon the research participants in terms of how Islamic-civic practice can be implemented in a pluralistic environment.

Interpreting civicness from Islam

In the narratives, there is ample evidence that a civic identity that is interpreted from Islamic teaching and practice is being emphasised as valuable by the interviewees and discussants. In other words, there is empirical evidence that an Islamic-civic identity is important in the everyday lives of the research participants and is held in higher regard than the salience of an ethno-cultural or an overly nationalistic identity. For example, within the first generation male discussion group, Farid stresses the lack of connection between being Muslim and a national, yet strongly emphasises the complementary relationship between being Muslim and civic. As Farid states:

> We don't feel like we're national, Irish national. Probably, we feel more civil. Like, vote civil rather than [vote] Irish.
>
> (Farid)

Idris opines that there is no conflict whatsoever between Islamic, national or civic identities. For this discussant, Islam equals respect and he states the following in this regard:

There is no real conflict between being a Muslim first because Muslim, if you are a true Muslim then you will respect everything of the country that you are living in. In Islam, you have to follow the laws of the country you are living in. So, this is a small thing, you have to follow the law of the country. You have to pay your taxes and if you are called to the army, then you have to go to the army.

(Idris)

Hurriyah, a first generation female discussant, states in relation to integration processes in Ireland that 'here [there] are some of us [Muslims] as well that are not ready to integrate, and everybody has the right to do what they want'. It could be inferred that this discussant is stating that an awareness of Islamic civicness is growing but that more needs to be done to expand on how Islamic identity can find the flexibility in its own teachings to relate to the European environment. However, such a process is both internal and external. Hurriyah stresses that 'we [Muslims] need to find the inner side of us and educate ourselves about certain things' (Hurriyah). In terms of whether civicness is inside Islam or whether it is distinctly separate from Islam, Hurriyah states the following narrative:

It's separated in the sense that even though you are a citizen there are some laws that still bound you, but you can't override that law as a Muslim. For example, you are a Muslim first before your citizenship. I am a Muslim first that comes before my citizenship. Then my citizenship comes next. To follow the rules of that citizenship, not to betray the government and everything that is already in Islam. Islam said, 'follow the rules of the land'. The only time you may not follow the rules of the land is when you are under threat to practise your Islamic religion. It'll [Islam will] move elsewhere because Allah said, 'he has created all the walls here for you to live in different places', so that's the only time you can't follow the rules of that law, but apart from that follow the rules of the law. So, in as much as we can do all this. Together, we'll see that we can live together side by side without any prejudice, but individually, we have a set mind that we are racist to each other, and then we use, for example, politics and religion to get into each other rather than finding the solution within ourselves.

(Hurriyah)

In the above narrative, Hurriyah claims that civicness is not inside Islam per say but is separate. However, the teachings of Islam insist that Muslims must obey the law of the land. For this discussant, this is vitally important. However, she also clarifies that in her subjective opinion, Islam comes before 'any legal citizenship' (Ibid.). In other words, Islamic identity takes precedence over formal civic identity or citizenship, yet Islam implements a degree of reciprocal respect for the laws of the land as long as those laws do not infringe upon the right to practise one's Islamic faith. If Islam is mistreated in a bounded nation state, Hurriyah claims that Muslims are permitted to move to another area, where the Islamic religion is given a degree of respect and freedom. This discussant would like people to collectively work towards social harmony, however, in her opinion, what prevents such ideals from forming is the racist mindset that forms part of the human condition, which manipulates political and religious ideology to sow disharmony among people. As a solution, she restates her conviction that individuals must reflect and conduct a process of self-examination to identify pathologies that lead to disrespectful action and the misrecognition of others.

Both female interviewees, Dahlia and Safeerah, are critical of Muslims who assimilate into Irish culture and neglect their Islamic identity. They refer to such people as Muslims by name but not in practice. For Dahlia, the neglect of an Islamic identity in Western democracies is unnecessary because, in her opinion, Islam provides the answer to integration in that civicness is inside Islam, which thereby enables Muslims to continue to spiritually recognise God and to civically participate as citizens in the public sphere. As she states on this point:

> Some Muslim people don't know this [being involved in the wider community, i.e. the civic component of Islam] is from the Sunna, from the Prophet Muhammad, this is the problem … they didn't know this [civicness] is inside Islam.
>
> (Dahlia)

Both female interviewees elaborate on the difficulties they face in terms of being members of a Muslim women's group, who act civically outside of their Muslim community by organising charitable events in their wider local area. On top of being critical about how Muslims in Ireland interact with the media and of other Muslims, who have assimilated into Irish culture and forsaken their Islamic identities, they actively promote Muslims to become active through a civic interpretation of the Islamic sources. For these two interviewees, many Muslims do not know that Islam promotes civicness and participation.

The female civic group has had to struggle against stereotypes in the wider society and have also gained little support from within their own Muslim community. Dahlia views Muslims in Ireland as 'isolated, they are just sitting in the corner' (Ibid.). However, the interviewees are trying to change perceptions and inform their community and wider society that Muslims can civically participate and contribute positively to their local community and to Irish society generally. Safeerah sums up the struggle encountered in Irish society and in their own Muslim community by stating that: 'we are fighting both'. This short statement is valuable. It suggests that their group is struggling against perceptions of the wider Irish society and against perceptions that remain in Muslim communities. For these women, their message is that Islam has a civic component that can be useful to those living in Europe, who wish to integrate and participate civically yet still maintain and even enhance a core Muslim identity.

Within the second generation female discussion group, Saiba differentiates between her recognition to God as a dependent child and how it progressed to be the foundation of her identity when she matured into an independent adult. Although Islam is her most salient identity, Saiba views civicness as emanating from her core religious identity. In this regard, she states that as a child she 'didn't think that she did' (Saiba) recognise God because her actions were co-ordinated and socialised by her parents. As she states about this constitutive power dynamic: 'at that time, I was just doing it because my parents told me to' (Ibid.). As a rebellious child, Saiba would give the appearance of acting-out her recognition to God, but in reality, she was not following parental instructions. She states about the act of fasting: 'even when I was fasting, I'd like fast because they told me to and then I'd like run away and go into the bathroom and eat food' (Ibid.). Saiba goes on to give a long narrative that examines how as an adult she agentically researched into Islam and began to see it as the 'foundation' of her identity (Ibid.). She narrates the following about this gradual self-realisation:

> I said 'I do accept God and I accept religion' and I did say like I mean [it] and then from then on like, everything I do even if I wasn't seen by other people I'd still feel conscious about it and be like you know 'God can see me' ... it's really hard to get to that stage where you're like totally conscious of everything, where everything I do I think mmm I do like basically for the sake of Islam. I mean, I'd always have it as my, my foundation, even when I'm in studies and when I like, anything I do, I'd always have a foundation of Islam and then even things I do for the civic, like my community, even if it's not benefiting Muslims, I'd still feel like it's benefiting people. Islam is humane, so it would always have an Islamic foundation to it.
>
> (Saiba)

The above narrative indicates that Saiba, as a young adult, rationally chose to use her individual agency to research what Islam was about instead of passively receiving socialising instructions from her parents. This process of acceptance is described as an internal feeling in which she, within herself, acknowledged God's existence. By accepting Allah, she describes how her actions took on a different meaning in that wrongful actions against oneself or others can be seen by God, even if acted-out privately. As an adult, Saiba believes that she is responsible for the actions she performs in private as well as in public. However, she also stresses that 'it's really hard' (Ibid.) to be continuously conscious of every action that one initiates and performs in everyday life. With that said, overall for Saiba, Islam is her most salient identity. It is her core identity, the foundation of herself. She correlates her foundational Islamic identity to her civic actions by stating that any civicness she performs can be related back to the teachings of Islam. For this discussant, Islam is a humane religion in which civic identity and action is embedded and promoted.

The civic example of Prophet Muhammad

The narrative data indicates how civicness emanates from an Islamic ethos. In the focused discussion groups, multiple discussants narrate how their civicness is highly influenced by hadith (or small stories) that elaborate on the religious and civic identity of the Prophet Muhammad in the multicultural and multireligious environment of Medina. In terms of narrative evidence within the first generation female focus group, Hurriyah states adamantly that the Prophet 'was civic' and that it is important for all Muslims to 'try to emulate his behaviour'. In her opinion, this implies a constant 'need to keep on training ourselves', especially since people in the Muslim community are 'still not copying him even though we're following the Sunna, which is his practices' (Ibid.). Overall, she is sure that 'civic[ness] is there' (Ibid.) and is actualised in actions conducted by Muslims.

In terms of how the second generation male discussants relate to the Prophet Muhammad and the Islamic-civic life he lived in the diverse environment of Medina, Masud is the first to respond to this topic in the discussion group: 'I understand what you mean'. Hussein then interjects into the conversation to clarify how immigrant Muslims can identify with the Prophet, who was 'from the city of Mecca and he went [migrated] to Medina'. This discussant speaks about the fact that Muslims in Ireland are from 'Arab countries and African countries' and have 'come to Ireland' just as the Prophet had ventured from Mecca to exile in Medina (Hussein). Through his narrative, Hussein seems to be making the claim that Islam has a strong civic element in that it encourages its followers to be social. In other words, 'mixing with other people is part of Islam' (Ibid.). Furthermore, he also determines that Islam promotes the need to 'respect other people, always' and to 'integrate with them [and] make sure everything's going smooth' (Ibid.). Overall, Hussein stresses that Islamic identity advocates and promotes civicness, such as participation and integration as well as having respect for the Other. Following on from Hussein's comments, Siddiq enters the discussion to make the claim that the relationship between Islam and civicness is intrinsically related to 'tolerance'. For this discussant, Islam and the Prophet's example illustrates how to interact and integrate in a pluralistic environment. As he states:

> It's tolerance and also God says in the Qur'an that 'we've made you from different tongues that you may learn from one another' and this is also something that Islam promotes when you go into [a] different culture.
>
> (Siddiq)

Aswad returns to the theme of Medina and pluralism by stating that he thinks 'it's because of ignorance' that there is a tension and confusion between Muslims and non-Muslims. He concedes that many Muslims themselves are 'ignorant' (Ibid.) of the civic message of tolerance and respect that resides in Islam. His criticism specifically targets the culture of Muslim-majority countries that misrecognise people. He states that:

> Muslims, a lot of them are ignorant. If you look at the Arab counties, look at Tunisia and Egypt. Tunisia has Christians living in it and also Jews. Okay, they have a tension. [Authoritative voice] 'They are Christians, they're Jews, they're the bad guys, never go near them'.
>
> (Aswad)

At this point, Azaan re-emphasises the point that tolerance is a fundamental aspect of living in a pluralistic society in which 'you're going to walk into people from every religion and culture'. For this discussant, living a 'day-to-day life' in a pluralistic democratic European state implies that you should be as 'tolerant as you can be' (Ibid.). Importantly, Azaan stresses how intersubjective social relations determine how people act towards one another and that people need to be tolerant and flexible in multicultural contexts, which are shared by a variety of people acting-out different cultures and beliefs. He succinctly states in relation to the necessity for toleration in a pluralistic society:

> If someone was to say something bad about you and you'd get offended by it or hurt by it, or whatever, why would you bother doing the same thing to someone else? I think even if you don't agree with it, it's valid and you may as well turn the cheek or accept it or stay away from the person rather than having to reel up all this confrontation because it is so unnecessary.
>
> (Azaan)

The last point about civic identity is made by Siddiq, who emphasises that the younger second generation, by growing up in Ireland and being knowledgeable about Irish-European culture, have a greater capacity to be civic and tolerant in a European environment than the immigrant first generation (Siddiq). This discussant states that Muslim youth, due to their social and cultural knowledge, have the means to find a way to connect their Islamic identity to life as lived in a European democratic society. This knowledge becomes a form of capital that enables youth to be more tolerant of Christian and secular social acts and also to discover new ways of interacting as Muslims in and towards a non-Muslim environment. Siddiq's enlightening narrative is as follows:

> I think our experiences growing up here in Ireland also allow us be more civic and more tolerant as well than the [first] generation that came here to live in Ireland, in my opinion anyway, because we are used to Irish culture, we are used to some of the things that you guys [the ethno-national Irish] think trivial with one another and that is also something that we pick up [from you] that our fathers and mothers probably won't be able to comprehend. For example, cursing around the house, or something like that.

We'd be used to hearing people swear in class or whatever, but our parents they'd be shocked at that. That's where growing up here has made us more tolerant [of different ways of life].

(Siddiq)

Conclusion

The art of sociology was founded on the study of religion. The founders of sociology, Weber and Durkheim, developed grand theories that remain relevant today. With that said, modern sociologists are not standing still. They are developing insights into religion and spirituality by combining classical theoretical thinking with empirical sociology. As stated in the introduction, sociologists of religion tend to utilise four theories to understand religion and its practice in the modern world. These are deprivation, socialisation, rational-choice and the theory of seeking. The empirical narratives in this study match and connect to all four theories in one way or another. However, of note is that narratives associated with deprivation and socialisation theories are emphasised more by the research participants in relation to everyday experiences of spiritual recognition.

Although this study utilises Honneth's (1995) secular theory of the struggle for recognition, through preliminary empirical research, it was decided that the theme of spiritual recognition could not be excluded from this study that focuses on a wide array of Muslim everyday experiences in the Irish-European context. From the streams of narrative in this chapter, we learn how spiritual recognition gives a keen sense of support to individuals and increases collective solidarity between religious adherents. Religion and its practice, especially by minorities under a securitised lens, is a comfort and coping mechanism that can positively develop and maintain an individual's positive relation-to-self and heal the hurt of everyday intersubjective life in which perception reigns over reality. It also brings people together. Religious practice has a regulative function that increases and strengthens collective solidarity, which is important for migrants and people of difference living in busy European cities that imbue secularist values. Overall, religion and spiritual recognition give comfort, help people cope with everyday life and are intrinsically social.

We also learned that educated Muslim youth, emanating from different ethno-cultural backgrounds, yet all living in the Irish-European context, are actively searching individually and collectively for a social common ground. These young people are actively filtering-out what they perceive to be the negative aspects of Irish culture and their parents' ethno-cultural traditions. By filtering out such *cultural baggage*, these educated young Muslims feel that they are closer to attaining the real and authentic Islam as determined by the Islamic sources. From the youth's viewpoint, this real Islam allows them to share and practise authentic Islamic values in a liberal European environment and be unimpeded by the perceived negative aspects of Irish and home country cultural practices.

From the streams of narratives, we also learn how civic identity and practice relates to authentic Islamic identity. There is a common misconception about Muslim youth and their Islamic practice in Europe. It is generally perceived that the spiritual search Muslim youth are undertaking to find an authentic form of Islam is pointing them towards developing a political and fundamentalist religious ideology, with the potential to lead Muslim youth down the dark path to terroristic actions in the name of Allah. This is false. As the narratives in this study show, Muslim youth have a strong primary Islamic identity followed by a civic participatory identity. This Islamic-civic dual identity counter balances the ethno-nationalist identities prevalent in Ireland and their home countries. In modern Europe, which is more intercultural and diverse, Muslim youth feel that their practice of an authentic Islam enables them to be effective citizens. In other words, these youth are interpreting their civic identities through their core Islamic identity. Islam enables them to be more active citizens by promoting their interaction with the wider community. In terms of empirical evidence, interviewees and discussants mention the influence of the civic example of Prophet Muhammad and how they wish to emulate his example of being Muslim and interacting civically with others. From the narratives, we learn that Muslim youth are filtering out negative ethno-cultural influences and searching for an authentic Islamic viewpoint and practice that promotes civicness and participation in an Irish-European context. By actioning this viewpoint and identity, this youth are building a common ground between themselves (unimpeded by their parents' culture) and also creating a bridge of belonging to the wider community they interact with on a daily basis.

The next chapter, Chapter 6, presents narratives that give an insight into the intergenerational relations within the Muslim community in the Irish-European context, especially in terms of how first and second generation family and community members perceive, critique and relate to each other.

References

Durkheim, Emile. 2001 [1915]. *The Elementary Forms of the Religious Life*. Oxford: Oxford University Press.
Furseth, Inger and Repstad, Pål. (eds.). 2006. *An Introduction to the Sociology of Religion: Classical and Contemporary Perspectives*. Aldershot, UK: Ashgate.
Honneth, Axel. 1995 [1992]. *The Struggle for Recognition: The Moral Grammar of Social Conflicts*. Cambridge: Polity Press.
Kuhn, Annette. (ed.). 2013. *Little Madnesses: Winnicott, Transitional Phenomena, and Cultural Experience*. London: IB Tauris.
Marranci, Gabriele. Sociology and anthropology of Islam: A critical debate. Chapter 16, IN: Turner, B.S. 2010. *The Sociology of Religion*. London: Wiley.
Modood, Tariq. 1998. Anti-essentialism, multiculturalism and the 'Recognition' of religious groups. *The Journal of Political Philosophy*. 6(4), pp.378–399.
Ramadan, Tariq. 1999. *To be a European Muslim*. Markfield, UK: The Islamic Foundation.

Rogers, Melvin L. 2009. Rereading Honneth: Exodus politics and the paradox of Recognition. *European Journal of Political Theory.* 8(2), pp.183–206.
Turner, Bryan S. Introduction: mapping the sociology of religion, IN: Turner, B.S. 2010. *The Sociology of Religion.* London: Wiley.
Volpi, Frédéric and Turner, Bryan S. 2007. Introduction: Making Islamic authority matter. *Theory, Culture & Society.* 24(2), pp.1–19.
Weber, Max. 1966. *Sociology of Religion.* London: Methuen.
Weber, Max. Religious groups (the sociology of religion). Chapter VI, IN: Weber, M. 1978. *Economy and Society: An Outline of Interpretive Sociology.* Oakland, CA: University of California Press.
Weber, Max. 2001 [1904–1905]. *The Protestant Ethic and the Spirit of Capitalism.* London: Routledge.

6 Intergenerational relations

Introduction

This chapter provides an insight into the process through which youth are socialised or 'grow into societal roles' (Furseth and Repstad 2006, pp.114–117), which are sanctioned and maintained formally through the local community and informally in the love sphere of the family.

To gain such an insight empirically, this chapter explores intergenerational relations from two group perspectives. Firstly, narratives presented show a first generation parental perspective of Muslim youth, in particular, how asymmetrical power is utilised to constitute the identity of the next generation as well as examining how elders protect the youth from negative cultural influences. Secondly, narratives are presented to show a second generation perspective of their elders, particularly in terms of how the youth critique rigid inflexibility, identify the impact of patriarchal power, and reflect upon the continuing influence of social norms and the ongoing pressure to be a 'good Muslim'.

While such intergenerational socialisation processes can be positively productive by constitutively shaping and maintaining values, roles and social cohesion, when these norms, internally prescribed in a minority community, become overly penalising and run counter to the wider social context, then the legitimacy of such constitutive power comes under challenge through forms of critique and resistance. These challenges can take the form of 'rebellion, defiance, or spitefulness' (Ibid., p.115) against the legitimacy of authorities that propagate the recognition and performance of expected social norms.

First generation perspectives

This section presents narratives that provide an insight into the first generation Muslim perspective of intergenerational relationships in the Irish-European context, particularly in relation to how parents and elders feel they have the positive power to constitute the next generation. Such action is openly debated by the older discussants in relation to the second generation's potential to agentically maintain an Islamic identity into the future and the first generation's protective stance towards the youth. This leads to narratives about how the parental protective

Constituting the next generation

Although many of the first generation interviewees and discussants critique their own Muslim community in relation to the existence of patriarchy, the continuing lack of support and leadership, and the existence of ethno-cultural and nationalistic tensions; an ongoing issue of concern and debate is how to constitute the younger generation in terms of instilling and maintaining an ethno-Islamic identity to counteract the pervasiveness and influence of Irish culture and its associated dominant identity standard. Within the first generation female discussion group, Ayan states that the confidence to be strong is disseminated from parents to children and that this is a core aspect of constitutive power wielded by parents in the home. In Ayan's opinion, parents give children the foundation to go out into the world confident in themselves:

> [A] strong mother can build strong children and I think I build good foundations for my children and when my daughter have a problem and the teacher talk with me, I said to the teacher in front of the Vice Principal 'I'm not going to teach my daughter to be a weak person'. I say that. So, I think it's really Muslim woman inside the house with the children, really she have respect, she have a power inside the house. She has real power. People outside the house may see you, us [Muslim women] with the scarf. They think 'we are inside the house, under the man'. No.
>
> (Ayan)

What is interesting about the above statement is that it directly tackles the stereotype or common public perception that Muslim women have no power or agency in the domestic sphere and are under the control and power of a patriarchal figure. Ayan disrupts this perception and gains the widespread agreement of the other female discussants. Through her narrative, she opines that the Muslim woman, who works in the realm of the private sphere as wife and mother, has respect and power, as she states 'the real power' (Ibid.), to productively influence and construct people and events. This discussant rebukes the common perception that the headscarf is a symbol of domination. She counters the perception that Muslim women are 'inside the house, under the man' (Ibid.). In Ayan's experience, her domestic life is filled with respect and power to positively aid and construct the lives of the people she loves for the benefit of herself and the familial structure. For this discussant, it is imperative that the first generation ensure that the younger generation recognise God and attain a way to be internally empowered. On this point, she states:

> [When] you travelling to God, you come for more power inside yourself and that's what give our beliefs in God. Give us the power to, in our life,

to do with the children, everything. So, we can convince our children when you have beliefs you can prepare them and give them this way for them, this power.

(Ibid.)

Similarly to Ayan, Meera confidently emphasises that 'our man treat us in the house like a Queen!'. Certainly, such a statement cannot be taken any other way but as confirmation that she feels recognised and respected by her spouse. However, constituting the next generation is a contentious issue. This is exemplified by the debate Sadiyya and Dahlia have about whether Muslim youth can find an *identity balance* between being Muslim and living in a European context. Dahlia is optimistic about youth agency but Sadiyya is pessimistically certain that 'we [the first generation parents] should be with them [the youth]' but 'if we left them alone, I don't think that [the youth can create an identity balance]' (Sadiyya). Dahlia confronts Sadiyya by stating that the ability of the youth to create this balance can be traced back to 'the parents' confidence'. This links youth behaviour and ability as being 'related to the parents' (Dahlia). Sadiyya agrees that the parents 'have to be, you know, behind them'. However, Dahlia seems to be giving more agency and responsibility to Muslim youth by suggesting that parental instruction is and should be 'faint'. On the other hand, Sadiyya is adamant that the older generation must be behind the youth actively directing them onto the right path. In other words, it is important for the older generation to be there for the youth and 'call them, to talk'. Dahlia agrees in relation to this statement about communication.

Overall, the discussion about the first generation staying with the youth becomes more complicated when the issue of returning to the home country arises. Although Dahlia views Sadiyya as being overprotective, she agrees that parents should provide support and communication to the younger generation. In relation to the remark that parents have to be with the youth, Dahlia replies to Sadiyya that she herself has 'thought of that all the time' (Dahlia). She then continues by providing an example of how her advice to her son instilled in him a strong Islamic identity and an ability to work co-operatively with others. However, the following narrative still accentuates Dahlia's opinion that Muslim youth have the agency to build and maintain their own identities in an Irish-European context:

[My teenage son], he's doing Jumu'ah [Friday] prayer in the school. Doing the Jumu'ah, imagine! And he ask the teacher for a room and the key and he divide [the tasks] between his friends, 'the key with you, the prayer on me, the adhan [call to prayer] for you'. Teamwork! To build your[self] and I keep on saying 'don't work by yourself, if you have your friends, Muslim friends, you have to work as a team. Enhance each other, don't work with your own only. You will collapse!'.

(Dahlia)

In response to this small story, Sadiyya re-emphasises the need to protect and guide the younger generation. She is very pessimistic about the future, especially in terms of Muslim youth being able to keep hold of their Islamic identity in a European environment. She foresees a future in which young Muslims have grown older and do not have parents to advise them. She negatively imagines this scenario:

> imagine that after twenty years if you don't have your friends, any other Muslim friends or Sheikh or if he don't go to mosque, if you [the parent] are not here [in life], I doubt that his Muslim community will continue.
> (Sadiyya)

Protecting youth from negative cultural influence

In line with Sadiyya's protectionist viewpoint, Idris, a first generation male discussant, opens up the conversation by indicating that parents have the constitutive power of 'being able to teach them [the youth]' to be critical of culture and how it relates to an Islamic identity. Farid agrees that such teaching is conducted to 'protect them'. For these two discussants, the need for protection is exacerbated by the issues that come to the fore when one lives in a Muslim-majority country versus living in the European context. Farid clarifies that in his home country 'we don't think about Islam' (Farid) because everybody is Muslim, but when in Ireland, in Europe, 'you try to teach' (Ibid.) your children an Islamic identity by getting them to learn the Arabic language and Qur'an. As he states, teaching his children an Islamic identity gives him a sense of happiness: 'I feel happier that my son or my daughter learns Arabic before they learn English. That's the [core] identity' (Ibid.). Farid then explains how he is concerned about the influence Irish culture has upon his children, particularly on their Islamic identity, which he has actively taken steps to convey and instil in his children. As a father, he feels that he must protect his children's Islamic identity from homogenising cultural influences. He states on this matter:

> I try to protect them because the only place we feel safe in Islam is the mosque. Outside the mosque, our children, they get lost. Especially when they go to school, they see the Irish people, they see the French people, the German people, all mix of culture of people, all of them have different culture, background, probably different religion.
> (Farid)

When asked about how he feels when his children leave the mosque and are influenced by Irish society, Farid states: 'you feel bad to be honest, of course, you feel bad' (Ibid.). The reason for such feeling is that he is keenly aware that his children 'will get influenced by Irish society' (Ibid.), thereby negating the work he undertook with his wife to promote an Islamic identity in the familial sphere. He emphasises the struggle he undertakes to ensure that his children are protected and that their Islamic identity remains intact and relevant. Such comments suggest that this discussant has become an overprotective father and that identity construction and maintenance are of prime concern: 'you try to teach them [their identity], like twenty-four hours you have to watch them' (Ibid.). He is anxious that, without practical influence, his children will 'get lost' when interacting with others in Irish society (Ibid.). When asked if he feels that his two young children are maintaining an Islamic identity, Farid answers 'oh definitely, definitely. We're trying hard to give them this' (Ibid.). Through his comments, one gets the sense that he is struggling, as a parent, to protect and ensure his children gain and maintain an Islamic identity in a non-Muslim society. Farid reflects on how an immigrant's life is harder in the absence of familial support:

> Like back in your [home] country, your background, the origin country, at least you have your family, you have your sisters, your cousins ... but here [in Ireland], you don't have [familial support]. You have you and your wife, you know otherwise, your kids will get lost.
> (Farid)

Such identity concerns for the younger generation are also vocalised within the first generation female discussion group. Dahlia states that she and other Muslim parents are cognisant and concerned about how non-Muslim children interact with their children in school. She states that non-Muslim children are negatively influencing Muslim children to be like them, i.e. 'forcing them [Muslim children] to this kind of initiation, this kind of argument' (Dahlia). She also states that although rare in primary school such interactions become more common in secondary school, a time of adolescence, representing the 'very critical years' of identity formation (Ibid.). For Dahlia and other first generation female discussants '[the young] generation is a big issue' (Ibid.).

An example of such concern emanates from Maja, who opens up about her own children's experiences. Although Maja clarifies that she likes to be a 'very close friend to the Irish people', she has noticed a negative angle to everyday social relations, which has become a 'problem' (Maja). She has noticed the powerful extent to which the imitation of Irish culture puts pressure on minorities, people of difference. For this discussant, social pressure to conform to the dominant culture and identity standard has become the 'biggest struggle' internally in the familial structure and externally in the wider social sphere (Ibid.). On this point, she states:

> They [non-Muslim children] are very good, but the problem, 'if you want to stay with me as a friend, you have to imitate me. If I drink, you have to drink, if I'm going to the pub, if I'm going to have appointment with whoever, you have to, otherwise if you don't, we have a problem with our relationship'.
> (Maja)

148 *Intergenerational relations*

Maja continues her narrative by focusing on the problems that her children encounter in school from other children due to their difference from the identity standard of the majority. She talks about non-Muslim children questioning her son as to why he is not allowed to eat ham. She recounts that discussions can turn nasty between these children and her sons. She mentions that 'sometimes if they [the other non-Muslim boys] are angry', they say to her son 'go home. Don't stay. Go home' (Ibid.). Such comments have forced Maja's children to defend themselves by replying: 'No! My dad, he's a doctor here, he's paying tax. We are working here. It's not your right to say to me "go home"' (Ibid.). Hurriyah echoes Maja's narrative by re-emphasising and accentuating the words 'go home to your country'. Elmira clarifies that these words do not suggest going home to your house but return to your home country, the foreign location where your parents originated from. She states in relation to this clarification: 'Homeland! Your roots, your roots' (Elmira).

Sadiyya has a more pessimistic thoughts on the future of Muslim youth in Ireland. In her opinion, she feels that life for the youth is 'not going to be easy' (Sadiyya). For this discussant, the first generation will always be fine because they are independent adults, however, she feels that the second generation will encounter 'a very big problem' (Ibid.) by having an Islamic identity and growing up in an Irish-European context. She has the view that some Muslim youth will reject an Islamic identity because of its minority status and because it is consistently overshadowed by the dominant identity standard of what constitutes social belonging, i.e. Irishness. Sadiyya supports her point by narrating a small story about her daughter's friend:

> For example, my daughter's friend, she told her [Mother] 'I don't want to be Muslim, because we are Muslim, I don't want to be Muslim anymore'. So, she's six years old. It's a problem. If she's in Sudan, she would never think about not wanting to be Muslim.
>
> (Ibid.)

Sadiyya also gives a personal account of the troubles encountered with her own daughter, who is influenced by the dominant culture and is undergoing stages of identity rejection. This narrative gives an indication about how she feels as a Muslim mother, who is struggling to raise her child as Muslim surrounded by an influential dominant culture. It also emphasises the protectionist care that Muslim parents give their children so as to aid them in acquiring an Islamic identity in the European context. There are indications that this protectiveness is strong by the fact that Sadiyya feels her daughter may lose her identity if she (as overseeing mother) is not close by:

> So, I think it's not very easy, but they [her children] try to feel something. We talk about Allah with them all the time and she know about God, but I know that if I'm not here it will not be that easy and maybe she will lose her identity, so this gonna be a very big problem, especially if we are

not with them and we can't be with them all the time, so I don't know, maybe sometimes I think that we have to go back [to the home country].

(Sadiyya)

Although the dominant culture is problematic for the first generation, they are also facing difficulties in the familial sphere itself in that their Islamic and ethno-cultural identities and practices, i.e. their *cultural baggage*, brought with them from the home country, is being challenged by their offspring. Within the first generation male discussion group, Idris speaks about his own familial experience. He confirms that religious practitioners, from the same religion, may have different ways of viewing the teachings of the religion and that 'in every religion' (Idris) there are contradictions or 'things that don't sit well together' (Ibid.). The seemingly contradictory elements of the same religious ideology are why scholars are needed to explain and interpret religion. In Idris' experience as a father, it has been his inability to explain such contradictions that has created 'a little bit of conflict' with his children (Ibid.). He openly details his struggle to explain key concepts to his children and has often found himself 'lost to explain something because I actually haven't thought about it in terms of identity or experience' (Ibid.). For this discussant, originating from a Muslim-majority culture means that there was no need to critically assess the cultural and religious practice he received and 'lived with all my life' (Ibid.). However, as Idris explains, in the Irish-European context, he has 'to explain it and that's a little bit difficult' (Ibid.). He remarks that his children, as European Muslims, are looking for more cognitive and rational explanations to solve contradictions in Islamic belief. However, this discussant has the viewpoint that some things cannot be explained by rational cognitive analysis because human spiritual belief lies 'above the mind' (Ibid.). On this point, he makes the following statement:

> When they [his children] ask me to explain it [Islam] and I don't know why and I have to go and search and sometimes I can't find an answer because it's not easy to find certain things that are not plain in every religion ... simple things like heaven and hell and the last day and all this stuff. And people that lived in this [European] society, they don't [believe this], it's more of the mind [cognitive/rational] thinking and mind cannot explain everything, because we have limitation [as humans]. So sometimes, spirituality is supernatural or above our mind, you know, you're lost to explain it.
>
> (Idris)

Similarly, within the first generation female discussion group, Elmira affirms that she is recognised by her family but that 'sometimes they don't' recognise her identity (Elmira). She continues her narrative by confirming once again that 'they [her immediate family] respect me' (Ibid.), however, she stresses that sometimes she feels misrecognised in her relations as a first generation Muslim communicating with a second generation son, particularly when sternly advising him on aspects of Islam. Elmira states that:

> Sometimes if I talk to my eldest son, he's twenty-five years old. I'd be a little bit strict about the Islam and that what they say to me. Sometimes he will say 'Mum, sometimes you offend me'.
>
> (Ibid.)

Hurriyah responds stating 'old, yeah', confirming that when speaking to her son, Elmira feels 'old true, like you are sixty years old' (Elmira). Sadiyya rephrases this as a feeling of being 'old-fashioned'. This accentuates the point that the youth feel that they represent the present and the future, i.e. modernity and how Islam fits into a modern post-traditional life. For Elmira, she feels that she is respected and recognised by her family, however, she also confirms that she feels misrecognised as representing an old-fashioned viewpoint and practice of Islam. She states that 'this is the main problem. It's like that' (Ibid.). Hurriyah interjects clarifying that Elmira's son has a new 'elaboration' of Islamic identity. Elmira then suggests that he also has a new reaction in relation to her 'opinion' and 'mentality'. She states in this regard:

> Yeah, he [her son] will tell me something like this because if you will tell him not to do something or to do that, he will tell me 'mom, you are really like sixty years old. You are from that generation before!'. This is what, you know, my experience is in my family.
>
> (Elmira)

Second generation perspectives

This section explores the narratives that give an insight into the youth perspective, particularly how the second generation are critical of the elderly propensity to be rigid and inflexible in terms of identity and practice. The narratives presented show how the youth, particularly young women critique patriarchal pathologies that continue to exist in the familial and communal spheres. This section also explores how the youth negotiate social norms they are expected to conform to and act-out in order to be perceived by others as 'good Muslims'.

Critiquing rigid inflexibility

Throughout the second generation interviews and discussion groups, there is a consistent critique of the rigidity and inflexibility of the first generation. For example, Daleela, a young female interviewee, states about intergenerational relations that there 'is a gap between the first generation and the second generation'. She then specifically links this generational gap to an inflexibility in values and beliefs by stating that 'they [the first generation] have set values and beliefs and they don't understand that you're growing up in a society that you can't be as rigid as they are' (Daleela). She is advocating for 'more communication between the generations and more flexibility' (Ibid.). It is important to note that this steadfast rigidity can pressurise the second generation to negotiate family values and beliefs alongside societal norms. As Daleela states, 'there is a lot of pressure from inside the community' (Ibid.). This pressure can come in the form of following a set life plan. For Aziz, 'coming from a Pakistani [family and heritage] you're either an engineer or a doctor'. On the other hand, Daleela views this pressure in terms of its ethno-cultural form and how it interacts with religious belief and identity. In this regard, she states:

> I'm speaking more about cultural pressure to believe a certain way, to live a certain way ... because their identity, they're, I suppose, they are first generation Irish but they identify more with the their home countries. You kinda need to be flexible, like for me not going to pubs was a big deal and I was like, this is not part of Islam or my culture. Like I was, from an early age, 'this is like wrong and I can't do it'. But you can, you can, kinda. You need to be able to at least go to a pub, be able to sit and be open-minded and accept that this is [Irish] culture, you need to be able to do that.
>
> (Daleela)

The narrative above gives a clear indication of the recognitive differences that exist between the Muslim first and second generations in Europe in that Daleela is clearly stating that the elders, even though they are resident in Ireland, are still very much connected to their home country and socialised by its ethno-cultural and religious norms. Consequently, their values and opinions are fixed and inflexible. In contrast, the younger second generation, who were born and/or have lived most of their lives in an Irish-European context, do not have a strong connection to such values and norms. The youth have transnational identifications to Europe and their home countries and are therefore more cognisant of the values and norms that emanate from both locations. As a result, they need a degree of flexibility to accommodate Irish culture into their lived experience. Daleela uses the example of the Irish pub, as an example of Irish culture that needs to be viewed by Muslims in a flexible manner. She advocates for Muslim youth to go beyond the use of alcohol and understand the interpersonal aspects of such environments. To be flexible involves action in terms of going to a pub and being open-minded about the social nature of Irish culture.

Another interviewee, Azad, also makes succinct statements about the generational divide. He specifically mentions that his perceptions are different from his parents and members of his extended family. These differences are not physical but are related to 'when it comes to ideas' (Azad). This interviewee feels isolated from first generation perceptions and viewpoints, i.e. how they view the world, the importance of their ethnic traditions and how to act-out an Islamic identity. This isolation is exemplified in the phrase: 'I just find myself a bit way-out from my family, from their own way of thinking' (Ibid.).

152 *Intergenerational relations*

Furthermore, he states 'I feel like I'm just living my own way [and] find it very difficult to fit into their group' (Ibid.). Such a divide manifests itself in disagreements about actions in that Azad disagrees with his family members about 'what they say or what they do' (Ibid.). This divergence may be related to how the first generation view the relationship between their ethno-cultural traditions and acting-out an Islamic identity.

Azad's difficulties also envelop wider relations. He comments on several difficulties that he feels exist in his Muslim community. These relate to a lack of leadership, a lack of facilities, the Arabic-English language barrier and the isolation felt by the younger generation. This interviewee claims to be speaking 'from the young perspective', which is 'a bit different' from that of the older generation as well as from non-Muslim youth (Ibid.). One of the main issues for him is the lack of leadership or 'somebody to look up to, like to follow' (Ibid.). In Azad's opinion, this issue has created negative feelings in young Muslims. He remarks that 'a lot of young people are frustrated' (Ibid.). As well as a lack of facilities, he makes some very important points related to the general feeling that the younger generation are excluded and isolated from their own community. He gives a linguistic example by stating that the Arabic language is used during the conduction of Friday prayers. For the most part, young Muslims raised in Ireland do not speak Arabic, therefore, these young people cannot understand what is said during Friday prayers. Azad is also highly critical of ethno-cultural traditions brought to the West by Muslim immigrants. He states on this point that:

> you'll find most of the time [at the mosque], the old people will be there, and not so much of the young people and part of it is maybe language barriers as well because the old folks they speak maybe Arabic of which the young guys here they don't and if they're to have, let's say, lecturers or something like that from the Middle East, and all be towards Arabic kinda thing of which the young guys kinda feel left-out. So, you can't really do much of the things. In a sense, the issues we face most of the time, it's a lot of issues but the main one is to be like, being left-out, like not being part of the whole, whole process because of the old guys, the old guys with their own mentality and then the young guys coming up kinda caught in the mix.
>
> (Azad)

In this narrative extract, Azad indicates the language difficulties that are faced by the younger generation in their own community in terms of practising religion. Most mosques still conduct prayer in Arabic, however, many young Muslims do not know how to speak it. The internal language barrier in the community accentuates the feeling of being left-out, despite the wish to have a deep comprehension of religious doctrine. Overall, towards the end of this narrative, Azad identifies isolation as a major issue that the young generation face 'most of the time' (Ibid.). In other words, the younger generation do not feel 'part of the whole' because the older generation are not willing to change or be flexible with their traditions, leaving the younger generation 'kinda caught in the mix' (Ibid.).

Within the second generation female discussion group, Rifa emphasises the difference between the generations in terms of identity and interaction. She makes the following statement about how her family hold tightly to ethno-cultural habits and do not want such practices to be tainted by or mixed with other traditions or innovative actions. In opposition to such a rigid stance, Rifa, who is of Algerian heritage, views Islam as a universal common ground that brings people together and actively enables the mixing of cultures and races:

> It's hard. I find it hard like, anything I learn I try to bring it to my family and if it's Islamic, they accept it but once it get to culture, they're like 'no way'. Like yesterday, I was having an argument with my Mum and so I was like 'I don't want to marry an Algerian or an Arab'. So, I was like 'what do you think?' and she was like, 'no way, I'm not accepting it'. I'm like 'Okay but Islam doesn't say anything about that. It doesn't say anything about the colour, about the race, nothing, Islam is just in more step [with modern times]'.
>
> (Rifa)

Isha supports Rifa's small story by stating that 'it [Islam] actually encourages you to mix'. Rifa replies in a high tone 'yes' and then puts forward her side of the argument, which is that 'once the person is Muslim, then it's okay to marry them' (Rifa). She disagrees with and rejects her mother's perspective, which aims to maintain culturally socialised norms and the esteem of others: she [her mother] was like 'yes, but if you go back home [after a having a mixed-marriage] and they'll be like [negatively], "there's Rifa!"' (Ibid.).

Through Rifa's narrative, the discussion moves onto the difference in how young female discussants are recognised by their immediate family members compared to their outer familial circle in the home country. In terms of having a new elaboration of Islamic identity, Fusaila states that 'you can deal with the [immediate] family'. Isha agrees and confirms that members of her immediate family will 'accept it'. However, Rifa returns to the conversation with her mother and highlights how her outer family will react after she has convinced her mother that a mixed-marriage is Islamically acceptable. She states regarding such familial politics:

> I'll make random calls and I'll try to change my mother's mind and she'll be like 'yes, okay fine, I agree' but then going to your grandmother [in the home country] and it's different and she's like [negatively], 'you'll have mixed kids'.
>
> (Rifa)

Critiquing patriarchy

Although first generation female Muslims view the domestic sphere as the location where constitutive power reigns, they do acknowledge the existence of limited occurrences of patriarchy performed by individuals in the community. For example, Saadiqa (1st Gen, F, Cit, FDG), confirms the existence of patriarchal culture in the Muslim community but adamantly emphasises that it occurs only in exceptional circumstances and is acted-out by individuals. She states: 'some men they treat their wives in bad ways but this is his personality. It's like an exception, an exception' (Saadiqa). As previously stated above, Ayan challenges the public perception that Muslim women who wear the hijab, are oppressed by male patriarchy in the domestic sphere. Of note is that this statement received total agreement in the first generation female discussion group:

> People outside the house may see you, us with the scarf. They think 'we are inside the house, under the man'. No.
>
> (Ayan)

In contrast to the above, Isra, a young female interviewee, strongly criticises familial and community recognition particularly in terms of the treatment of females. She advocates for flexibility in terms of the remit of actions that can be performed by young Muslim women in the family and communal spheres. Isra narrates a small story related to the rejection and limiting of young Muslim women who wish to partake in social and artistic activities such as sporting activities and acting. She states in relation to this issue:

> We did an acting class in groups and there were some young Muslim girls who was taking part and then, you know, they were told that they cannot do it because of the religion and stuff like that … it's a problem, it's really a problem. A lot of young Muslim woman want to take part in football and stuff like that but they were rejected because of the community, because of their family and they were told 'you cannot do this because of this way and this way'.
>
> (Isra)

In this narrative, Isra is expressing her view that women are being misrecognised in family and community structures. This misrecognition is not physical but a misrecognition of identity in that the agency of Muslim women to take part in sport and artistic activities is being impeded by the religious interpretation of powerful others, who prohibit Muslim women from performing such actions. Isra describes this as rejection. She stresses that young Muslim women are forcefully advocating for the right to play sport and to partake in a variety of social activities. However, this is deemed forbidden (haram) by the patriarchal powers in the family and community, who dominate the articulation and acting-out of permissible (halal) actions and social norms.

Isra also narrates a small story related to her own familial experience. This story is evidence of the *recognitive-power dilemmas* she encounters in her everyday life. She must find a space between the need to be recognised by both her friends and family, yet also negotiate her identity in relation to the expected social norms that inform and constitute these differing social groups:

> for example, [if] my family see me not wearing scarf and going around and wearing trousers, it will cost me problem because I can lose the relation [between] myself and my family because of my dress and all that and again when I see in my friends, they all dress and they look nice. I like the fashion, the way they are. I will try to be like the way they are and then again, at the same time, I have to hide it. So, it's really a big problem between the family and the new generation [of young Muslims].
>
> (Isra)

In addition to the above, Isra continues her criticism of her community by emphasising the plight of Muslim women in relation to communicative participation in the public sphere. She states that 'there is a lot of young Muslim women, who can't be active because our community believe if you're a woman and you're Muslim, you cannot talk in public' (Ibid.). This view that Muslim women are prohibited from speaking publicly creates a sense of fear when being resistively active and vocalising critical opinions to a wider audience. As Isra explains, 'those women they're scared if they say "okay, I'm going to stand up for my religion and my society"' (Ibid.). Isra has no trust in her Muslim community to remedy the issue. She therefore advocates for the Irish government and a universal legal framework to step in and defend Muslim women's rights to public expression. It should be kept in mind how complex this recognition dilemma is for Muslim women, who do not want to lose respect from God or from their loved ones and community. They do not want to be discriminated against by their own kind yet also strive to attain external recognition from the wider social sphere.

Isra continues by stressing that the feeling of fear plays a significant factor. She remarks that 'they [Muslim women are] scared to do it [to speak out publicly]' (Ibid.). This interviewee feels that her agency is curtailed by the lack of legitimised authority she has as a woman to interpret the Qur'an and other Islamic sources. For Isra, power comes from the ability to interpret the religious sources, and thus, as a Muslim woman, she is powerless to defend her position as she does not have the legitimacy from others to conduct such interpretative actions. This gendered legitimacy deficit and corresponding exclusion from interpreting Islamic jurisprudence prevents her from agentically partaking in struggle. As she states in this regard:

> the only problem that I cannot do is, I cannot explain the holy Qur'an in and out. If I really know the religion explanation, I would stand up and fight but I don't know it.
>
> (Isra).

156 Intergenerational relations

Isra opines that Muslim women will only overcome this fear if they are either protected and supported by the universal application of law or by an advocate in the Muslim community itself, who is 'strong and says, "I'm standing in the community and I will do something about it"' (Ibid.). However, this young interviewee acknowledges that such a strong woman, who advocates for female rights in the Muslim community, 'ain't me' (Ibid.). She then specifically narrates her own experience about being misrecognised in her community by stating that she herself was told 'not to speak out' (Ibid.) in public about the issue of Female Genital Mutilation (FGM). She was thus verbally disrespected for speaking up about women's concerns in the community.

> They [Muslim women] don't feel like speaking out, they're scared because they are woman and the religion didn't allow it [speaking out publicly]. I was told by a powerful man in the community not to speak out. I was told that I'm a [unknown word] because I'm speaking in public about FGM. So, those [Muslim] women they're scared to be discriminated within the [Islamic] community.
>
> (Ibid.)

The above criticisms echo and reinforce Saiba's resistive statements presented in Chapter 5, which advocate that religious adherence and practice should be primarily an individual autonomous choice and not forced upon individuals against their will. For Saiba, religiosity as individual freedom is conducive to creating and maintaining self-confidence, whereas patriarchal domination that enforces social norms upon an individual's will, destroys self-confidence and reduces the capacity to internally accept religious belief and practice. Saiba's statement is also worth restating in this chapter as it concisely reflects many of the narrative statements made by young Muslim women in this study by advocating strongly for individual freedom, resistance and a need to rebuke patriarchal oppression in all spheres of life:

> Once you not doing it because other people expect you to do it, or because it's the norm and you accept it within yourself, I think you'll find it much easier to answer questions of like oppression and do you feel oppressed? You just say 'no' or other times where I think people that are, have to wear the hijab or have to practise certain ways, they'd be like 'I'm not oppressed but like why?' and they wouldn't have reasons because technically they are, they're being forced to wear it and if you believe in it [Islam] yourself, I think you'll feel a lot more confident in yourself.
>
> (Saiba)

The judgements of others and the pressure to be a 'good Muslim'

The streams of narratives from the second generation discussion groups provide an important insight into the judgements of others and the social pressure that young Muslims encounter in relation to conforming to social norms and being perceived by others as correctly practising Islam as a 'good Muslim'.

For example, discussant Isha differentiates between the acceptance of her immediate family versus the non-acceptance she feels from her 'outer family', i.e. the extended family resident in Ireland, throughout Europe and in the home country. Bisma (2nd Gen, F, Den, FDG) agrees with this differentiation of familial acceptance. Isha expands on her previous statement by stating its recognitive importance in that 'they', the extended outer family, 'they're different' and 'they see you differently'. Saiba also agrees with this differentiation and reflects that it is caused by a lack of knowledge and a distorted perceptual picture of Muslim life in Europe. She remarks about how her outer family recognise her from a distance:

> because they don't see you day to day, they'd just be like, they know they have a picture of you, of what the norm is, like a little innocent Muslim girl there [in Europe], and then when you're like, if you have an opinion [said firmly], they'd be like 'but she's just a kid like', you know.
>
> (Saiba)

Fusaila picks up on Saiba's comments about the outer family positioning their own children towards or against a particular behaviour. She states laughingly that the outer family members advise their own children: 'you be like [them] there ... and don't be like that girl' (Fusaila). She then concisely outlines what differentiates the inner immediate family from the distant outer family. She states firmly that 'we are accepted by our immediate family but then your outer family, they will use you as an example to their kids' (Ibid.). It is at this point in the conversation that Saiba identifies a behaviour the outer family frown upon. She states that the second generation youth are 'filtering-out the negative culture' and, in her opinion, it is perceived by the extended family as 'a bad example' (Saiba). Fusaila then voices what the outer family say to their children about such actions: 'they'd be like "don't be like them"'. The above narratives, from young female discussants, position the outer family as viewing actions such as filtering-out, perceived to be negative culture, as a bad example for their own children to follow.

The sisters also elaborate on the issues they have encountered in terms of how they are recognised by their extended family in the home country. Both struggle to be recognised by their outer family due to identity differences. For example, Isha states that her outer family 'think we're not Tanzanian enough. They see us as being Irish' (Isha). Rifa comments on the possible reason for such views being held by the outer family. She remarks: 'that's the culture though' (Rifa). Fusaila adds that the outer family more often than not see the sisters as 'not even Irish' but as 'European'.

In the second generation male discussion group, in terms of family influence, Yusuf looks towards his home country familial relations in Libya. First of all, he states that when he goes 'back to Libya', he can see the differences between his father's family, who are 'not too strict' in their religion (Yusuf) and his mother's family, who are austere in their adherence to an Islamic identity (Ibid.). Yusuf aligns himself to his mother's family, who pray and go to the mosque regularly. He describes how members of this section of his family are 'always' shaping his identity by 'giving you advice, you know, anything they see wrong, they just always correcting you' (Ibid.). This aids the development of his Islamic identity. However, his father's side of the family are lax in their practice and are 'kind of mesmerised' (Ibid.) that Yusuf, on visiting from Europe, will go and pray in the local mosque. The differences between both sides of the family are narratively explained in the following small story:

> Whereas if I go to my dad's [family] side, and you know, I go to pray in the mosque, which is only five-minutes away, they wouldn't want to go to the mosque, 'ah, it's such a trek and five minutes away'. They take it for granted because it's so close. But for me [in Ireland], I have to drive you know fifteen-minutes down the road, it'll be like an hour walk and so I go to the mosque [here in the home country]. So, they're kind of like, they're kind of mesmerised. You know, they don't really [get it that] 'this guy he's coming from Europe, he's coming from Ireland but he's going to pray in the mosque, really?' you know, but if I don't go to the mosque with my mum's side [laughter], I get in deep trouble, yeah.
>
> (Yusuf)

Returning to the female discussion group, Mahala (2nd Gen, F, Den, FDG) narrates her experience of being misrecognised by others for not following the social norms expected of a young Muslim woman. This is closely related her Turkish origin, not wearing the hijab and having light-skin. She begins by differentiating herself from the other hijabi-wearing discussants: 'I'm different from them' (Mahala). Such divergence may be most apparent in her opinions about community recognition. She openly states to the other discussants how she feels. She states: 'I don't have a community per se' (Ibid.). The reasons for not feeling a sense of belonging relates to how she is misrecognised by other Muslims in her community. She details how she gets 'the reaction from people's faces' (Ibid.) when they come into contact with her father and herself together. Her father has 'good ties' (Ibid.) with the community and is respected. However, through facial gestures and communication, Mahala has come to know that she is not respected by certain sections of this community. She explains to the other discussants that:

> I know I'm not acc[epted], not I know but I've, some people actually told me [to my face], I know but I am not accepted because I am different.
>
> (Mahala)

The difference she talks about is varied. She is a Muslim woman but follows a Sufi interpretation of Islam and does not wear the hijab. Furthermore, she has

Intergenerational relations 159

a light skin tone in contrast to her father. For this discussant, the knowledge that she is not accepted for who she is by other Muslims 'hurts' (Ibid.), especially since such disrespect can easily be compared to how those same people interact positively with her father. She states the following about this painful situation:

> because I am different and just that kind of hurt when they say to Dad, 'is this your daughter?', and I'm like 'yeah', and you kinda see the disappointment in their face because, I mean, my Dad is dark as well, because in Turkey we have different looks, like he's kinda brownish [in skin tone]. So, I can feel that they're very surprised for him to have me as a daughter, but yeah, I'm not accepted. I wouldn't feel that I'm accepted and I wouldn't feel comfortable in that mosque as well.
>
> (Ibid.)

Continuing their critique, Rifa is vocal about the problems she perceives exist in the Arab Muslim community where one negative action that disrupts expected social norms automatically identifies you as 'that bad person'. Fusaila acknowledges and clarifies that many people in the Muslim community in Ireland are critical of Arabs because they have too much control over social norms that determine correct Islamic practice. Rifa responds strongly to Fusaila by generalising that the Arab community is not accepting of change, especially in respecting the capacity of individuals to transform themselves into something better. She states the following narrative in reply to Fusaila:

> even if you change, no matter how much you change, you're still that bad person from years ago. So, it's kind of 'okay, we'll talk to you and everything' but you're still seen as that bad person no matter how much you change, which I really hate that about the Arab community.
>
> (Rifa)

After the above statement, Saiba makes the point that such dynamics in the community make it hard for people's transformations to be accepted and 'that's why we leave our own communities like' (Saiba). Moving to another geographical location or to another group enables the finding of acceptance, freedom and a break with the past. The sisters and Rifa, who together are emigrating from Ireland to the UK, all agree with the above statement. For Saiba, leaving one's community means one can 'be like' oneself. She correlates moving to a new community with gaining freedom from the past and attaining a 'clean slate' (Ibid.) that is free from the expectations and judgements of others. Saiba makes the following statement, which Rifa agrees with adamantly:

> I wanna, I wanna be new, I wanna have a clean slate in the community over there in the UK.
>
> (Saiba)

Conclusion

This chapter has shown the intergenerational perspectives of two groups in the Muslim community towards each other. Through streams of narrative, we learn that the first generation is concerned about youth identity. The older generation is concerned that by living, interacting with and being highly influenced by European society and culture, the youth will assimilate and dilute their identities into a European way of being, and thereby lose connections to the home country and its specific ethno-Islamic cultural identity and heritage.

It could be said that Muslim parents and elders are undergoing an integration dilemma involving the finding of balance between isolation and assimilation for themselves and their children. This is a common concern and worry for first generation immigrants to a new country. To prevent the assimilative dilution of identity, we learn that the first generation are taking active steps to socialise their children and constitute their identities. In other words, they are passing on their *cultural baggage* to protect and shield their children from the perceived to be negative influence of European cultural habits and different ways of life.

We also gain an insight into this intergenerational relationship from the younger perspective. Although the youth are socialised by the older generation during the years of dependent childhood, their narratives suggest that, upon entering early adulthood and socialising with others from different ethno-Muslim backgrounds, they have initiated a process of identifying and resisting elements from the cultural bag that are viewed as rigidly inflexible, patriarchal and against the norms and behaviours of the Islamic sources and the Irish-European social context. As the narratives show, these young Muslims, who are forging a new European Muslim identity, must contend with the negative judgements of others, not only from wider society, but also from inside their own familial and communal relations. The first generation utilise their powers of influence to create youth, who can be recognised as good *traditional* Muslims. And in this process, the youth feel the pressure to live up to the traditional ethno-Islamic ideal of the 'good Muslim'. However, we learn from the narratives that for European Muslim youth this passed-down identity is viewed as an impediment to gaining recognition from God, other Muslim youth, and from the wider society. It can be stated that the younger generation are creating and acting-out a post-traditional Muslim identity that serves their recognitive needs in the Irish-European context.

Muslim youth, individually and collectively, have had to resolve everyday social dilemmas and forge a new non-traditional, Islamic-civic identity that can operate effectively in the European social context, and at the same time, remain faithful to and enhance recognition to religion, family and community. As the empirical narratives in this chapter have shown, through such creative action, Muslim youth in the Irish-European context have rejected an isolationist, as well as assimilationist, being and forged a new identity that merges Muslimness and citizenship to aid the struggle to attain recognition from multiple social spheres of everyday interaction.

Intergenerational relations 161

The next chapter of this book, Chapter 7, is a discussion chapter that teases-out the main findings of the research by combining the information from preceding chapters into a holistic picture demonstrating the complexity of recognition relations in everyday life. Firstly, this chapter refers back to the empirical narratives to illustrate how recognitive relations are embedded and acted-out within varied and complex power relations. In this regard, three dynamics of power are identified and examined, i.e. power-over the actions of others in terms of domineering and constitutive power as well as bottom-up resistive power. This chapter then examines how the research narratives challenge the security paradigm. And lastly, by reflecting upon and synthesising the information presented, the chapter ends by concisely evaluating the overarching insight of the book.

References

Furseth, Inger and Repstad, Pål. (eds.). 2006. *An Introduction to the Sociology of Religion: Classical and Contemporary Perspectives*. London: Ashgate.

7 Resolving recognitive-power dilemmas

Introduction

This chapter discusses the main findings that have emerged from the research, which utilised Axel Honneth's typological framework of recognition to explore the everyday Muslim experiences in the Irish-European context. The prime aim of this chapter is to concisely discuss the preceding chapters to tease-out the findings of the research and demonstrate the complexity of recognition and its relationship to various formations of power. The discussion is conducted in two sections. Firstly, the complex intertwinement between recognition and power is explored, particularly with an eye on the varied and complex relations of power that envelop relations of recognition. Domineering, constitutive and resistive power are examined in detail and related back to how such powers impact upon recognitive relations in multiple spheres of life, i.e. in the family, the Muslim community, the legal sphere of citizenship, and the wider sphere of public interaction. To give the research findings theoretical and empirical support, this section refers back to, and shows how the social theoretical insights, provided for in the initial chapters of the book, link to the *streams of narrative* conveyed in the empirical chapters.

The second section shows how this research challenges the security paradigm and its risk aversion that has wrongfully stereotyped Islam as terroristic, and reified Muslim populations as suspect across Europe. Taking the knowledge that has been learned about struggles for recognition and the impact of power relations, the concluding section concisely evaluates the overarching insight of the research, which relates to how Muslim individuals and collectives resolve everyday dilemmas so as to find a way *to be* in the Irish-European context.

The intertwinement of recognition and power

As Honneth's (1995) theoretical frame and the empirical narratives illustrate, recognition is a subjectively innate need and an intersubjectively constructed dynamic of social interaction, which is a fundamental and necessary aspect of the human condition. It is verified by the empirical narratives that positive and negative recognition affects an individual's relation-to-self and overall sense of self-worth. However, it must be acknowledged that recognition does not occur in isolation but is continuously acted-out within and enveloped by complex power dynamics. In other words, there is no outside to relations of power. The following discussion explores these dynamic relationships by examining how everyday recognitive experiences relate to three forms of power. In terms of top-down relations, power-over others is the most prevalent, comprising two diverging components, *domineering* and *constitutive*. The third formation is a form of bottom-up power enacted by individual and collective agency, which manifests within and resists forms of top-down arbitrary interference. Following the work of Allen (1999, 2008, 2010) such a bottom-up agentic power is referred to in this study as *resistive*.

Domineering power

Recognitive relations across social spheres are enveloped by power dynamics and the narratives in this study give a valuable insight into how recognition and power relate to each other. This section examines domineering power, acted-out through pathological behaviour, in three spheres of interaction, i.e. in the wider societal public sphere in terms of discrimination, in the family and community love sphere in terms of patriarchy, and lastly, in the legal sphere in terms of exclusion through the stratification of citizenship.

Public discrimination

It has been identified that domineering power exists to a large extent in the wider societal public sphere in the form of discrimination. Using Petit's definition of arbitrary domineering power (Petit 1997) referred to in Chapter 3 of this book (see p.62), it is possible to state that it is common knowledge that such discrimination is domineering because it arbitrarily interferes with a person's capacity to be oneself in the wider social sphere, and thereby restricts freedom and choices in that sphere of interaction.

Furthermore, discrimination as domineering power fails Petit's eyeball test (2012), i.e. to be able to 'look another in the eye' without reason for fear or deference (Chapter 3, p.62) by the fact that it is an attempt to publicly shame individuals, who are different to prevailing social norms. The empirical narratives reference how everyday discrimination, in the public sphere, is a common experience and how surface-level traits are shamed because such attributes differ from the dominant identity standard that has become the culturally socialised norm in Irish society. The fact that an individual may be a citizen, and be legally the same as others in society, is negated by the supersession of what makes people different to each other. Such public discrimination can be acted-out as physical attacks or non-physical verbal and gestural denigration. Furat's small story about her friend having her hijab ripped off her head in public is a cogent example of such public shaming (Chapter 4, p.87).

The narratives indicate that it is Muslim females who bear the brunt of such domineering power, and are positioned on the front lines when it comes to acts of discrimination, whether related to Islamophobia, race or ethno-cultural prejudice. Muslim women's surface-level traits, particularly wearing the hijab and racial features, make them clear targets for public discrimination, or, as it is called in the narratives, the *prejudice of first impressions* (Ibid., pp.85–92). Such hostility negatively affects an individual's confidence to be oneself in society. A variety of narratives in this study illustrate this situation, such as Dahlia and Safeerah's small story about a female Filipino friend, who took her hijab off because she lacked the confidence to be visibly differentiated from others in public (Ibid., p.89), as well as Maja's small story about perceiving disrespect from a hotel receptionist (Ibid., pp.94–95). Hurriyah narrates how such experiences of everyday domination negatively affect an individual's relation-to-self and sense of worth, which carries the likelihood of leading to self-isolation and depression (Ibid., p.94). Importantly, from the first generation female focus group, there is also narrative evidence that women are struggling against domination by working collectively to prove to others that they, as female Muslim citizens, can civically participate and contribute to their wider community and society. Even though such women would like respect for their particular surface-level traits, they advocate that what should be normatively judged by others ought to be their particular meritocratic abilities and achievements that productively contribute to their local community and society.

An interesting aspect of this form of societal domination is that the narratives from the research participants, continuously connect everyday public discrimination as being fuelled by media misrecognition. From the narratives, media in general is perceived as having a negative impact upon Muslim populations in Ireland and Europe by subjecting them to forms of misrecognition such as sensationalist stereotyping, categorisation and reification. It is then perceived that this creates misunderstandings about Islam and Muslims. Predominantly, Islamophobia and racism are perceived to exist in Irish society because the media has influenced and pressurised everyday people to have a negative attitude towards Muslims. An example of this is Furat's small story of being shamed in her house as she watched television with her friends (Ibid., pp.77–78). The empirical narratives suggest that an unhealthy relationship, devoid of trust, exists between Muslim communities in Ireland and mass media outlets – national and international. Masud has the view that he lives in a suspect community, whose lived experience is tarnished by sensationalist media (Ibid., pp.74–75). The empirical data shows that Muslim youth are quite vocal about this stale relationship and are actively questioning the media's portrayal of their lived reality. Representation is also a problematic aspect of the relationship in that there is, in the Irish context at least, a definite non-representation of people of difference in mainstream media formats, such as in television and radio. Although Ireland has become a plural heterogeneous society, with all citizens and residents contributing taxes towards state broadcasting costs, people of difference still lack visible representation in state media, which predominantly promotes the dominant identity standard of Irishness.

Patriarchy

It has also been identified that pathological domineering power exists, to a minimum extent, in the private love sphere in the form of patriarchy. By once again utilising Petit's definition of domination (Petit 1997), it is possible to state that it is common knowledge that patriarchy arbitrarily utilises a mixture of Islamic prescriptions and ethno-cultural traditions to interfere with the female capacity to participate and contribute to everyday life. It thereby restricts a woman's individual freedom and range of choices in multiple social spheres. Such hard-to-see abuse (physical and non-physical) fails Petit's eyeball test (Petit 2012) because it is carried out by male familial and community actors in the private sphere. It creates shame by detrimentally affecting a person's positive relation-to-self and sense of worth, which reduces self-confidence and exasperates psychological difficulties and social death. First generation female narratives confirm that such patriarchal domination exists in the Muslim community, but maintain that it is not systematic, but minimally and arbitrarily conducted in rare and exceptional circumstances (Chapter 6, p.154). In contrast, young female participants are more vocal about how such domination over-regulates social action in the familial and community spheres and how it is subtly acted-out through regulating and preventing everyday social interaction, or in rare cases, through extreme pathological interaction in the form of Female Genital Mutilation (FGM), forced marriages and 'honour' killings.

Such forms of negative domineering power, conducted and legitimised by males against females in the love sphere, inextricably relates to the interaction between Islamic identity and traditional ethno-cultural social norms. There is evidence that uneducated first generation Muslims, who come from low socio-economic backgrounds, retain a diluted Islamic identity that is heavily socialised by home country ethno-cultural traditions and practises (Ibid., pp.149–150). This *cultural baggage* can contain domineering forms of patriarchal traditional culture that commonly evades critical assessment. Domineering power in the form of patriarchal pathologies are clearly equated, throughout the narratives, with ethno-cultural traditions, and are noticeably distanced from a perceived to be pure form of normative Islamic identity that promotes closer attention to the Islamic sources (Ibid., pp.150–159). Although, in parental minds, the passing of a home country identity to future European generations may be deemed a vital form of constitutive power, it can conversely be perceived by educated Muslim youth in Europe as a form of domineering power that limits flexibility and constrains Islam from being applied contextually and in a productive manner. This point of view is voiced by second generation discussant Saiba, who advocates that confidence in religious belief resides in its autonomous and rational practice free from domination (Ibid., p.156). This issue is prominently reflected in the

166 *Resolving recognitive-power dilemmas*

young female narratives as exemplified in Isra's small story that recounts how she must hide her identity to resolve a dilemma between how she recognises her socialised familial norms and the interaction she conducts with her friends in the wider public sphere (Ibid., p.155). This interviewee also points to how young Muslim women feel excluded socially from participating in sport and acting classes due to the particular way in which leading family and community members interpret the relationship between Islam and culture (Ibid., p.154).

An important aspect of this empirical study is that second generation female narratives give a clear insight into how domination is maintained through the link between power and knowledge. In other words, patriarchy is maintained by the male control of Islamic jurisprudence (Ibid., pp.155–156). This intermeshing of power and knowledge excludes female agency and limits women's capacities to resist being negatively impacted by a mixture of Islamic and ethno-cultural socialised norms, legitimised by males for the sake of control and privilege. The above is exemplified, from a young female perspective, by Isra, who is critical of the patriarchal domineering power that controls and determines a particular interpretation of Islam, and thereby prevents young Muslim women from participating democratically and contributing to a range of social activities. For example, taking part in acting and sporting activities, as well as vocalising their opinion in the public sphere against FGM. Isra stresses that she has a strong Islamic identity but that her struggle is essentially over the legitimate interpretation of Islam, which is controlled overwhelmingly by males in the familial and community spheres (Ibid.). Her point is that knowledge is power. Isra states that she has come in contact with many young Muslim women, who are scared of the patriarchal domination over them, which is exacerbated by the lack of female input into the interpretation of Islamic jurisprudence (Ibid.). In other words, Muslim women lack control over the interpretation of Islamic knowledge that would enable the formation of resistive power to counteract forms of domineering patriarchal culture. Such input would also aid the development of mechanisms to struggle against demeaning male pathologies, and enable Muslim women to constitute themselves and be recognised as autonomous human beings, who productively contribute, not only to their family and ethno-Muslim communal spheres, but also to their local area and wider society.

Furthermore, a number of young female discussants criticise the Muslim community for its overly critical, judgmental and regulatory view of female behaviour that restricts transformational change and growth. There is narrative evidence that gender issues form an important and continuing concern for young female participants, particularly in relation to patriarchal power and the pressure to conform to socialised norms. For example, Mahala narrates that she feels she is not accepted by elements in her Muslim community. She vocalises her painful experiences of verbal and gestural abuse due to her different Islamic practices and also for not wearing the hijab (Ibid., pp.158–159). Interviewee Daleela and other young female discussants speak of their experiences in their Muslim communities in Ireland, where young Muslim women lack the flexibility to be themselves due to the pressure to conform to a particular interpretation of Islam, as well as the over-regulation of everyday behaviours (Ibid., pp.150–151).

Exclusionary civic stratification

The third form of domineering power identified relates to the creation of an unequal civic stratification and exclusion in the legal sphere of interaction. It is the state that regulates citizenship status on behalf of all citizens and, in this regard, the state wields domineering power-over the governability of others in relation to their legal status. This power is negative as it has led to the stratification of people into different civic status groups. For example, denizens are in a less secure position than recognised full citizens, who have been conferred with full rights and obligations to others. Coming back to Petit's definition of domination (Petit 1997), it is possible to state that it is common knowledge that exclusion through the stratification of citizenship is antidemocratic in that it runs counter to the *all-affected principle* of fairness and equal treatment. Although citizenship is a necessary institution that has power-over others in terms of being productively constitutive, the application procedures for attaining citizenship have become arbitrary in many European democratic states, especially in terms of the normalisation of lengthy time-scales to process received applications, the informational deficit experienced by applicants, and how applications in the Irish context are judged under the sole discretion of the presiding Minister of Justice and Equality. Such arbitrary procedures interfere with an individual's capacity to live a stable democratic life, marked by full participation and contribution to the public sphere.

Without doubt, civic stratification creates undemocratic social and political exclusion, as well as limiting the range of choices and actions an individual can make. Civic stratification fails Petit's eyeball test (Petit 2012) because such restrictions are commonly known to shame people by excluding them from the performance of full democratic participation. An uncertain status, such as denizenship, detrimentally affects a person's positive relation-to-self and sense of worth. It reduces self-respect and the ability to see oneself as a morally responsible person capable of participating fully, that is civically, socially and politically, in the democratic public sphere.

The above argument is supported by participant narratives, which indicate that legal recognition has an unequal dimension, in that the nation state has used its domineering power-over others to stratify individuals into a variety of civic status types. Such stratification can be viewed in terms of how the research participants narrate their experiences of long-term residency, or denizenship, in Ireland. The empirical evidence substantiates that the uncertain denizen experience differs significantly from the more secure experience of citizenship. The status of full citizenship is equated with positive internal feelings and external reciprocity, boosting confidence in participation and enabling new opportunities; however in contrast, denizenship is viewed negatively as an insecure temporary residential status with limited social and political rights and obligations to others, and most disturbingly, as a status that can be arbitrarily rescinded.

Numerous research participants provide narratives indicating the negativity of an uncertain civic status, which isolates one's public voice and is given less credence than the recognition of full citizenship (Chapter 4, pp.96–103). Hurriyah links such negative experiences to a sense of frustration in not being recognised as a human with accompanying rights and obligations (Ibid., p.100). In fact, this study had difficulties convincing denizens to participate in the research because of the fear that any negative public statements made against their legal status may jeopardise pending applications for full citizenship. It is also possible to determine that legal misrecognition has the power to disrupt familial recognition. The experience of Aziz conveys how applying for citizenship can be a drawn-out process taking ten or more years, leaving individuals and families under an insecure status for lengthy periods of time (Ibid., p.97). Another cogent example of this is Furat's small story about how, due to a technical irregularity on a citizenship application, a close friend was forced to move to her father's home country and leave the certainty of her home life in Ireland (Ibid., pp.97–98).

In practical terms, denizenship status also financially impedes the opportunity to educate oneself as university fees are high for third-country nationals. Adeeb's small story illustrates how an uncertain legal status restricts sub-citizens from the human right to attain an education (Ibid., p.99). Freedom of travel is also restricted. Of note is that the Irish government did recognise the plight of such individuals and families by bringing in amendments to speed-up the citizenship application process and reducing university fees for denizens. Taking the empirical data into account, the narratives vividly illustrate how denizens have less freedom and opportunity to be themselves in Irish society, due to their limited rights and obligations to others, a responsibility unfairly and unequally carried by fully recognised citizens. This civic stratification has been created by the domineering power of a democratic nation state that views universal legal citizenship as applicable to select individuals and disregards the democratic *all-affected principle*, which expresses the normative viewpoint that all humans in a bounded state, who meet basic criteria, should be recognised equally as having reciprocal rights and obligations to each other.

Just as denizenship status came under sustained narrative criticism, the status of full citizenship itself was also reprimanded in the research. Despite the positive comments about reciprocal legal recognition, the narratives suggest that such a status is commonly viewed as too abstract in that it is inherently weak when applied to the practicalities of interaction in everyday life. Although it is important to be recognised universally as a human being with the same rights and obligations to others, such a status remains imperceptible when interacting on a daily basis with others. For minority groups, this is acutely problematic in that full legal recognition is deemed to have more value as a procedural formality, to be utilised when communicating with state services,

Resolving recognitive-power dilemmas 169

than as an everyday practical status in which people can be acknowledged for their universal human value.

A variety of narratives, particularly from female participants, emphasise how particular traits take precedence over the universal value of being a human citizen in everyday interaction. These narratives highlight the dialectical tension that exists between abstract universal legal recognition and the societal recognition of traits, abilities and achievements. The nation state's power-over the institution of citizenship has warped its fundamental essence by connecting it to a particular ethno-cultural and nationalistic conception of identity. By submerging human universalism beneath more visible particular traits, a dominant identity standard is forged that legitimises predefined traits and norms that have come to be taken as the essential components of Irishness. The result of this is that instead of an individual being recognised as an equal citizen universally to others in practical everyday life, minority individuals and groups suffer prejudice as second-class citizens because their particular traits differ from the preordained dominant identity standard.

This is exemplified in the narratives relating to prejudice, which show how Muslims, particularly females, consistently feel that their traits are judged negatively before any acknowledgement and acceptance of their full status as citizens. In power terms, it can be stated that legal recognition is too abstract to wield effective use in everyday realms of interaction and is continuously eclipsed by the recognition of what makes people particular to each other. Therefore, one can say that a dominant identity, formed by immersing universal sameness under a range of particular traits, has an oppressiveness over minorities, who, despite being conferred as citizens differ from the sanctioned traits deemed to form the essential components of Irishness. The narrative evidence substantiates this viewpoint. A clear example is Furat's small story about her workplace, and her experience of having a 'constant background fear' that her particular foreignness is a deprivation in relation to interacting with coworkers, who hold dominant traits deemed to be closer to the official Irish identity standard (Ibid., pp.106–107). Even though she is an Irish citizen, in such occupational situations, Furat feels that she does not have the power to openly criticise the wrongful actions of others because 'that person is the Irish person, I'm the Muslim, you know, the foreigner' (Ibid.).

Through Honneth's theoretical frame and the empirical narratives, we learn that Muslims in the Irish-European context struggle to resolve a number of issues relating to the interaction between recognition and power. Such *recognitive-power dilemmas* relate to domineering power that manifests as public discrimination in the wider public sphere, patriarchy in the love sphere, and exclusionary civic stratification in the legal sphere of citizenship. The empirical evidence confirms Honneth's argument that such forms of misrecognition detrimentally affect a person's positive relation-to-self and sense of worth, reducing confidence and the ability to be oneself in different social spheres of life. Alongside identifying that power-over others takes a domineering form, as the next section outlines, it can also take on a more productive and socialising role by positively constituting identity.

Constitutive power

While power-over others can be domineering, as Foucault famously realised and expounded, such power can also be constitutive in that it can shape, maintain and be productive for action and identity (McNay 1994, Foucault 2002). This section uses narrative evidence to concisely explore two examples of constitutive power relating firstly to the state's regulative power-over citizenship, and secondly, to the intergenerational productive power that shapes identities by utilising and promoting spiritual recognition in the Muslim family and communal spheres.

Shaping the 'good citizen'

As the empirical data illustrates, though the state's regulatory control over citizenship can be domineering, its overall power in this legal arena is predominantly constitutive by being productive of identity. State administrative bureaucracies move and transform sub-citizens into fully recognised citizens with equal rights and obligations to others. This means that the state has the constitutive and productive capacity to transfer and shape people from one civic status to another – from asylum-seeker to denizen, and then from denizen to the 'good citizen'. These transformations rely on the regulation of action and identity with the eligibility to move from one status to another commonly verified by citizenship tests, which determine whether an individual has reached the official standard of the 'good citizen'. Worthy of note is that uncivil actions by sub-citizens, even small missteps, such as accumulating driver penalty points, can detrimentally impact on whether one is recognised by the state as a morally responsible person. It is argued here that such status movements constitutively shape and mould an individual's identity by conferring stronger recognition, and enabling those who have been fully recognised to socialise more with others and express themselves with confidence through individual and/or collective action.

A good narrative example of this emanates from Abdul, who as a denizen, confined his social interaction to the bounded space of his local Muslim community and associated mosque in Dublin. However, on being conferred with full citizenship by the state and gaining rights and obligations to others, Abdul felt more confident to interact in the wider social sphere (Chapter 4, p.102). This example is pivotal to understanding how the state's power to regulate and confer citizenship status can be both negatively domineering, yet also positively constitutive and productive of action and identity.

Shaping the 'good Muslim'

Another form of constitutive power identified by the narratives relates to intergenerational interaction, particularly in relation to the promotion of spiritual recognition with the aim of shaping the 'good Muslim'. This form of power is closely linked to the sociology of religion's socialisation literature, which examines how people are raised with the expectation of continuing various actions and identities that have become legitimised in familial and communal spheres. Although such norms can be domineering, they can also be positive for identity formation.

For example, within the first generation female discussion group, the discussants view their role in the family as positively productive by feeling that they have the constitutive power to construct the private family environment and to manage how the next generation interpret and practise Islam in the Irish-European environment. Of note are narratives from older female research participants, who as wives and mothers, continuously stress that they wield productive and constitutive power in the family. This power comes in the form of communicative action to construct and maintain the identities of other familial members. It is perceived to be the constitutive power to construct and regulate how these family members relate to their multiple identities. For example, Ayan views herself as not being under the control of a man but having the 'real power' as wife and mother (Chapter 6, pp.144–145). In another example, discussant Dahlia narrates how she gives advice to her children and can see how the youth are working together to carve out an Islamic identity, which is specific to the Irish context. She describes her power as positively influencing her son to unlock a new European Islamic identity (Ibid., pp.145–146).

In terms of who wields constitutive power, it is commonly thought that parental influence holds sway over the actions and identities of upcoming generations. Meaning that the first generation, as parental authorities, hold the reins of socialising power, which can be domineering and/or productively constitutive. However, there is ample narrative evidence showing that as dependency ebbs and the youth evolve into independent beings, they develop the capacity to intersubjectively influence the identities of their elders and parental figures, particularly in relation to the development of a new interpretation and practice of Islam in the Irish and broader European context. Depending on time and context, both generations can influence each other in terms of identity construction and behavioural expectations.

As an example, the sisters, Isha and Fusaila, see their agentic constitutive power as having a very strong influence on their parents and even on the broader Muslim community. They perceive that they have been able to change how their parents interpret and act-out an Islamic identity that is contextualised for the European environment (Chapter 5, p.133). Similarly, Nurdeen also relates how he has influenced his mother and wife to filter-out home country cultural practices and return to a perceived to be purer form of Islam (Ibid.). These examples convey the crucial point that although the first generation generally retain the reins of socialising power, as their children transition to adulthood, it is confirmed that both generations have the potential to influence each other in terms of identity construction and maintenance.

Noticeably, much of the constitutive power exchanged between the generations relates to spiritual recognition and how to shape the other and oneself as a 'good Muslim'. As Chapter 5 elaborates on, although such a transcendental form of recognition can be an institutionally domineering form of power-over individuals and groups, in this study, the research participants overwhelmingly view their individual expression of spirituality as positively constitutive, in that it acts as a coping mechanism to deal with the complexity and hurt of everyday intersubjective interaction. From a secular viewpoint, the narrative evidence suggests that such esoteric recognition, referred to as a 'referential instinct', can be associated with the Winnicottian concept of transitional phenomena (Winnicott 2005, p.177). By constituting a potential space that is creative and playful, spiritual recognition as a transitional phenomenon has an illusionary aspect that enables people to escape the instability and immanent hurt of intersubjective life. Furthermore, this abstract sphere and religious expression can also be seen, in a Blochian sense, as a revolutionary act of recognition that makes individuals and collectives capable of transcending the uncertainty and *darkness of the lived moment* inherent in intersubjective relations and look towards the hope of a utopian 'Not-Yet' (Bloch 1964, 1986).

Vitally, individual and collective recognition to God must be separated from recognition to man-made religious institutions. Secularism has tended to view religion as an ideological trap that has enabled religious institutions to dominate and sustain power-over a populace through the control of theological interpretation. In contrast to the above, and in line with the sociology of religion literature, the narratives in this study confirm that spirituality, in its individualised form, has a beneficial constitutive affect on a person's relation-to-self and primarily acts as a comfort against the misrecognition suffered in everyday life. Just as a child receives comfort from various transitional objects, such as a blanket or teddy bear, adults also receive comfort in the expanse of cultural obsessional practices, or *little madnesses* such as religion, art, sport and science (Kuhn 2013). The narrative evidence illustrates cogently that such transitional phenomena stimulate individuals and collectives to have positive feelings and emotions, such as comfort, happiness, relief and satisfaction. These potential spaces stand in contrast to everyday life by being devoid of struggle, hurt and hardship. The connection between spiritual recognition and Winnicottian transitional phenomena is supported by narratives that reference how recognition to an abstract object can bring relief from struggles and pressures related to misrecognition and the judgements of others (Chapter 5, pp.116–122). Through abstract recognition, struggles sparked by the complex external arena of everyday life can be internally reflected upon and released, thereby enabling the soothing of being. Similar reflections also occur through meditative practices like mindfulness and counselling techniques, such as psychoanalytic talk therapy.

In terms of narrative examples, Yusuf refers to how recognition to God through prayer can act as a human coping mechanism in which physical and psychological tension can be released towards a deity, who is perceived as the all-powerful creator of everything and the ultimate controller of judgement (Ibid., pp.118–120). Although everyday problems can be let go through the recognitive act of prayer, the narratives also indicate that individuals attain strength and power from spiritual acts of recognition, which can then be redirected back into aiding positive interaction in everyday life. This form of empowerment can be equated to recharging a battery. Not only does spiritual recognition give a purpose in life but it can act as an empowering mechanism against forms of misrecognition. For example, Ayan states that her individual recognition to God makes her 'strong' so that she feels that she can 'fight' and 'do anything' (Ibid., pp.117–118). She views her matriarchal power as created by and sourced from God. In similarity to each other, Dahlia, Sadiyya and Azaan, all view their spiritual recognition to God as tempering various negative psychological feelings and emotions, such as depression and homesickness (Ibid.). In this regard, their acts of recognition give them a positive mental attitude, which can then be utilised to cope with complex spheres of interaction composed of recognition and misrecognition. As the narratives illustrate, when upset by oneself or others in a particular sphere of interaction, adherents can enter the solitude of the spiritual to reflect upon their lives, recharge, and then confidently return to the complexity of intersubjective relations.

It is clearly outlined above how power-over others can constitute and form identity. Nation states set the rules for gaining citizenship and regulate action and identity so that sub-citizens can eventually reach the standard of the morally responsible 'good citizen'. Denizens and asylum-seekers must meet set criteria, follow the law, and be morally responsible to attain the highest civic status. Receiving citizenship confers rights and obligations but also transforms identity and boosts a person's confidence to interact in the public sphere. Constitutive power also resides in the love sphere of the family and ethno-religious community, with Muslim parents socialising their children into their way of being a 'good Muslim'. The first generation are using their adult power to constitute the identities of the next generation. This is viewed as a positive act in that elders are passing down their form of spiritual recognition and gifting the youth with a useful comfort mechanism for enduring intersubjective life. The narrative evidence verifies that Muslim youth do gain comfort from spiritual recognition. However, upon reaching adulthood, the upcoming generation can reverse the flow of constitutive power and begin to resist, influence and socialise the identities of their parents and communal elders. Through this process, we gain an understanding that resistance manifests, not only against domineering power, but also against powers that are working to productively constitute identity. Relying on the narrative evidence, the next section investigates and discusses identifiable resistances to forms of domineering and constitutive power.

Resistive power

As outlined above, power-over others can take a domineering and/or constitutive form and deeply influence individual and collective action and identity. As humans, we struggle to attain positive social recognition and remain firmly positioned within relations of power. However, as Foucault practically showed through his own grounded struggles, resistance to top-down power can be created (Hoffman 2013). This section explores how agentic resistances manifest, particularly in relation to recognising authority. This resistive power is linked to second generation integration processes in which, to avoid total assimilation (involving the loss of one's prime identity) and isolation (involving the overprotection on one's prime identity), young Muslim individuals and collectives have developed an alternative way *to be* in Irish society. This refers to a balanced integration strategy that can maintain an Islamic identity and, at the same time, retain and enhance positive recognitive relations to others in different social spheres. However, it also implies that distinct social norms and practices originating in private and public social arenas are resisted by returning to the correct teachings of the Islamic sources. To action this resistance, young Muslims are filtering-out negative forms of Irish and home country ethno-cultural norms and practices from their identity repertoire so as to unobstruct the perceived normative practice of Islam and enhance recognition in different spheres of social interaction.

Resisting familial and communal traditions

For second generation youth to find a space as Muslims in the Irish-European environment, they must strategically resist particular social norms and practices that emanate from the spheres of the Muslim family and community. The empirical narratives verify that the young research participants view Islam as their most salient identification. However, complications arise by the fact that there are many divergent forms of Islam practised by differing ethno-national individuals and groups in the Irish state. Such diversity creates complexity but it also, through intersubjective communication, enables educated Muslim youth to identify everyday practices that are a mixture of ethno-cultural and Islamic traditions.

Unlike the first generation, who have held tightly to traditional forms of ethno-cultural Islam, leading to tense power struggles in the community, the youth view such Islamic variations as an impediment to internal and external cohesion. As expressed in the interviews and focus groups, the youth hope and aim to find an Islam that will provide a common ground for all Muslim youth to actively interact and practise together, irrespective of ethnic or national affiliation. In reaction to the first generation's traditional Islam, the second generation have begun to search for the normative ideal of Islam. In other words, to practise Islam as they perceive it ought to be practised with specific reference to the Islamic sources, the Qur'an and Sunna. This universalised Islam is consistently referred to in the narratives as the pure or real form of Islam that is filtered of negative ethno-cultural and nationalistic aspects (Chapter 5, pp.123–134). In this regard, the second generation narratives illustrate the perceived negative impact of culture and the growing trend among young educated Muslims in the Irish-European context to filter-out what is perceived to be in opposition to the newly adopted way of understanding and practising Islam in a non-Muslim country. This filtering process takes place in the course of everyday life with the aim of reaching a purer form of Islamic identity that is perceived as more effectively facilitating and enabling mutual recognition.

This identity movement is an alternative way of integrating into wider social arenas of Irish society, yet at the same time, maintaining and strengthening connections to faith, family and religious community. This novel process enables integration without total assimilation or isolation. It is the Muslim youth's answer to *resolving recognitive-power dilemmas* encountered in the Irish-European context and, there is evidence to indicate that second and third generation Muslim youth across Europe are replicating this process to meet their own contextual requirements. This bottom-up integration strategy is referred to by the research participants in this study as *integration without dilution*. By returning to a purer form of Islam, Muslim youth can see a viable way to integrate into European society as Muslim citizens and thus be recognised as contributors, and at the same time, maintain and strengthen an Islamic bond to family and community members. Such a movement relies on identifying traditional norms and practices that are perceived as going against the normative tenets of Islam and create impediments to interacting in wider social spheres. This study has identified that second generation Muslim individuals and collectives are promoting the above actions and are actively passing this new viewpoint, process of filtration and associated identity, to the next generation (Ibid., p.134). Such intragenerational influence is focused on the deconstruction of existing cultural norms and practices that have solidified over time into socialised identities. Alongside this, the youth are forming and maintaining what is deemed to be a revitalised Islamic identity. This identity places greater emphasis on key religious sources and on the deep civic and democratic examples emanating from Islamic texts, particularly the Sunna, which is comprised of numerous stories showing the everyday practicalities of how Prophet Muhammad lived an exiled life in the multicultural and multireligious context of Medina. The processes outlined above are deeply fastened to the need for recognition, which resides under the umbrella of complex power relations. It is argued that this identity movement is a form of resistive power against pathological social norms emanating from the family and Muslim community, which impede holistic social interaction. Examples of such pathologies include FGM, marital abuse, forced marriages, and 'honour' killings.

Corresponding to McBride's (2013) work, such agentic resistances against domineering and constitutive top-down power can be connected to the recognitive struggle over authority that legitimises what is deemed to be normal conduct for everyday people. This is very much visible through the narratives of the female research participants, who vocalise how they slowly yet actively resist the powers-over them in the private love sphere and in their Muslim communities. More specifically, there is evidence that Muslim youth, particularly well-educated Muslim women, are beginning to redirect their recognition away from local authority figures, such as male family members,

Imams and traditional scholars, and are actively using a new interpretation of Islam to counteract male patriarchal domination and parental constitutive power. This involves the act of redirecting recognition to alternative Muslim authorities and public networks that utilise a counter-interpretation of the Islamic sources, which advocate against forms of domineering and constitutive power. However, although resistances exist and are growing in number, the male interpretative control over Islamic jurisprudence makes such struggles a slow and difficult process for women, especially for those less educated and who remain socially isolated.

The narrative evidence highlights that the above transformations, facilitated by the rise of online fatwa markets, are being actively discussed and debated by Muslim youth. As exemplified by the narratives within the second generation female focus group, Muslim youth in Ireland are debating among themselves whether Islamic jurisprudence and its interpretation by non-European Islamic scholars, remains statically fixed-in-time or whether it progresses-through-time in a manner cognisant of context (Chapter 5, pp.127–129). When the strong pan-European links between various Muslim youth groups is taken into consideration, it becomes highly probable that this same debate is taking place in other European contexts. It is at this point that Ramadan's (1999) work in relation to the reformation of Islamic jurisprudence comes back into play, particularly in relation to the concept of *ijtihad* or critical reasoning, which enables trained scholars to produce Islamic rulings more cognisant of context. Such rulings facilitate a greater degree of flexibility in how Islam is interpreted and acted-out in a post-traditional modern society. The re-emergence of *ijtihad*, a contested concept, enables young Muslims to feel that their Islam is not a controlled ideology enforcing domineering power-over them but, is instead, positively constitutive in terms of being respectful of individual and collective autonomy. In other words, it empowers Muslim youth to utilise online fatwa markets and, through their free rational choice, to select verified rulings that suit the context of their lives as lived in Europe. The digital age of the internet has ushered in a new era in which young Muslims are less dependent on family figures and nearby religious authorities to direct them onto the right path to practising Islam. Islamic websites collate indexes of rulings from all over the world on specific topics, which can then be adopted by Muslim youth depending on whether such Islamic rulings suit contextual needs. Young Muslims in Europe are searching the internet for flexible guidance. However, this searching can end in disappointment as Saiba's experience illustrates when she unsuccessfully tried to resolve the issue of handshaking (Chapter 5, p.128).

Although reforms are slow-in-coming, they show how change, however incremental, to the interpretation of Islamic jurisprudence facilitates how Muslim individuals act-out their identities in the European context. Be that as it may, as Ramadan (Op. cit.) has critically acknowledged in relation to Islamic jurisprudence, the majority of Muslim scholars based outside Europe cannot adequately facilitate the specific contextual needs of an increasing population of Muslim youth. The reason for this is that such distant scholars

Resolving recognitive-power dilemmas 177

lack a comprehensive knowledge of the European contextual environment. Following Ramadan's advocations, essential reforms to Islamic jurisprudence and its interpretation must be continuously struggled for by the Muslim grassroots. Alongside this, European states must actively promote and support the education and training of European-based Islamic scholars, who are open to utilising critical reasoning, i.e. *ijtihad*, to provide flexibility and contextualised Islamic rulings for Muslim youth throughout Europe.

It is argued above that the identity transformation, unearthed by this research, is an agentic form of resistance to familial and community norms and practices. The move to what is perceived to be the real Islam is seen to be beneficial for enhancing identity and social interaction. As Muslim youth perceive it, such change enables them to *resolve recognitive-power dilemmas* that detrimentally impact everyday interaction and enable them to gain positive recognition from multiple spheres of social life. For example, it is perceived that their actions in this regard enable the attainment of a higher recognition to God, a more cohesive and united familial environment, as well as the retaining and strengthening of communal bonds through the creation of a common ground between Muslim youth.

Overall, such resistive power conducted through an identity movement, enables Muslim youth to use religious sources to produce and constitute an Islamic identity that correlates positively to the everyday Irish-European context. By returning to what is perceived to be the normative condition of their religion, i.e. Islam as it should be interpreted and practised, as advocated by the key sources, Muslim youth have gained an interpretive resistive power to counteract and struggle against the historical intertwining of ethno-cultural traditions and Islamic values. A conflation that matured in the home country environment and arrived in Europe through the mental and physical *cultural baggage* of the first generation. This interaction between Islam and culture is capable of establishing domineering power-over others legitimating and enforcing patriarchal acts in spheres of everyday life. To disrupt this fusion, Muslim youth have utilised their individual and collective resistive power to remake a universalised Islamic religious identity that emphasises and promotes civic interaction. By doing so, the second generation have gained the capacity to integrate without diluting core identities as well as successfully resolving dilemmas that block or impede the attainment of positive recognition in various social spheres of everyday life.

Resisting societal norms and practices

As shown above, the second generation are resisting a variety of familial and Islamic community social norms and practices that do not co-ordinate with a pure form of Islamic identity and do not facilitate the flexibility to be oneself in the wider public sphere. Running alongside this is resistance to societal norms and practices, particularly towards the dominant identity standard that has come to constitute a static Irishness and inhibits the recognition and performance of a positively contributive Islamic identity. Throughout the empirical chapters, there is narrative evidence to suggest that resistive agency struggles against forms of top-down domineering and constitutive power but from a position within these relations.

For example, the narratives indicate that research participants, particularly young females, have gained resistive power through the act of reasoning, reinterpreting and reflecting upon the relationship that exists between norms and practices transacted between various Islamic and ethno-cultural identities in the European context. Such forms of resistance do not occur in isolation, but manifest in solidarity with others. Thus, it can be stated that the Muslim youth in this study have agentically used their Islamic solidarity to each other to find a position for themselves in wider society as *Irish Muslims*. By interacting with others, educated Muslim youth have come to acknowledge the difference between home country ethno-cultural traditions (commonly viewed as Islamic by the immigrant first generation) and the normative practice of a pure Islam that is filtered of negatively identified traditional norms and practices that have either originated from Ireland or the home country. In turn, the youth are harnessing an Islamic identity that is civic and enables Muslims to participate and contribute to the value-horizon of society. It allows them to be recognised positively for *who they are*. Such defiance leads to a practical curtailment of ethno-cultural and nationalistic aspects of identity alongside the interactive link between Islamic and civic components. Young Muslims are not trying to assimilate to the dominant static conception of Irishness but are making concerted efforts to develop, as Pędziwiatr (2010) calls it, a *Muslim civicness*. By this he means an identity that is based around the normativity of Islamic identity and participatory citizenship that actively challenges securitised notions of Islam as terroristic and Muslims as suspect.

In the narratives, there is evidence that young Muslims do view Ireland positively and have developed a unique Irish identity. In contrast to the dominant identity standard, which is overly nationalistic and rooted in ethno-cultural traditions, the second generation are in the process of constructing a new form of Irishness that relies on the civic components shared by Islam and citizenship. Many of these youth lack the possibility of being Irish in its prevailing form, which is associated strongly with being Christian, Caucasian and ethnically Irish. As an alternative working solution, Muslim youth are actively promoting a new conception of Irishness that falls back on the civic aspects of Islam and citizenship. They see themselves firstly as Muslims, who are secondly citizens of Ireland. This is where the promotion of an *Islamic-civic* identity is fruitful for the task of gaining recognition in the wider societal sphere.

With regard to the development of an Islamic-civic identity, the narratives show that Islam is the most salient identification among the research participants. As is clearly evident in Chapter 5, Islam is the core foundational identity, which acts like a prism through which other identities are viewed and enacted. It can be argued therefore that all other identities revolve around and are regulated by this prime religio-moral identity. For example, civic identity is perceived as an element inside or as originating from Islamic teaching and practice. This new elaboration of identity, an Islamic-civicness, is agentically operationalised by educated Muslim youth to resist and counteract forms of identity that do not create a facilitating environment to resolve dilemmas in everyday life. This double-barrelled identity gives Muslims the ability to be themselves in multiple spheres of everyday social interaction.

In line once again with McBride's focus on the recognition of authority (2013), such resistance is closely related to recognitively redirecting legitimacy from traditional authorities to a plurality of decentred counter authorities, which advocate for and promote the civicness of Islam and its utilisation in the European democratic sphere. This process is conducted in a practical manner by filtering-out what is perceived to be negative cultural practices and searching for a pure form of Islam that heeds to the Islamic sources and has the capacity to extract key civic examples and principles from the Islamic historical record.

The most illuminating examples of an Islamic-civic identity emanate from female research participants, particularly from the first generation female focus group, where a strong emphasis is placed on their Islamic-civic identity to convey to others in their local Dublin district that Muslim women can use individual and collective agency to contribute positively to their locality (Chapter 5, pp.136–137). This is evidence to show that Muslim women are using positive power, flowing from their religious identity and legal recognition as full citizens, to empower, resist and change socialised norms and the skewed perceptions of Muslim females.

The struggles outlined above are inextricably linked to the need to be positively recognised as an individual, who despite being the same yet different to others, can productively participate and contribute to society. However, to do this, one must resist the dominance of norms and pathological practices that warp the ethical and meritocratic recognition of universality and particularity. For example, the research participants, particularly females, recount their various experiences of discriminatory prejudice (Chapter 4, pp.83–92), relating to the pathological action of misrecognising visible surface-level traits before any acknowledgment of a person's unique abilities, which reside underneath the surface. Although the narratives provide a spectrum of experiences relating to social denigration, it must be acknowledged that the research participants do not passively accept and kowtow to such disrespect and domineering power. In fact, the narratives show that individuals use their resistive power to counteract discrimination and regain recognition and a positive relation-to-self. Small stories by Aamil (Ibid., pp.81–82) and Isra (Ibid., p.91) highlight how Muslims have taken agentic action to counteract discrimination, whether related to Islamophobia, racism or sexism, and by doing so, have protected themselves and others by reclaiming recognition and maintaining their sense of self-worth.

In positive terms, there is a general perception among the research participants that Irish society is progressing towards a more meritocratic society where traits are respected, yet overall, abilities and achievements are the merits that are recognised and valued as contributing to the value-horizon of society (Ibid., p.111). Such views show a deep understanding of social justice relating to the equal chance of being recognised for one's abilities and achievements ahead of how one's surface-level characteristics differ from the established identity standard and its associated norms and practices. Although past cultural configurations in Irish society placed a high value on the recognition of particular traits that conformed to socialised and dominant norms, practices and identity standards, modern pluralistic Ireland is progressing towards a more democratic and meritocratic assessment of people, in which abilities and achievements are gaining more traction in terms of what should be ethically recognised and how the differential particularity of others is assessed in a post-traditional society.

The empirical narratives identify *cultural transitional phenomena* as the socially interactive microspheres in which meritocratic ability and achievement gain recognitive primacy over the pathological misrecognition of differing surface-level traits. Worth mentioning are two narrative examples related to art and sport. First is Isha and Fusaila's small story about attending an art exhibition. The sisters recount how upon entering an exhibition at an art gallery, they felt hostility as their headscarves identified them as Muslim. This created an initial awkwardness. However, through communication, the sisters gained recognition as artists from other like-minded people (Ibid., pp.92–93). Despite both sisters having suffered forms of pathological misrecognition in Irish society due to their differing skin colour, religion and ethnicity, both verify that they feel recognised positively by others through the transitional phenomena of art, which provides a common ground to interact with others over a shared love. In such a playful potential space, an interest and/or ability in art is recognised by the community as beneficial and contributory.

The second example relates to narratives from Masud, who is a highly skilled soccer player. He narrates that, although his identity differs from those he plays with, it is his ability that is recognised and respected on the pitch (Ibid., p.93). Soccer's playful space enables Masud and his abilities to supersede his particular traits that stand in difference to the dominant identity standard of Irishness. For this discussant, his particular traits always have positive relevance in such situations in that spectators of the game get the opportunity to see a Muslim athlete contribute positively to both local and national communities (Ibid., pp.93–96). It is significant that Masud contrasts the recognition of his abilities on the pitch to the everyday discrimination he has experienced against his visible traits off the pitch. In these situations, his visible traits are misrecognised and his unique abilities remain unseen. Through these narrative examples, the transitional phenomena of art and sport have been identified as common cultural arenas in which individuals, who are the same legally yet different in terms of surface-level traits, can mutually play together in a meritocratic microsphere with the equal chance of having their underlying skills and achievements recognised as valuable.

Resolving recognitive-power dilemmas 181

As the above sections show, Muslim everyday experience in Europe is complex. Alongside the struggle to attain positive recognition from others, Muslims, particularly the youth, contend with a variety of power formations, which impact different recognition spheres, i.e. the family, the Muslim community, the legal sphere in relation to citizenship and the wider sphere of public interaction. Forms of power-over impact Muslim individuals from top-down. Both domineering and constitutive power exude significant influence in controlling the actions and identities of individuals and groups across different social spheres. On the one hand, domination promotes misrecognition and pathological control. On the other, constitutive power is positively productive of identity and action in that it can aid development, but also in certain situations and contexts, hinder it. Despite these challenges, the narratives clearly show that Muslims, particularly the second generation, harness individual and collective resistive power to agentically counteract forms of top-down power. Through such action, Muslim youth are able to attain a space to develop a new Irish-European identity that fuses Islamic-civic practices, which thereby enables them to gain positive recognition from multiple intersubjective social spheres. Muslim youth are taking what they need and avoiding what they do not need from the cultural bag of their parents and from European culture, and in so doing, they have established a creative process that innovatively leads to the gradual formation of a new *European Muslim* identity.

Challenging the security paradigm

By reflecting upon the preceding chapters, it can be determined that the individual and collective Muslim experience of recognitive-power relations in the Irish-European context is highly complex. The utilisation of Honnethian recognition theory, alongside narratives of everyday experience, provides a vivid insight into this lived complexity, and by doing so, challenges the security paradigm, which is highly influential in framing how we perceive and act towards Muslim populations in Europe. The following section discusses how narratives of everyday experience, multidimensionally framed into distinct spheres of recognition, i.e. the Muslim family and community, the legal sphere of citizenship, and the wider sphere of public interaction, provides a more complex and nuanced understanding of Muslim life and experiences in Ireland, which can be universally translated to the wider European context.

The multidimensional frame and narrative focus of this study provides a unique emancipatory perspective that runs counter to the dominant security paradigm residing in the European literature that is too narrowly concerned with viewing Muslims in Europe through the lens of political extremism. Despite the securitisation perspective tackling important and sensitive issues, such as Islamic fundamentalism and youth radicalisation, it provides little reflection on everyday Muslim experiences in Europe. It must be noted that Islamic fundamentalist views are held and propagated by a small minority and do not reflect the practical everyday lives of the majority of Muslims living peacefully and productively throughout Europe. In the influential and interconnected fields of academia, politics and media, political extremism and terrorism is a popular topic that has significant potential for exploitation. As the narratives illustrate, such fields create media stereotyping and academic overgeneralisations, which have a propensity to link the Islamic religion and its followers to terrorism. As experienced by other minorities, like the Irish residing in the UK throughout the turbulent twentieth century, Muslim people have been made into the go-to suspect community (Hickman, Thomas, Silvestro and Nickels 2011).

This study counteracts the security paradigm by deploying an advocacy and participatory counter perspective, with emancipatory intent, to give a more nuanced understanding of the everyday experiences of Muslim individuals and groups in the Irish-European context. It is a more rounded holistic approach, which provides the research participants with a space to describe the complexity of their recognitive-power relationships and to critique forms of misrecognition. The aim of providing a more nuanced view of everyday Muslim life constitutes a significant challenge to the security paradigm, which generalises and reifies Islam as terroristic and views Muslims as suspect.

It can also be argued that such a holistic sociological approach, particularly the multidimensional view of recognition and its interaction with power relations, permits security experts, media personnel and academics to gain an alternative comprehension of the dynamics that influence the spread of Islamic fundamentalist ideologies and the growth of radicalisation among Muslim youth in various European nation states. By attaining a more refined understanding of the experiences that occur in multiple recognition spheres and identifying the dilemmas that manifest in such arenas, valuable insights are gained into how identity is influenced, constructed and maintained intersubjectively by a religious minority in Europe.

Pivotal in challenging the security paradigm is enabling research to show that Muslim communities in Ireland, as well as across Europe, are not isolated communities – where the risk of insecurity ferments – but civic communities comprised of active citizens, who engage and participate in their societies. Notably, the narrative empirical evidence in this study contrasts significantly with the Taylorian viewpoint (Taylor 1992) that minority groups simply seek to have their particular culture and beliefs endorsed by a majority. In this study, the research participants provide a clear narrative account of how they, as individuals belonging to Muslim communities in the Irish context, are actively striving to be recognised positively in different spheres of everyday life. They want to be seen for *who they are* in multiple social spheres, which involves being recognised positively in their sameness and difference to others.

The importance of being recognised as the same as others is reflected in narratives that criticise the civic stratification of citizenship and advocate for the need to be seen and treated equally, in similarity to other citizens that are recognised as morally responsible human beings. Such narratives, which advocate for equality, participation and contribution in and towards wider society, rail against the premise that minority groups are concerned solely with the recognition and valuation of their particular cultural norms and belief systems. Being legally the same as others in terms of being treated equally, and conferred with the same rights and obligations to others, is an extremely important form of recognition narratively advocated for by the research participants. Its everyday importance is identified in criticisms of how perceived difference supersedes equal recognition or sameness to others in the legal and wider societal spheres. This is exemplified by the narratives in Chapter 4, which identifies pathological interactions in terms of legal exclusion as civic stratification and societal discrimination as the *prejudice of first impressions.*

There is the argument that the majority have ethical responsibilities to recognise the differences of minorities in relation to culture, belief and identity. Certainly, as this study shows, the research participants want their cultural life and beliefs to be respected in Irish society, however, it must be understood that these ways of life and social norms are also contested by members in these communities. The empirical narratives convey the complexity of recognising difference, which is more commonly related to how individuals and groups differentiate between surface-level traits as well as underlying individual meritocratic abilities and achievements. In line with Honneth's typology, the narratives support that Muslim individuals and groups expect their particular way of life to be respected by others. However, overall, the narrative evidence places more emphasis on objective recognition of individual abilities and associated achievements. This recognition may be indirectly influenced by particular ways of life, yet closely aligns to the continuing rise of a meritocratic society in which individuals and groups are recognised and esteemed for their contribution to the value-horizon of society. Such meritocratic recognition is promoted through culture. This point is exemplified in the small stories of Masud and the sisters, who narrate how their underlying individual abilities and associated achievements are socially recognised in the arenas of sport and art, yet at the same time, their surface-level particular racial and religious traits are discriminated against due to being different to the dominant identity standard that still holds sway in the culture of Irish society.

The empirical narratives associated with the Irish case pose a serious challenge to the security perspective by making visible the fact that Muslim individuals and communities are not isolated cultural enclaves that pose a potential security risk, but are human beings, actively seeking positive recognition in multiple spheres of everyday interaction. By breaking down the isolationist myth, this research shows that for Muslims in the Irish-European context, it is the objective recognition of individual abilities and contributory achievements that individuals normatively strive for in the wider societal sphere of interaction. Considering that such recognition struggles are universal and constitutive of being human, then these translate to the experiences of Muslims throughout Europe. This is an area of further research to be progressed and disseminated by the advocacy and participatory approach so as to challenge and weaken the risk-averse ideological security viewpoint that Muslims are suspect and Islam constitutes a terroristic and cultural threat to European values and democracy.

Conclusion

This section concisely summarises the pinnacle point emanating from this study that has attempted to synthesise a grounded philosophical frame with empirical narrative sociology. Recognition is an intrinsic part of the human condition that can be defined as a basic need, which implies that individuals and collectives struggle to be recognised by others in multiple spheres of everyday life. However, as the *streams of narrative* vividly illustrate, recognitive relations take place within a complex array of power dynamics that can be both domineering and/or constitutive. In this regard, the interaction between recognition and power has a deep impact on individuals and the possibility of receiving recognition and maintaining a positive relation-to-self. To attain such ethical acknowledgement, individuals must negotiate the complex powers that reside in each sphere of everyday life, which has the authority to legitimate social norms and practices determining standards of normal action and identity. Such a complex interaction leads to social dilemmas in how one can be recognised as true to oneself in multiple spheres of life that are controlled and regulated by powers propagating differential norms, actions and identities.

Such everyday complexity is the pinnacle sociological finding unearthed and made visible by this study and the term *recognitive-power dilemmas* is a product of the research that describes the interweaving of recognition and power dynamics that generate everyday dilemmatic situations between varying (sometimes competing) norms, actions and identities. In terms of being oneself and living an autonomous life as human, the narrative evidence suggests that Muslims in the Irish-European context, particularly the youth, are struggling to *resolve recognitive-power dilemmas* so as to find a positive recognition balance between familial, communal, legal and wider social spheres of interaction. To do this, individuals and collectives deploy and utilise agentic forms of bottom-up resistive power to challenge domineering and constitutive powers that carry the capacity to pathologically impede the ethical recognition of one's being in context.

The next chapter, Chapter 8, concludes the book by summarising the main findings of the research, assessing how it contributes to the existing literature, determining the study's influence on integration knowledge and policy, and lastly, recommending avenues for future research to explore.

References

Allen, Amy. 1999. *The Power of Feminist Theory: Domination, Resistance, Solidarity.* Boulder, CA: Westview Press.
Allen, Amy. 2008. *The Politics of Our Selves: Power, Autonomy, and Gender in Contemporary Critical Theory.* New York: Columbia University Press.

Allen, Amy. 2010. Recognizing domination: recognition and power in Honneth's critical theory. *Journal of Power*. 3(1), pp.21–32.
Bloch, Ernst. 1964. *The Spirit of Utopia*. Redwood City, CA: Stanford University Press.
Bloch, Ernst. 1986 [1959]. *The Principle of Hope*. Volumes 1–3. Cambridge, MA: MIT Press.
Foucault, Michel. 2002. *Power: The Essential Works of Michel Foucault 1954–1984*. Volume 3. London: Penguin.
Hickman, Mary J., Thomas, Lyn, Silvestri, Sara, Nickels, Henri. 2011. *'Suspect Communities'? Counter-Terrorism Policy, the Press, and the Impact on Irish and Muslim Communities in Britain*. London: London Metropolitan University.
Hoffman, Marcelo. 2013. *Foucault and Power: The Influence of Political Engagement on Theories of Power*. London: Bloomsbury.
Honneth, Axel. 1995 [1992]. *The Struggle for Recognition: The Moral Grammar of Social Conflicts*. Cambridge: Polity Press.
Kuhn, Annette. (ed.). 2013. *Little Madnesses: Winnicott, Transitional Phenomena and Cultural Experience*. New York: IB Tauris.
McBride, Cillian. 2013. *Recognition*. Cambridge: Polity Press.
McNay, Lois. 1994. *Foucault: A Critical Introduction*. Cambridge: Polity Press.
Pędziwiatr, Konrad. 2010. *The New Muslim Elites in European Cities: Religion and Active Social Citizenship amongst Young Organized Muslims in Brussels and London*. Germany: VDM Verlag.
Petit, Philip. 1997. *Republicanism: A Theory of Freedom and Government*. Oxford: Oxford University Press.
Petit, Philip. 2012. *On the People's Terms: A Republican Theory and Model of Democracy*. Cambridge: Cambridge University Press.
Ramadan, Tariq. 1999. *To be a European Muslim*. Markfield, UK: The Islamic Foundation.
Taylor, Charles. 1992. The Politics of Recognition, IN: Gutmann, A. (ed.). 1994. *Multiculturalism*. Princeton, NJ: Princeton University Press.
Winnicott, Donald W. 2005 [1971]. *Playing and Reality*. London: Routledge.

8 Conclusion

Introduction

Shadowing 1930s populist politics, over the last thirty years, alt-right political formations have incrementally risen to the surface of mainstream politics and gained a significant foothold and influence in the US, throughout Europe and across the globe. By countering co-operation and progressiveness, such populist politics is regressively slip-sliding democratic countries into extreme nationalism, isolationism and aggressive trade policies while, domestically, igniting and promoting sectarian tensions against individuals and communities, who differ from the dominant identity standard. In this new world order, misogyny, racism, ethnocentrism, xenophobia and religious discrimination become acceptable, and normalised to the point of informing policy. With each day, the lived experience of minority groups becomes precarious. This can be seen in the US, where African-Americans, Muslims, Mexicans, illegal immigrants, LGBT+ communities have been denigrated and Othered as either potential criminals or terrorists. The situation is not limited to the American context, as the ideology of the alt-right has spread and taken root across Europe and to other regions of the world. The reinstallation of this regressive form of divisive and unethical politics jeopardises democratic progress, future economic well-being as well as the recognition and respect for minority individuals and groups.

In such times, the importance of a critical approach to sociological investigation comes to prominence. Critical social theory, with its emancipatory intent supported by empirical methods, can identify and present the everyday experiences of unrepresented minorities. It can show the universalism in the particular. It aims to understand being, hold power to account, and keep the hope and potential of democratic progress alive. The research in this book has attempted to walk along this ethical path. The empirical aspects of this study were complemented by Axel Honneth's comprehensive recognition theory (Honneth 1995), which, despite being developed nearly thirty years ago, remains applicable to progressing a deeper understanding of the human condition and acting as a frame for empirically exploring Muslim everyday experiences in twenty-first century Europe. Despite deficits in relation to the theory's conception of power, which were rectified and buttressed through the work of other critical theorists; overall, Honneth's theoretical insights proved pivotal for forging and progressing the direction of this research. His influence on this work is comprehensive in terms of showing the importance of recognition experiences in multiple spheres of everyday life, outlining a typology of recognition and misrecognition, and describing how the movement of recognition impacts an individual's relation-to-self with misrecognition leading to a struggle to regain a positive relation-to-self. He also provided vital insights in relation to social pathologies and the importance of Winnicottian social psychology. This work stands on his shoulders and it is hoped that its empirical angle informs the continuing development of Honnethian recognition theory. In particular, this research is beneficial by providing insights into how subtle forms of disrespect, power and resistance exist in the familial sphere as well as showing the importance of adopting a more complex understanding of power to enable recognition theory to comprehensively reflect everyday social life.

To conclude the book, this chapter firstly summarises the new knowledge discovered by the research. It then determines how this study contributes to the existing academic literature as well as concisely outlining how it influences policymakers and impacts European integration policy. Finally, recommendations for future research are listed and the book ends with some brief concluding remarks.

Unearthing new knowledge: summarising the research

This qualitative study, which utilises grassroot narratives and is framed by Axel Honneth's multidimensional modes of recognition (love, legal respect and social esteem) demonstrates the complexity of recognition relations by making visible a deeper understanding of the experiences of Muslim individuals in the Irish-European context, who use the language of recognition to convey their everyday struggles in various social spheres.

This study deployed the tools of philosophy, sociology and psychology so as to bring forth new understandings about the lived experiences of Muslims in Europe. The book's findings emanate from European Muslims themselves. It is their story, in their own words, presented through a *steams of narrative* technique. It is these grounded insights about Muslim everyday life that constitute the research. The author's role was to facilitate and enable grounded philosophy and everyday narrative to come in closer contact, to intertwine and productively synthesise. Through this interaction transformations can be identified and even enabled. This novel approach allows new knowledge and insights to surface in relation to Muslim life in Europe.

One of the most pivotal findings of the research is how the everyday narratives from the research participants resistively challenge the security paradigm perpetuated in popular discourse by media institutions, academia and governing powers. The security perspective narrowly views Muslims in Europe (and across the globe generally) through the distorted lens of political extremism. It is well-known that sensationalism is a tool deployed to sell media products yet similar techniques and perspectives are used, alongside the fear of terrorism, in academic and policy circles, to build profile, gain scarce funding and to progress a nativist securitisation ideology. To provide justification for unpopular action, such discourse thrives on using the Other as a scapegoat. In the past, various ethnic and religious groups have been instrumentally positioned without consent. Irish, Jews and African-Americans have all fallen victim to the imposition of such blanket stereotyping in different time-periods and contexts. In the early decades of the twenty-first century, it is Muslims, immigrants and refugees that are being used and scapegoated by domineering powers to justify undemocratic political action. Through this regressive repetition, we come to learn that the thwarting of universal democratic principles and values requires the need to blame and fear the Other.

In contrast to the above ideology, this study makes concerted efforts to learn about everyday Muslim experiences from Muslims themselves – in their own words. This study explores how Muslims, however diverse, experience recognition and feel perceived by others in European society. The grassroots multidimensional narratives of subjectivity that form this study fuse together to provide an objective everyday holistic understanding. By focusing on ontological recognition experiences, the universalism of Muslims as human beings comes into view. This perspective is so often lost in studies that focus on Islamic terrorism and radicalisation in isolation. The approach of this research is philosophically broad yet manages to give a grounded perspective of recognition experiences from within multiple social spheres. By doing so, it rails against description and disrupts the one-dimensional securitised view of Islam and the unsupported generalisations of Muslims as terroristic and suspect. This research highlights that the narrow securitised perspective that tarnishes whole Islamic communities is an injustice to the lived reality of Muslim life in Europe, which is positively productive and contributive.

The Muslim narratives in this research not only disrupt the security narrative but also actively challenge isolationist accounts of Muslim existence in the European context. This study's grounded empirical approach confronts the standardised view that assumes religious minority groups simply seek to have their particular culture and associated beliefs positively endorsed by a majoritarian populace. In this view, the Muslim is isolated in their familial and communal environments with no meaningful social interaction with others in wider society. Muslims are thus perceived as being siloed in the practice of a particular identity and struggle only for the majority to recognise the legitimacy of this way of life. In contrast, the narratives in this research convey how intersubjectivity and social interaction are both pivotal aspects of the human condition. Humans strive to be recognised as the *same*, in terms of being fully recognised as legal citizens endowed with universal rights and obligations to others, yet also as *different* to others, in terms of having meritocratic underlying abilities and associated achievements recognised as contributing positively to the generalised value-horizon of society.

The research highlights the complexity of human nature that strives to be recognised in both its universality and particularity.

The multidimensional perspective of this study focuses on social interactions, which take place in the love, legal and wider societal spheres, and in so doing, a deeper understanding of the complexity of everyday life is enabled. It provides a space for research participants to vocalise their perceptions of misrecognition and thereby identify social pathologies that run counter to being positively recognised as a participatory citizen and contributory individual. It verifies that forms of disrespect and misrecognition permeate multiple social spheres to varying degrees. The participant narratives, particularly small stories, confirm that misrecognition does negatively affect an individual's relation-to-self leading to a struggle to regain recognition and a positive relation-to-self. Such struggles vary with context and can manifest in violent or non-violent action.

These everyday insights into Muslim life in Europe make visible the connection between misrecognition and power. Aided by the participant narratives, this study has identified three forms of power inherent to social spheres, which impact upon Muslim everyday life in the Irish-European context. The powers identified include the existence of *domineering* power, in terms of public discrimination in the wider societal sphere, patriarchy in family and communal life, as well as exclusionary civic stratification in the legal sphere of recognition. Also identified is the existence of *constitutive* power in terms of the regulatory and penalising process performed by governmental and legal powers in productively shaping individuals into the mould of the 'good citizen'. Running alongside this, in the family and communal environments, is the intergenerational dynamic of shaping the 'good Muslim' by the act of regulating the correct way to conduct spiritual recognition to an abstract deity. Importantly, this study also identified the existence of grounded *resistive* power, particularly by Muslim youth, against specific socialised norms and identities legitimised and controlled by traditional authorities in the family, community and wider social spheres. This power is often left unexplored in studies of Muslim populations in Europe as it is a bottom-up reaction against restricting and controlling top-down power. Of note is that this grounded form of power emanates from within and bursts-out from the grip of domineering and constitutive influence.

This study has made it philosophically and empirically apparent that recognition and power intertwine in a complex manner. At times this relationship is plainly visible and identifiable, yet this interaction can also manifest in subtler forms in everyday life and break to the surface only when faced with individual and collective resistance. The research shows conclusively that individuals (and groups) need and strive for positive recognition from others in everyday life yet they must also negotiate the powers inherent to each social sphere of interaction. Complicating things further is that these formations of power (along with their corresponding social norms and identities) regulate, compete, and sometimes clash within and across spheres of interaction. This is the complexity of everyday life, which creates dilemmas for individuals and groups, who intersubjectively strive to gain positive recognition from others in various interactive arenas. This is particularly pertinent for those people who differ from what is deemed and perceived to be the dominant standard of normal.

A compelling sociological finding unearthed from the research relates to resistive power. It has been identified that Muslims in Europe, particularly Muslim youth, utilise individual and collective agency to resist domineering social pathologies and forms of constitutive power. They thereby create a space to enact a new Muslim identity that corresponds in a positive manner to various intersubjective social spheres. The research identified that there is an ongoing identity transformation, from the particular to the universal, taking place in the Irish Muslim community. This process is concerned with attaining universal recognition and outlines the possibility of a similar process taking place or developing throughout Europe. The research showed that this identity movement predominantly relates to second generation Muslim youth, who are actively attempting to return to what is perceived to be a purer form of Islamic identity by filtering-out negative forms of ethno-cultural tradition that are viewed as distorting the correct practice of Islam and spiritual recognition to God. It relates to universal recognition in that this process is a way to resolve recognition dilemmas that manifest in a variety of social spheres. In line with McBride's (2013) work on recognition and authority, such actions are a form of resistive power in that young Muslims in Ireland and across Europe are agentically resisting and struggling against particular inflexible social norms and static identities that manifest in the love sphere as well as in wider social arenas. This is actioned by bypassing traditional authority figures and redirecting legitimating recognition to a plurality of alternative decentred authorities. Advanced media technology facilitates such resistance and enables young Muslims to contest the inflexible social norms and rigid socialised traditional identities that formulate what it is to be a 'good Muslim'.

For young Muslims, intersubjective communication and collaboration makes visible the path that leads to a return to what is perceived to be the real Islam. By following this route, Muslim individuals learn to work collectively to strengthen their recognition to God, enhance and create a common ground to their Islamic family, friends and community, and uncover the civic practices of Islamic tradition that enable the attainment of recognition as active Muslim citizens. This identity transformation helps Muslim individuals and groups avoid total assimilation and isolation by enabling the creation of a balanced integration strategy, referred to by the research participants as *integration without dilution*. This alternative grounded form of integration strategy enables Muslims to intersubjectively interact in the Irish-European context but with the benefit of maintaining and even strengthening their core foundational Islamic identity. It does so by placing more emphasis on *Islamic-civic* identity rather than a religious identification that synthesises with and accentuates ethno-cultural or nationalist markers. In essence, Muslim youth are constructing their own way *to be* in Europe. As the empirical case study has shown, they have become *Irish Muslims* by constructing their own unique Irish identity with its own assortment of values, norms and everyday actions. In Hegelian terminology, it could be stated that these young Muslims are *thesis* (Irish-European) and *antithesis* (foreign Muslims) but have been able to reconcile their being into a *synthesis*, i.e. they have transformed into Irish-European Muslims.

Discovering that the research participants are attempting to resolve social dilemmas buttresses the findings of this study allowing for a unique and unified argument. Following Petherbridge's constructive criticism (Petherbridge 2011, 2013) about the relationship between recognition and power, the empirical narratives illustrate that Honneth's ethical recognition struggles can and should be connected to Foucauldian power struggles, which in turn highlights the complexity of everyday life. In this study, the term *resolving recognitive-power dilemmas* conveyed the complex intertwinement between recognition, power and everyday life. This phrase emphasises how individuals strive for positive recognition, yet simultaneously, they must negotiate the authoritative domineering and constitutive powers (and the corresponding misrecognition and social pathologies associated with such power) that reside and control social circles. Such powers regulate norms and identities that formulate what is considered normal as well as what is worthy of value and replication. It is important to stress that although this book has focused on the particularity of Muslim life, it unearths the universalism of being human. Through the use of an ontological frame and empirical *streams of narrative*, where subjectivities construct an objective outlook, this book uncovers a deeper understanding of the grounded dynamics of intersubjective relations. Importantly, the insights and processes described in this work pertain not only to Muslim individuals and groups alone, in isolation, but have significance for all human beings, who in different spheres of everyday modern life strive to attain their being in context, a process involving a negotiation and resolution between the dynamics of recognition and power.

Contributions to literature and policy

This study makes strong contributions to the philosophical and Muslim studies literature as well as showing a grounded perspective on integration, which should aid policymakers in forming representative and efficient policies at local and national levels throughout Europe.

As mentioned, this study is highly influenced by Axel Honneth's multi-dimensional typology of recognition, which framed the empirical aspects of the research. Of note is that much of the research and academic output that relies on the theme of recognition tends to be either philosophical theory development or a legalistic International Relations (IR) approach to understanding the dynamics of state recognition. It is surprising that although Honneth's recognition theory strives to ground philosophy in order to make it more socially relevant, to date, there have not been many sociological studies that empirically utilise it. The research presented here fills this gap. By combining recognition theory and narrative sociology to learn about everyday experiences of Muslim life in Europe, this unique research has contributed significantly to the philosophical literature that focuses on the theory of recognition. This is the first book to illustrate the possibility and potential of *Applied Recognition Studies,* in the hope that it influences and enables recognition theorists and sociologists to find further common ground to advance similar interdisciplinary research and collaboration.

Alongside contributing to the philosophical and sociological literature, this book also contributes to the nascent field of Irish Muslim studies as well as to the wider European literature. As outlined in Chapter 2, there is limited research on minority Muslim populations in the Irish context as well as in other peripheral European states. The Irish Muslim studies literature that does exist tends to be overly descriptive or ideologically compromised. This study productively adds to the scant and limited Irish literature. It also contributes holistically to the European literature. Instead of viewing Muslim life one-dimensionally – for example, investigating in isolation forms of discrimination in the public sphere – the design of this research facilitates a multifaceted approach enabling the exploration of everyday experiences in different spheres of life. By doing so, it builds a more comprehensive picture of Muslim life and makes a strong contribution to knowledge. Furthermore, this study also brings new insights about Muslim life in Europe, especially in relation to the themes of recognition, power, intersubjectivity and identity. Such an alternative approach challenges and disrupts the security paradigm that has dominated the European Muslim studies literature, which remains reactive to Islamic terrorism in Europe. By exploring the grounded dynamics of universal recognition experiences, this research becomes translatable to other contexts and it is hoped that a new generation of social researchers will take up the challenge to further extend this critical approach so as to uncover new knowledge and more nuanced sociological understandings about minority life in the European context.

Alongside developing the existing literature, this study also contributes to aiding the formation of integration policy at local and national levels throughout Europe. The grounded narratives in this research give a unique insight into how Muslim individuals view integration in the Irish context, where the importance of intersubjective interaction and identity is recognised, but where the Irish policy of intercultural integration remains rhetoric with little influence or impact on everyday life. A significant finding of the research is that the narratives show a resistance to existing integration policies in Europe that demand and promote either total assimilation, like France's secularism policy, or the isolationism and ghettoization of multiculturalism.

In this study, the research participants narratively advocate for a form of integration, which protects their most salient and active identities. They seek to integrate but without compromising or diluting core identities. This means they want to keep and strengthen valued identities and, at the same time, productively integrate with society. This research shows that the research participants are taking steps to accentuate an Islamic-civic identity that better facilitates integration by attaining legal and societal recognition yet also protecting valued identities from dilution or even extinction. This study supports the argument that for integration policy to be effective, it must take the concerns and opinions of minorities into account. It is hoped that this research, which makes dormant knowledge visible and retrieves a bottom-up perspective on integration, will influence and impact the attitudes of the decision-making powers at local and national levels throughout Europe. The everyday narratives in this book have the potential to aid policymakers make informed decisions when constructing and promoting integration policies, which, as this book argues, should ethically meet the intersubjective needs of all those affected.

Recommendations for future research

This study retrieved a deeper knowledge of the Muslim experience in Europe by examining empirically how Muslims perceive recognition relations in everyday social spheres. By doing so, new understandings were opened-up in terms of how recognition and power relate to social struggle and how multiple identities interact to *resolve recognitive-power dilemmas* in everyday life. It can also be argued that this unique study stimulates further research avenues. The following are four recommendations for future research, in no particular order or hierarchy of importance, which have the potential to progress and open-up new critical directions.

Firstly, because this study focuses on universal themes related to recognition, power and identity, the qualitative findings are transferable beyond the case study of Ireland to experiences of Muslim individuals and communities throughout Europe. Further research is needed to explore this transferability. This study can act as a template for other qualitative studies that aim to acquire new knowledge into the everyday recognition experiences of Muslim individuals and groups living in Europe.

Secondly, in terms of empirical expansion, the qualitative findings from this study can and should be accompanied and corroborated by quantitative methods of analysis. Such additional techniques and mixed-method results would enable wider coverage and more generalised findings in relation to Muslim recognition experiences in Europe.

Thirdly, while this study focused entirely on the Muslim Other, sociologists may deem it worthwhile to combine recognition theory and narrative sociology to gain a clearer understanding of how other minorities perceive and relate to the European recognition order. For example, future research could explore the recognitive experiences of individuals and groups within and across European nation states, who do not align with the dominant identity standards by having a differing religious affiliation, ethnicity and culture, citizenship status, or gender and sexual orientation. As this study shows, applied recognition theory is beneficial for exploring the everyday lives of individuals and groups, who are hidden, subaltern and Othered. It is therefore important for researchers who utilise a critical approach, to simultaneously deploy philosophical and empirical tools to enhance emancipatory intentions, challenge dominant paradigms, and uncover the complexity of everyday life for oppressed and unrepresented people.

And lastly, this study provides new insights and an alternative viewpoint for those working in the narrow confines of the security paradigm as well as for the IR field more generally. With the advent of civil strife in Syria and Iraq, and the rise of Islamic radicalisation among a small number of Muslim youth in Europe, this study provides relevant insights that deepen the knowledge and understanding of youth radicalisation and its occurrence. It does so by exploring alternate themes such as recognition, power and identity. The empirical narratives of this study show that young Muslims in the Irish-European context are open to transformation and are actively searching and working towards identity change. Despite beginning positively, this identity and integration process can leave searchers open to manipulation, especially when communicating and interacting with negative influencers locally or over the Internet. Unfortunately, the openness that initially enables positive identity transformation and facilitates progressive civic integration, can also be hijacked by others to sidetrack well-meaning Muslim youth onto a more ideological track. This tragically leads to the negativity and dehumanising influence of Islamic extremism. It is imperative that future research strive to gain a clearer understanding of this derailing process. That is, how European Muslim youth are influenced towards divergent avenues of action and identity formation with one path leading to a contributive Islamic-civic identity and the other to a radicalised, potentially terroristic, Islamic fundamentalism.

Concluding remarks

The universalism of this book illustrates how recognition, power and identity intersect in everyday cultural life and verifies that humans, whether Muslim or non-Muslim, are not static entities but remain dynamic, fluid beings, in constant forms of transformation due to the intersubjective interaction conducted with others in the context of everyday life. As this study illustrates, the identity movement undertaken by Muslim youth in the Irish-European context proves that although such a shift may be perceived as natural, when viewed through a recognitive lens, it becomes apparent that these transformations are an identity construction aiming to resolve everyday social dilemmas in context.

It is important to note that this identity transformation also impacts upon the European secular-religious divide and the integration issues emanating from it. As outlined in the Introduction to this book, to avoid falling back into a nativist regressive politics, Jürgen Habermas devised a normative solution that advocated for the achievement of European integration and democratic solidarity by ensuring all people living in Europe become citizens, who can then direct their loyalty and allegiance to an abstract pan-European legal framework. For Habermas, a constitutional patriotism would enable all people in Europe, whether religious or secularist, to productively interact and live together in solidarity and, at the same time, bypass nativist machinations and the exclusion of the Other. Notably, Habermas identified that secular and religious citizens can recognise each other, intersubjectively interact, and rationally communicate about important social issues by prioritising participatory civicness as a key component of European identity. However, has Habermas' ideal gained any traction? On the one hand, from a top-down perspective, a pan-European constitutional framework has not developed. Alongside economic recession and the rise of the alt-right, the European project continues to suffer a democratic deficit by remaining under nation state control and aloof from its citizenry. On the other hand, the empirical narratives in this book show, from a bottom-up perspective, the first signs that the secular-religious divide is being slowly traversed by Muslim youth through their use of a participatory civic identity that is informed by Islamic tradition. As the grounded narratives vividly convey, young Muslims are developing an active and participatory Islamic-civic identity that has the components and potential to bridge the secular-religious divide that has come to define a post-traditional European public sphere. Only time will tell if this identity can communicate effectively and attain the recognition it deserves.

This research into everyday recognition dynamics throws up an additional pertinent question in relation to 'how forms of disrespect towards Muslim minorities and people of difference can be reduced in various spheres of life?'. Reflecting the stance of critical social theory, the answer is found in acknowledging the importance of mutual intersubjective relationships. It will be up to differing individuals and groups across European society to develop a shared sense of mutual responsibility towards each other so as to come to a better understanding and recognition of each other. To accomplish this, intersubjective interaction and communication is vital, yet its volatility and unpredictability will inevitably lead to further struggles for recognition. What is important, however, is whether such struggles for recognition are respected and given tolerant consideration. If such an ethical stance is adopted and people begin to learn about themselves by recognising the normative expectations of others, social justice in each sphere of everyday life will find firmer ground. This iterative process will give a higher degree of freedom to individuals to self-realise their being, which on a daily basis interweaves and traverses a variety of complex intersubjective spheres of experience. The creation of such a *facilitating environment* (to use a Winnicottian term) opens-up the potentiality for individuals and groups to self-realise the complex dynamics of their identities and to tolerate the identities of others. In this way, by taking responsibility for changing the interpersonal dynamics of cultural recognition, we incrementally transform culture itself and ethically direct its trajectory toward a brighter more inclusive future. To end, it is appropriate to return to Axel Honneth's work to retrieve a quote that reflectively encapsulates how cultural change is an important aspect to consider in relation to the expansion of ethical recognition and solidarity in post-traditional societies:

Social-structural upheavals in developed societies have so greatly expanded the possibilities for self-realisation that the experience of individual or collective difference has become the impetus for a whole new series of political movements. In the long run, their demands can only be satisfied once culture has been transformed so as to radically expand relations of solidarity.

(Honneth 1995, p.179)

References

Honneth, Axel. 1995 [1992]. *The Struggle for Recognition: The Moral Grammar of Social Conflicts.* Cambridge: Polity Press.

McBride, Cillian. 2013. *Recognition.* Cambridge: Polity Press.

Petherbridge, Danielle. (ed.). 2011. *Axel Honneth: Critical Essays: With a Reply by Axel Honneth.* Leiden, Netherlands: Brill.

Petherbridge, Danielle. 2013. *The Critical Theory of Axel Honneth.* Lanham, MD: Lexington Books.

Appendix

Table A.1 Pseudonyms and attributes of interviewees

1st Generation	2nd Generation
Adeeb	Aamil
Akhtar^	Adam
Dahlia*	Ayyub
Firaq	Azad
Hakim	Aziz^
Iqbal^	Daleela*
Kaleem	Furat*
Mazhab	Isra*^
Nabeel^	Mahir
Nazir	Nurdeen
Saad	
Safeerah*	
Sayyid	
Ubaid^	
Yaseen	

* = Female, ^ = Denizen

Table A.2 Pseudonyms and attributes of discussants

1st Gen. Male	1st Gen. Female	2nd Gen. Female	2nd Gen. Male
Abdul	Aisha	Bisma^	Aban
Amir	Ayan	Fusaila	Aswad
Farid	Dahlia	Isha	Azaan
Idris	Elmira	Mahala^	Hussein^
Labeeb^	Fazia	Rifa	Masud
Rashid^	Ghazalah^	Saiba	Nejeed
	Hurriyah	Sumayya^	Siddiq
	Maja		Yusuf
	Meera		
	Saadiqa		
	Sadiyya		

^ = Denizen

Index

9/11 attacks 2, 16, 25, 77, 79, 88

abilities 55, 57, 58, 59, 60, 67, 188; and social recognition in Ireland 92–94, 95–96, 112, 164, 169, 179–180, 183
academic literature (European) 12, 14–15, 37, 188, 192; focus on advocacy and participation 18–23, 37, 182; focus on security 15–18, 22, 37, 181–182, 187, 188; *see also* Irish Muslim studies
achievements 55, 57, 58, 59, 60, 67, 95, 112, 164, 169, 179–180, 183, 188
Adorno, Theodor 46
advocacy: academics' focus on 14, 18–23, 37, 182
Afghanistan 15, 25
Ahlul Bayt Islamic Centre 25
al-Maktoum Foundation 25
alcohol 109, 110, 129, 151
Allen, Amy 33, 64–65, 68, 163
Allen, Chris 31
alt-right 1, 186, 195
An Garda Siochana 30
Anderson, Joel 46
Anwar, Muhammad 18, 37
Apel, Karl-Otto 46
art 154, 180, 182
asylum seekers 25, 170, 173
authenticity 123–124; Islam versus culture 124–134, 140
authority: in Islam 124, 127–128, 129, 165–167, 175–177; and power 65–67, 68, 165–167, 174; and recognition 65–67, 68, 190

Ballyhaunis Mosque 25, 26
Belfast Agreement (1998) 24
Benjamin, Jessica 49, 51
Benjamin, Walter 11
Black Lives Matter 45
Bosnian War (1992) 15
Brexit 1
Brussels 21
Burma 75

Canada 17
Carr, James 29–37, 64, 111
Catholics / Catholicism 55, 104; schools 83–84
Cavan 26
Central Statistics Office (Ireland) 30
citizenship: Habermas on 3–4, 7–9; immigrants and 3–4; Muslims and 20–21, 22, 96–99, 102–106, 112, 135, 167–169, 170, 173
civic participation 76, 80–82, 103–106, 112, 134–140, 141, 154–156, 164, 167, 170, 177–179, 182–183, 190, 192–193, 195
civic stratification 97–99, 102–103, 112, 167–169, 182–183
civil rights movement 55–56
Clash of Civilisations 15
Clonskeagh mosque complex 25
Cold War 1
constitutionalism 3–4, 6–9
constitutive power 162, 170–173, 176, 181, 184, 189
Cooke, Maeve 64
Coolsaet, Rik 16
critical social theory 3, 6, 9, 13, 17, 18, 38, 43, 46, 67, 186, 195
Crusades 1

culture: contributions to 1, 92–94, 95–96, 112, 180; filtering out 127, 129–134, 140, 157, 171, 174–175, 179, 190; generational views of 143–159, 160, 174–175; harm to 1; and identity 109–111, 112, 124–134, 140, 143–159, 160, 174–175, 177–179; Islam versus 124–134, 140, 143–153, 156–159, 160, 165–167, 174–175, 177–179; misunderstanding 82, 91–92; and recognition 46, 92–94, 95–96, 112, 195
Cuthbertson, Ian M. 16

De Schutter, Helder 97
denizenship 73, 96–99, 112, 167–169, 170, 173; and access to opportunities 99–103, 112, 167–169
deprivation theory 114, 115, 116, 140
development: and security 17
discrimination 72; everyday 85–92, 94–96, 112, 163–165, 169; in Ireland 30, 31–37, 76–77, 80, 83–99, 111–112, 163–165, 169, 179, 180, 183; and power 32–37, 163–165, 169; structural exclusion 83–85, 111–112
disrespect: and legal recognition 56; and love recognition 52; and religion 115; and social recognition 60, 91–92, 94–96; *see also* misrecognition
domineering power 162, 163–170, 181, 184, 189
Dublin, Muslims in 26–27, 37, 131
Dublin City 26
Dublin City Mosque 25
Dublin City University 17
Dublin Islamic educational facilities 26
Dublin Islamic social and political institutions 26, 29
Dublin Islamic Society 25
Dublin mosques 25–26, 29
Dún Laoghaire-Rathdown 26
Durkheim, Emile 114, 140

Economic and Social Research Institute (Ireland) 30
education: discrimination in 83, 112; and legal status 99–101, 112, 168
educational institutions, Islamic: in Dublin 26; in Ireland 27, 28
Egypt 103
emancipatory paradigm 3, 10, 14, 17, 18, 22, 30, 37, 182, 186
employment: discrimination in 90–91

Equality Authority and Tribunal (Ireland) 30
Esposito, John L. 15
European Security Strategy 16
European Union 1, 3–5

familial disruption: due to legal status 97–99, 112, 168
fear 1, 188
Feinberg, Joel 54
Female Genital Mutilation (FGM) 156, 165, 166, 175
Fingal 26
first generation Muslims 21; on civicness 134–137; on constituting the next generation 144–146, 160, 170–173; in Dublin 26; on legal misrecognition 96–97, 99, 100, 101–103, 107–108; relationship with second generation 10, 12, 81, 105, 111, 124–129, 131, 133–134, 137, 143–159, 160, 165–167, 170–173, 174–175, 177; on religious solidarity 122–123; on religious support 116–118, 120–121; on social misrecognition 73–82, 83–92, 107
Flynn, Kieran 27–28
Foucault, Michel 32, 33, 61–63, 68, 170, 174, 191
France: headscarves in schools 18; Muslims in 18, 19, 101–102, 192
Frankfurt School 46
freedom of movement: and legal status 101–102, 112, 168
Fromm, Erich 46
Fukuyama, Francis 15
Furseth, Inger 114, 124

Gardaí: discrimination in 84–85, 88
Gartner, Heinz 16
Germany: citizenship in 3, 7; Muslims in 7, 19
Goody, Jack 19
Gulf War (1990) 15

Habermas, Jürgen 46, 62; on citizenship 3–4, 7–9; on constitutionalism 3–4, 6–9; on the European Union 3–5; on immigration 3; on Islam in Europe 5, 6–7; on nationalism 3–4, 8–9; on secular–religious divide 4–9, 194–195; on supranational entities 3–4, 9; on tolerance 6
hadith 121, 138
Hajj 122, 124–125

Hammer, Thomas 55
handshaking 128, 176
headscarf *see* hijab
Hegel, Georg Wilhelm Friedrich 43, 46, 47, 48, 49, 53, 57
Hellyer, H.A. 19
hijab 83, 84, 86–92, 93, 108, 121, 144, 154, 155, 158, 163, 164, 166, 180
History of Islam in Ireland 28
Hoffman, Marcelo 61–62
Honneth, Axel 10, 11, 12, 43, 44–45, 46, 47–60, 67, 114, 140, 162, 181, 186–187, 191, 195–196; criticisms of 60–61, 62–68, 115–116; and power 62–68, 169, 186–187, 190, 191
Horkheimer, Max 46
Huntington, Samuel 15–16

identity 12, 18, 20–22, 72, 115, 192, 194–195; civic 104–106, 134–140, 141, 168, 170, 177–180, 190, 192–193; difference 109–111, 112–113; generational views of 143–159, 160, 170–173, 174; Islamic versus cultural 124–134, 140, 143–153, 156–159, 160, 165–166, 174–175, 177–179, 190; and misrecognition 79, 85–96, 106–109, 112–113, 181–184, 190; and recognition 45, 67–68, 92–94, 95–96, 105, 115, 184, 190
identity balance 145
ijtihad 20, 124, 128, 176, 177
Immigrant Council of Ireland 34
immigrants 1, 2, 14, 24, 188; and citizenship 3–4, 96–99; *see also under* Ireland, Muslims in
immigration: Habermas on 3–4
institutionalisation 37; *see also* educational institutions; mosques; social and political institutions
intersubjectivity / intersubjective relations 49–51, 52, 56, 57, 58, 65, 67, 112, 120, 127, 139, 171, 172, 173, 174, 188, 189, 190, 192, 195
IRA 24
Iraq 25, 194
Ireland: neoliberalism in 30, 31; transformation of economy 25; transformation of society 23–24
Ireland, Muslims in 23–26, 37; age 24; and civic participation 76, 80–82, 103–106, 112, 134–140, 141, 154–156, 164, 167–169, 170, 177–180, 190; demographics 24–25; discrimination towards 83–96, 111–112, 163–165, 169, 179, 180, 183; ethnicity 24; gender 24; immigrants 24, 25, 27, 29, 96–99; Islam versus culture 124–134, 140, 143–153, 156–159, 160, 165–167, 174–175, 177–179; legal status of 96–111, 112, 167–169, 170, 182–183; marriage 24; media misrepresentation of 73–80, 111, 164–165, 181–184; nationality 24; occupation 25; refugees 27; religious solidarity 122–123, 140; religious support 116–122, 140; *see also* first generation Muslims; second generation Muslims
Irish government: Department of Education 101; and institutional racism 30–37, 111–112; studies 28
Irish Muslim studies 12, 27–37, 38, 192
Irish Research Council for Humanities and Social Sciences 28
Islam 114; and civic participation 134–140, 141, 154–156, 164, 177–179, 192–193; Habermas on 5, 6–7; misunderstandings of 75–76, 80–82, 91–92, 164; versus culture 124–134, 140, 144–153, 156–159, 160, 165–167, 174–175, 177–179
Islamic Cultural Centre of Ireland 25
Islamic Foundation of Ireland 25
Islamic fundamentalism 15, 16, 181–182
Islamophobia: conflation with racism 31–32, 37; in Ireland 29, 31–32, 164, 179
isolation 7, 9, 118, 136, 174, 188; academics' focus on 14; and legal status 97

Jihad Jane 78
jihadism 1, 17, 22
Journal of Muslim Minority Affairs 28–29

Keohane, Kieran 24
Kerry, County 26
Khan, Adil 28, 29
Kuhling, Carmen 23–24

legal misrecognition: affect on self 102–103, 112, 167; in Ireland 72, 96–103, 106–109, 112, 167–169
legal recognition 53–56, 66, 67, 115, 183; and civic participation 103–106, 112, 170, 192–193; and self-respect 54–56, 112; *see also* legal misrecognition

Lentin, Ronit 34
LGBT+ 45, 186
London 21, 131
love recognition 47, 48–52, 66, 67; and disrespect 52
Lowenthal, Leo 46
Lukes, Stephen 61

mahram 128
Marcuse, Herbert 46
Marx, Karl 46
McBride, Cillian 65–67, 68, 175, 179, 190
McConnon, Eamonn 17
McNay, Lois 61
Mead, G.H. 47, 49, 53, 57
media misrepresentation 72, 73–82, 111, 164–165, 182, 187–188
misrecognition 44, 46, 47, 52, 56, 60, 67, 187, 189; *see also* legal misrecognition; social misrecognition; spiritual misrecognition
misrepresentation *see* media misrepresentation
misunderstanding 74–76, 82, 91–92, 164
mosques: in Dublin 26, 29; in Ireland 25–26, 28, 29
Muhammad, Prophet 75, 88, 125, 128, 175; and civic participation 134, 136, 138–140
Murdoch, Rupert 74
Muslim Brotherhood 29
Muslims: academic literature (European) on 12, 14–23, 181–182; and civic participation 2, 76, 80, 103–106, 134–140, 141, 154–156, 167–169, 170, 177–180, 190, 192–193; fear of 1–2; Islam versus culture 124–134, 140, 143–153, 156–159, 160, 165–167, 174–175, 177–179; legal misrecognition of 96–102, 106–109, 112, 167–169, 170; Othering of 2, 3, 9, 15, 17, 19, 20, 22, 29, 186, 188; recognition experiences of 9–10, 12, 92–96, 187; social misrecognition of 72, 73–82, 83–96, 107, 111–112, 154–159, 160, 179–180, 181–184; spiritual recognition 116–123, 140, 156–159, 160, 165–167, 170–173; as a threat 2, 15–17, 181–182; *see also* Dublin, Muslims in; first generation Muslims; Ireland, Muslims in; relations between first and second generations; second generation Muslims
Muslims in Ireland *see* Ireland, Muslims in

nationalism: in Europe 3–4, 8–9, 19; Habermas on 3–4, 8–9
neoliberalism: in Ireland 30, 31, 32–37
non-recognition 44
Northern Ireland 55

object relations theory 49
Offe, Claus 46
Other / Othering 2, 3, 9, 15, 17, 19, 20, 22, 29, 186, 188

Pargeter, Alison 16
participation: academics' focus on 14, 18–23, 37, 181–182; Muslims in Dublin 27; Muslims in Ireland 76, 80–82, 103–106, 134–140, 141, 154–156, 164, 167–169, 177–180
Patel, Ismail 31–32
patriarchy 154–156, 160, 165–167, 169
Pędziwiatr, Konrad 21–22, 37, 178
Petherbridge, Danielle 62–64, 68, 191
Petit, Philip 62, 163, 165, 167
police: discrimination in 84–85, 112
political Islam 16
Politics of Difference 44
Politics of Universalism 44
populism 1, 13, 186
power 61–62, 192, 194–195; constitutive 162, 170–173, 184; domineering 162, 163–170, 184; patriarchal 154–156, 160, 165–167; and racism in Ireland 32–37; and recognition 12, 43, 62–68, 162–163, 169, 184, 187–191, 193; resistive 162, 173–181, 184
prejudice of first impressions 86, 89, 90, 92–94, 95, 164, 183
Prevent 16
Protestants / Protestantism 55

Qur'an 20, 116–117, 123, 138, 146, 155, 174

racism 136; conflation with Islamophobia 31–32, 37; in Ireland 29, 31–37, 77, 80, 86, 112, 164, 179; and power 32–37
Ramadan, Tariq 20–21, 37, 128, 176–177
rational choice theory 115, 124, 140

recognition 9–10, 184, 187–191, 192, 194–195; and culture 46, 92–94, 95–96, 195; and identity 45, 67–68, 92–96, 105, 112–113, 184, 187–191; Muslims in Dublin 2; and power 12, 43, 62–68, 162–163, 169, 170, 184, 189–191, 193; *see also* legal misrecognition; legal recognition; love recognition; social misrecognition; social recognition; spiritual misrecognition; spiritual recognition
recognition order 9, 27
recognition theory 10, 11, 12, 43–45, 46–60, 67–68, 115, 181, 186–187, 191–192; criticisms of 60–61, 62–68, 115–116; and power 62–68, 186–187
recognitive-power dilemmas 91, 155, 162–185, 191, 193
refugees 1, 2, 27, 188
relations between first and second generations 10, 12, 81, 105, 111, 124–129, 131, 133–134, 137, 143, 160, 165–167, 170–173, 174–175, 177; first generation on 143–150, 160; second generation on 150–159, 160
religion *see* Catholics / Catholicism; Islam; Protestants / Protestantism; spiritual misrecognition; spiritual recognition
religion versus culture 124–134, 143–153, 156–159, 160, 165–167, 174, 177–180
religious solidarity 122–123, 140
religious support 116–122, 140; affect on self 120–122
Repstad, Pål 114, 124
residence rights 72, 96–99
resistive power 162, 173–181, 184, 189, 190
rights 53–56; *see also* residence rights; social opportunity rights
Rogers, Melvin L. 115–116
Rousseau, Jean-Jacques 43
RTE 74
Rundell, John 50
Rushdie, Salman 18

St. Vincent de Paul 104
Sakaranaho, Tuula 28, 29
Salafi female converts 29
Scharbrodt, Oliver 28, 29
Schmidt, Alfred 46
second generation Muslims: on civicness 137–140, 177–179; in Dublin 26; on filtering out culture 127, 129–134, 140, 157, 171, 174–175, 179, 190; on Islam versus culture 124–134, 150–153, 156–159, 160, 174–175, 177–180, 190; and Islamic identity 20–22, 110–111, 124–134, 137–140, 150–153, 156–159, 160, 170–173, 174–180, 190; on legal misrecognition 97–100, 101–102, 106, 108–109; on patriarchy 154–156, 160, 176; relationship with first generation 10, 12, 81, 105, 111, 124–129, 131, 133–134, 137, 143–159, 160, 165–167, 170–173, 174–175; on religious 118–120, 121–122; on social misrecognition 74–82, 83–96, 154–159, 160, 177–179; on spiritual misrecognition 156–159, 160
secular–religious divide: Habermas on 4–9, 194–195
security: academics' focus on 2, 14, 15–18, 22, 37, 181–182, 187; challenging the paradigm 162, 181–184, 187, 188, 192, 194; and development 17; and online extremism 17
self: and legal misrecognition 102–103, 112, 167; and religious support 120–122; and social misrecognition 78–80, 86, 89, 94–96, 111, 112, 164, 165; and spiritual recognition 120–122, 172
self-confidence 51–52, 89, 95, 117, 120, 121, 156, 165, 169, 173
self-respect 54–56, 67, 102, 105
sensationalism, media 73–74, 78, 164, 187–188
Shanneik, Yafa 29
Shia Muslims: in Ireland 24, 29
shisha 129–130
Smyth, Lisa 66
social and political institutions, Islamic: in Dublin 26, 29; in Ireland 27, 28, 29
social esteem 47, 57–60, 67
social misrecognition: affect on self 78–80, 86, 89, 94–96, 111, 112, 164, 165; in Ireland 72, 73–82, 83–96, 107, 111–112, 154–159, 163–165, 177–180, 181–184; among Muslims 154–159, 160, 165–167
social opportunity rights 72, 99–106
social recognition 57–60, 66, 67, 192–193; in Ireland 92–94, 95–96; *see also* social misrecognition
socialisation theory 114, 117, 124, 140
spiritual misrecognition 156–159, 160, 165–167

spiritual recognition 114–116, 140, 170–173; affect on self 120–122, 172
Spitz, Rene 49
sport 130, 154, 180, 183
Steinhausler, Freidrich 16
stereotyping 73–80, 164, 182, 188
Sufi Muslims 156; in Ireland 24
Sunna 20, 125, 136, 138, 174, 175
Sunni Muslims: in Dublin 27; in Ireland 24
supranational entities: Habermas on 3–4, 9
Syria 194

Taoiseach, Department of the 28
Taylor, Charles 12, 43–44, 182
terrorism / terrorists: fear of 1, 2, 188; fetishisation of 17; Muslims as 2, 15, 16–17, 22, 74–75, 77–80, 87–88, 90, 181–184, 186, 192; *see also* 9/11 attacks
theory of seeking 115, 140
Thompson, Simon 44
tolerance: Habermas on 6; in Islam 138–140
traits 45, 55, 57, 58, 59, 60, 67; and legal misrecognition 106–109, 112, 169; and social misrecognition 85–86, 93–94, 95–96, 163, 164, 179–180, 183
Tralee 26
transitional objects/phenomena 50–51, 92–94, 95, 112, 115, 120, 124, 130, 172, 180

Travellers: in Ireland 45, 60
Turner, Bryan S. 123–124

United Arab Emirates 25
United Kingdom 1; Muslims in 18, 19, 75; security policies in 16, 17
United States 75, 186; security policies in 17
University College Cork 28

Volpi, Frédéric 123
Vox-Pol 17
vulnerability and racism in Ireland 32–37

War on Terror 22, 23
Weber, Max 114, 140
Winnicott, D.W. 49–51, 120, 172
workplace: discrimination in 90–91

youth: identity 20–22, 79, 85, 92–94, 95, 106–107, 108–109, 110–111, 113, 124–134, 137–140, 143–156, 160, 170–173, 174–176, 177–180, 190, 194; Islam versus culture 124–134, 140, 143–153, 156–159, 160, 174–175, 177–180, 190; and patriarchy 154–156, 160, 165–167, 176; radicalisation 16–17, 20, 22, 181, 182, 194; spiritual recognition 115, 156–159, 160, 170–173
Ypi, Lea 97

Zurn, Christopher 57

Printed in the United States
By Bookmasters